Remarkable Survivors

ALICE T. DAY

Remarkable Survivors

Insights into Successful Aging Among Women

THE URBAN INSTITUTE PRESS
Washington, D.C.

Library of Congress Cataloging in Publication Data

Day, Alice Taylor.
  Remarkable survivors: successful aging among women/Alice T. Day.
    p.   cm.
  Includes bibliographical references.
  1. Aged women—United States—Social conditions.
  2. White women—United States—Social conditions.
  3. Social surveys—United States.   I. Title.

HQ1064.U5D388   1991   90-26598
305.4—dc20   CIP

ISBN 0-87766-491-9 (alk. paper)
ISBN 0-87766-492-7 (alk. paper; casebound)

Urban Institute books are printed on acid-free paper whenever possible.

Printed in the United States of America.

9 8 7 6 5 4 3 2 1

Distributed by:
        University Press of America
4720 Boston Way   3 Henrietta Street
Lanham, MD 20706   London   WC2E 8LU   ENGLAND

THE URBAN INSTITUTE is a nonprofit policy research and educational organization established in Washington, D.C., in 1968. Its staff investigates the social and economic problems confronting the nation and government policies and programs designed to alleviate such problems. The Institute disseminates significant findings of its research through the publications program of its Press. The Institute has two goals for work in each of its research areas: to help shape thinking about societal problems and efforts to solve them, and to improve government decisions and performance by providing better information and analytic tools.

Through work that ranges from broad conceptual studies to administrative and technical assistance, Institute researchers contribute to the stock of knowledge available to public officials and private individuals and groups concerned with formulating and implementing more efficient and effective government policy.

Conclusions or opinions expressed in Institute publications are those of the authors and do not necessarily reflect the views of other staff members, officers, or trustees of the Institute, advisory groups, or any organizations that provide financial support to the Institute.

For
Caroline C. Taylor
Born 1901

CONTENTS

Tables

Figures

FOREWORD

Life for the elderly in this country can be difficult due to social isolation, economic hardship, failing health, or all three. This is even more the case for women than for men because of women's longer life expectancy, lower earning power, and greater likelihood of living alone.

Policies aimed at increasing the quality of life for elderly women may serve to enhance the quality of life for us all, including those whose work productivity is affected by the pressing need to care for aging parents. The author of this book argues that American communities are changing in ways that decrease elderly women's opportunities for independent activity and intimate social interaction, two of the keys, she concludes, to successful aging. Although social policies may not be able to reverse larger demographic trends that may adversely affect the well-being of the older women, they can reduce the social and economic costs of premature dependency among the elderly. For example, greater public services that facilitate the mobility of the elderly could enhance the quality of life for all ages by increasing the elderly's independence while at the same time freeing up family members to work in the labor market.

A major contribution of this book is that it complements quantitative analysis of aging by seeking to understand, through intimate one-on-one interviews, the ingredients to successful aging among elderly women and, more importantly, how these ingredients interact to shape the chances for aging well or poorly. The author's recommendations on how to foster more successful aging among women in their seventies and eighties are meant to serve as a guide to community- and national-level policymakers, but also to us all, on how we can set the stage now for an old age that does not necessarily lower our social, economic, or emotional quality of life nor that of those around us.

William Gorham
President

PREFACE

In a real sense, women in their late 70s and 80s are pioneers in unchartered territory. They are having to confront the challenges of aging, such as long periods of widowhood, living alone, and diminishing physical stamina, within a society that has not yet fully come to terms with the fact that it is aging.

The lives of older women portrayed in this study reflect the transformation created in American society by the unprecedented increase in life expectancy and the growing proportion of elderly in the population. The magnitude and momentum of these trends have been largely unanticipated, and, for the most part, have occurred within the experience of older people alive in the United States today. The English social historian Peter Laslett (1984:379) has written: "We are in a condition which has to be described by such unsatisfactory terms as 'cultural lag,' even of 'false consciousness.' We are now being challenged in fact to make a determined effort to be our age, our social age."

Matilda White Riley, sociologist, and, for over a decade, associate director of behavioral and social research at the National Institute on Aging, Washington, D.C., sees these demographic changes as particularly significant for the family relations of older people. How can today's families, she asks, fill people's pressing needs for close human relationships—in the late as well as the early years of adult life? Changes in the last two decades, she has argued, compel us to "rethink our traditional view of kinship" (Riley 1983:439–54). The extraordinary increases in longevity have literally altered the "configurations" of kinship structure. No longer can we view the family in the same light as we did in the past, that is, as an institution in which frail, dependent elders will automatically receive security and care.

New patterns of kinship have both strengthened the family and made it more vulnerable as a source of emotional and practical support. On the one hand, stated Riley (1983:439–54), "kinship structure has become more extensive and complex, the temporal and spatial boundaries of the family have been altered, and the opportunities for close family relationships have proliferated," while on the other hand, the exchange of mutual support—within and between the generations—is less certain. Family relationships are no longer prescribed as strict obligations. Rather, said Riley, "they must . . . be earned—created and recreated by family members over their long lives."

This book is about the impact of these profound changes on the lives of a particular group of older women, those born during the years 1900–1910, who, when interviewed in 1987, were in their late 70s to late 80s. It is a book about a group we are all well acquainted with, "our foremothers," women who could be our own mothers, aunts, grandmothers, or great-grandmothers. Or, who, if you are a white, ever-married woman in your late 70s or 80s, could be a woman much like you. Moreover, although over half the women in this study were living alone in 1987, the great majority were not isolated, but were maintaining active social lives with extended family and friends. Therefore, this book is also about the people who matter in their lives—the husbands, daughters, sons, sisters, brothers, granddaughters, grandsons, nieces, nephews, and friends with whom they share close personal ties, and the obligations of kinship or long-standing friendship.

ACKNOWLEDGMENTS

During the 18 months that I wrote this book, I received much support that not only helped to advance the project but improved the manuscript's contents and made the work more enjoyable.

Research for this study built upon a national survey of older American women conducted in 1978. The women were interviewed at three different times—in 1978 when they were 66 to 77 years old, in 1987 when the survivors were 77 to 87 years old, and in November 1988, when I talked to 20 women from the 1987 study in their homes.

The research for the 1987 study was funded initially from September 1, 1986, to December 31, 1988, by a two-year grant (nos. R01 AG06207-01 and -02) from the National Institute on Aging (NIA), Washington, D.C. Kathleen Bond, then Project Officer for the Social-Behavioral section of NIA research grants, provided information and encouragement.

The NIA grant was funded through The Urban Institute, which supplied office space, support services, and congenial colleagues. I am particularly grateful to Stephen B. Hitchner, Jr., Senior Vice President, and H. Morton Grant, Executive Business Manager, for their support in the research process and their assistance in getting the book under way.

Funding for the qualitative fieldwork, conducted October to November 1988, was provided in part by BRSG RR 05982, awarded by the Biomedical Research Support Grant Program (BRSG), Division of Research Resources, National Institutes of Health. The Urban Institute supplemented the BRSG funding by assuming the general administrative costs. From December 1988 to October 1989, I received a stipend from The Urban Institute as an off-site consultant to prepare the first draft.

Over the last year and a half, I have worked on three continents and received hospitality from a number of sources. From January to June 1989, Professor Robert Gregory, of the Department of Economics, Research School of Social Sciences, The Australian National University (A.N.U.), Canberra, provided me with office space and facilities as a Visiting Fellow in the A.N.U.'s Centre for Economic Policy Research. From September to October of that year, Jane Marceau, Professor of Public Policy at the A.N.U., arranged another Visiting Fellowship for me in the A.N.U.'s Public Policy Program. From January 15 to February 12, 1990, I was privileged to be a Resident Scholar at the Rockefeller Study and Conference Center, Bellagio, Italy. In each of these places, the space provided and the contact with colleagues offered a stimulating and supportive environment.

The sample for this book's study, for which I served as Principal Investigator, was originally developed for a fertility study undertaken in 1978 under the direction of Jeanne Clare Ridley, Professor of Demography, Georgetown University, Washington, D.C. The fieldwork for both that survey and this one was conducted by The Institute for Survey Research (ISR), Temple University, Philadelphia, under the direction of Koray Tanfer, then Research Director at ISR. Jeanne Ridley and Douglas A. Wolf, then Senior Research Associate at The Urban Institute, participated in the developmental stages of the present study.

I am indebted to Professor Marjorie H. Cantor, Third Age Center, Fordham University, New York, N.Y. and Joy Spalding, then Research Director, National Citizens Coalition for Nursing Home Reform for ideas about the research design.

Among those at The Urban Institute who have made substantial contributions to the research, Douglas Wolf assisted in developing the initial grant applications and preparing the final research report, for which he wrote a section describing a multivariate analysis of transitions in mortality and institutionalization among women in this sample. Tracy Goodin compiled the qualitative data from the interview schedules, and Terri Murray monitored the budget and processed the grant applications and research reports. In addition, I am grateful to three Senior Research Associates at The Urban Institute, Marilyn Moon, Thomas McBride, and Douglas Wolf, for reading the entire manuscript and encouraging me to persevere in crafting the contents and striving for comprehensibility. The contributions of Felicity Skidmore, The Urban Institute Press, and Molly Ruzicka to editing the volume also deserve mention and my appreciation.

Several colleagues at The Australian National University helped substantially along the way. Valerie Braithwaite, Lecturer in Psychology, worked with me in developing the initial scales for psychological well-being. Debra Hinton of the Computer Services Centre devoted herself meticulously and unstintingly to the programming. I am particularly indebted to Ian Diamond, then Senior Research Fellow, Department of Demography, Research School of Social Sciences, for his time and assistance in designing the statistical procedures. His sensitive understanding of old people in Great Britain greatly enriched my own thinking about the conditions of old women reflected in these American data. Lincoln H. Day, Senior Fellow, Department of Demography, Research School of Social Sciences, accompanied me on the fieldwork trips and helped with the analysis of household structure and family composition. His companionship and lively ideas added immeasurably to the pleasure and quality of the work.

Finally, of course, I owe whatever important insights about successful aging there are in this book to the women in this study. The changes in their lives in the decade following their late 60s and 70s have provided a concrete picture of the challenges of aging for women in American society today. Special thanks go to the 20 women I visited personally—for welcoming me into their homes, for sharing their problems and pleasures, and for wanting to convey something of value from their own experience to women of all ages. The insights are theirs. The responsibility for any misconceptions in conveying these insights is mine.

INTRODUCTION

American women in their late 70s and 80s are a remarkable group of survivors in terms of the times they have lived through, their orientation toward childbearing, and their resilience in the face of the changes associated with aging.

Women in this age group lived through a period of turbulence and enormous social change: there were two world wars and the Great Depression; the automobile became the primary means of private transportation; a national system of social insurance was established, giving a majority of older people in the United States a minimum level of income security; and advances in medical technology led to extensions in the average length of life, increasing the likelihood that a woman who survived into her 60s could expect to live on well into her 80s. In their young adulthood, women now in their 80s produced a distinctive pattern of fertility, something of a "Quiet Revolution" (Dawson, Meny, and Ridley 1980), with average family size limited to unprecedentedly low levels. At a time well in advance of the widespread availability of modern methods of birth control, such rigorous family limitation required a high degree of self-discipline and motivation.

By the time they had entered their late 70s and 80s, a majority of the 589 women in this book's study had experienced major changes in marital status, in their capacity to manage daily activities, in their networks of close relationships, and in their living arrangements. Over half of those not already widowed by 1978 had lost their husbands, and 9 percent of those interviewed in 1987 (N = 53) had lost a total of 64 sons and daughters. More than two-thirds had lost close family members other than a husband, such as a brother or sister, and 3 in 10 had lost friends and neighbors.

On the other hand, a substantial minority had experienced additions as well as decrements to their social networks. Forty-two women had remarried, and, in the 10-year period between the two interviews, 49 had added one or more adult children to their families. Three in 10 had formed new, emotionally supportive relationships. Overall, despite major changes in their families, physical capacities, and access to the mainstream of social life, nearly 7 in 10 said they were in good to excellent health, and over half said they could manage all daily activities without help.

FOCUS ON "SUCCESSFUL" AGING

A major purpose of this book is to lend insight into the characteristics of "successful" aging among this group of women. I explore the meaning of aging successfully, the factors associated with it, and the kinds of social settings and social policies that might be seen to foster satisfying aging among the elderly population.

This search to describe and account for "success" in aging draws upon both subjective attitudes and objective behavior. What are the distinctive features of those women interviewed in 1987 who describe their lives with a sense of contentment, rather than despair? One hypothesis is that a sense of autonomy (that is, the capacity to be independent and to direct one's own life) and a penchant for activity (that is, the capacity to maintain an interest in and an active orientation toward social relations and community affairs) are both important contributors to achieving satisfaction in old age.

IMPLICATIONS FOR POLICY

In his address to the United Nations General Assembly in December 1988, Mikhail S. Gorbachev (N.Y. Times, Dec. 8:A16) noted that "the greatest philosphers sought to grasp the laws of social development and find an answer to the main question: How to make man's life happy, just and safe." The ultimate concern of this book is the application of this question to women in their ninth decade.

This study raises many issues that are beyond the reach of the data to resolve. We are still a long way from finding a magic bullet to make old age "happy, just and safe." However, the national scope and representativeness of the sample from which the data are drawn provide the opportunity to examine successful aging in a wide variety of circumstances and family contexts. The initial sample was selected at random from over 27,000 households across the United States. Unlike many studies of aging, there was no disability criterion. Thus, the sample includes women reflecting a broad range of health statuses, functional capacities, household structures, family relations, and caregiving arrangements. Major exceptions to this diversity involve the exclusion of women in three categories: black women, women who never married, and those too ill to be interviewed. The book examines the implications for policies on aging of excluding these women from the definition of success.

I conclude with an overview of the contribution of this research to understanding persistent gaps in our efforts to meet the challenges of "our social age," and the directions that might be taken to rectify our collective myopia about the conditions that would contribute to extending the stimulating, socially integrated years of life.

A TALE OF TWO WOMEN

The oldest hath borne most; we that are young
Shall never see so much, nor live so long.

—William Shakespeare, *King Lear*

This first chapter opens with a glimpse into the experiences of two women who were study participants. I visited Mrs. Silvestri and Mrs. Farnsworth[1] in their homes in November 1988, 16 months after they had been interviewed in the second of the two social surveys in this study. We talked informally at length about their interests, activities, and families, and about what aging successfully means to them.

The chapter introduces successful aging within the framework of two concrete lives. The stories illustrate the great diversity in outlooks and circumstances among women born at the turn of the century. The lives of these two women also raise many issues in relation to the very old that concern families, professionals, and policymakers today. I begin with Mrs. Silvestri.

Mrs. Silvestri:
"You make yourself happy."

"I mean, there's no secret to it," said Mrs. Silvestri, when I asked her opinion about the key to successful aging, "as long as you keep healthy. One thing I pray when I go to bed—for the health of my children and the health of me. Never pray for money. If you are healthy, you can always make money."

She went on without hesitation to describe her formula for success, illustrating her points with detailed anecdotes from her own life:

"Listen, it's this way. . . . Now, I have cataract, see, and I go to the doctor, sometimes once a month, sometimes twice a month. Sometime, he says to me, 'Your eyes are doing very well.' " Here, she paused to bring out her calendar to show me the dates and times for several months of all her future appointments with the eye doctor. "When I'm there, I have to call this number. Would you believe, they have taken me home by cab!

"In other words, I mean, as long as you make yourself happy. I mean, it's no use worrying about something. Some people are such worry warts that they worry themselves to death and then it doesn't amount to anything. . . . So why worry, you know, and that is it."

"It's nice to be alive"

At age 79, widowed 12 years, living alone in a modest, three-room vacation cottage in a wooded rural area of a southeastern state, Mrs. Silvestri is mentally and physically fit; does all her own housework; goes to her local senior citizens club five days a week; participates in all concerts, socials, and trips sponsored by the club; attends Our Lady of the Lake Catholic church up the road every Sunday; and, in her own view, is very happy and feels, "it's very nice to be alive."

She has a daughter and two sons of whom she is proud: They have fine families, she says, and have done well in their chosen professions. Their pictures are wedged in amongst the untidy jumble that covers every available surface in her home: books, magazines, newspaper clippings, plant cuttings, and craft work of all descriptions— artificial satin roses, knitted pot holders, tea towels, and paint-by-number pictures.

Mrs. Silvestri sees her house as at once the key to her economic security and a major source of her capacity to live as she chooses: "What helps most is that my home is paid for. So I have no mortgage."

Her children, she says, all want her to stop living in the little cottage and come to live with them, instead:

" 'Mum, why don't you sell the place down the lake—come. . . .'
'But I love this place. Your father built it, and I helped.' Believe me, I know the difference between a Phillips screwdriver and a regular screwdriver.

People in the city, they want to live in the suburb. I'm living in the suburb. Why should I go back to the city!"

A year earlier, when asked on the survey, "Why do you want to stay at home with outside help, instead of moving in with one of your children or a relative?" she had replied, "I like to do all different things. I like to have things around—books, crafts, knitting, and my children would not put up with that. I just want to do my own thing—when I feel like doing it, in my own home."

Mrs. Silvestri's rewards, moreover, are not merely personal and private. She has received public recognition for her contribution to the community. Awarded the Senior Citizen's Award of the Month, she is the proud possesser of a letter from former President Ronald Reagan, commending her for her efforts in behalf of the senior citizens clubs of her state.

In contrast to Mrs. Silvestri's bright outlook is that of Mrs. Farnsworth, described next.

Mrs. Farnsworth:
"People don't pay any attention."

"You got me at the wrong time," said Mrs. Farnsworth, when we had dispensed with opening pleasantries and settled down to talk. "I've had the two new hips put in. And this one here, I'm afraid I'm going to have to have done over. The pain's terrible—more when I put my weight on it. So I'm planning on going back to [northern state] to be with my daughter.

"He," she said, gesturing toward her husband sitting opposite us, "had a stroke and doesn't know what's going on here. He was in the hospital seven and a half weeks [starting] in April. He came home, 23rd of May. He's able to do things, but don't want to. So he's going to have to . . . and I can't do anything."

Later, when I asked if she had any views about the sorts of things older people can do to get the most out of their later years, she replied with a short, "Not much."

"I've been so disgusted and discouraged to wind up like this"

Also turning 80 and widowed from her first husband for about the same number of years as Mrs. Silvestri, Mrs. Farnsworth lives in the same community, only about two blocks away. She is not on her own and living in her own home, however. Eleven years ago she remarried and moved away from the northern state where she had spent all her previous adult life, in order to join Mr. Farnsworth in the mobile home he owns in the woods. In so doing, she left behind 4 adult children by her first husband, 10 grandchildren, and 5 great-grandchildren. "My children and everything is all up there." Although, in marrying Mr. Farnsworth, she acquired 4 stepchildren who live closer at hand, she regards them more as enemies than as allies:

"He's got four children, but they won't do anything for him. When he was sick—so sick in the hospital, his daughter came down and she stayed with me for a week. And what they were doing was planning on contesting his will—and what they wanted and what they didn't want—and what belonged to them and what didn't. That's when I started to get upset. His son came and he wanted to go through the trailer and see what he could get. And he was still my husband! They're after what they can get. I haven't felt good since he came home from the hospital.

They were down, Sunday, and her husband asked me, who was going to take my check, my Social Security check. I said, 'I'm going to take it!' But, boy, what business!"

Unlike Mrs. Silvestri, who views her life with an upbeat sense of creativity and personal fulfillment, Mrs. Farnsworth sees herself as on a downhill slide, burdened with intractable problems that make her feel weary, depressed, and defeated. When I asked her just before I left whether there was anything particularly important to her that she would like to record, she replied, "I don't really know. I've been so disgusted and discouraged to wind up like this."

Mrs. Farnsworth describes her problems in terms of three major strands: health, husband, and homesickness. First, she says her own health problems are a major deterrent to doing what she wants to do. She does not go out at all except to do the necessary household chores and for doctor's appointments:

"I've had nine surgeries. I've had part of my bowel out. I can't take regular arthritis drugs because they upset my stomach. I've had an ulcer.

I take painkills, but they make you feel lousy . . . codeine. . . ."

I've been trying to drive. I think that's what's the matter with me. We have to go all the way up to [town] for shopping, even to do the laundry. I make him go with me because I can't lift things, even the laundry."

On top of her own discomfort and physical handicaps, Mrs. Farnsworth finds that, particularly since her husband's stroke in April 1988, he has become withdrawn, inattentive, and "ugly"—more of a burden than a source of comfort and help. She never refers to him by name, only in the third person:

"I think he's leaning on me too much and expects too much of me. I just can't keep doing it.

He doesn't seem to pay attention that I can't walk around here.

Five weeks I've been after him to vacuum the rug. I can't do it anymore. Well, he did it the other day, finally.

I have to do the cooking—and I go out there to get supper, and, oh,
my leg. I stand there crying and he'll just sit there. And he'll say, 'Is
it ready yet?' He depends too much on me. He won't help. He won't
do nothing. I've got arthritis all through. I've got a pinched nerve in
my neck, so the chiropractor has been helping me quite a bit. So I
went up there this morning and I got a few groceries. He came back,
slammed them on the table and sat down. You'd have thought he'd
have put them away. There wasn't many there. Didn't straighten out
the kitchen or anything. He just wants me to do it!"

Mr. Farnsworth is quite deaf. I asked whether anything could be
done about it. Mrs. Farnsworth says that he has a 25-year-old hearing
aid that does not work. She has spent $3,000 of her money on new
hearing aids for him, but he refuses to use them:

"He's very stubborn. He says to me one day, 'I am the boss.' I says,
'Well, you're not bossing me. I'll do as I want.'

After he was widowed, he lived here six years alone. He's always
throwing that in my face. It wasn't my fault that he lived here six
years alone, but he says, 'I lived here six years alone and I got along
all right.' "

For Mrs. Farnsworth, the worst feature of Mr. Farnsworth's condition is the marked deterioration it has brought about in their relationship. What she sees as his total indifference to her needs makes
her feel completely alone. She illustrates this by recounting what
happened when she had her recent hip replacement. Rather than, as
in the past, having the surgery done in the state where she comes
from, and where she has her daughter and other family members
around her, this time she had it done in the community where she
has been living since she married Mr. Farnsworth:

"I'll never have another one done alone down here. If he felt like
coming up, he'd come. And I had a beautiful nightgown that I got for
myself and a robe to match, and I said to him, 'Take it home and just
rinse it out.' And he left it in the men's room up there. Never got it
again. He paid no attention to me. I'd ask him for like a comb or
something like that—he don't pay no attention, and he still doesn't.
Oh, it's been wicked. Nobody knows!

If I don't get up in the morning . . . if I don't feel like getting up . . .
he never comes to the door and asks me if I'm all right. I'd lay there
dead for a day or two before he'd come to. I can't live like that."

A third area of trauma for Mrs. Farnsworth has been moving away from her home and family. Health problems and marital distress aggravate her homesickness and sense of isolation. To my question, "How is this community as a place to live?" she responded:

"Oh, I hate it! They are the most unfriendly people that I ever seen in my life. I had to have a plumber come here when he [husband] was in the hospital—a young feller, and he said, 'Where are you from?' I said, '[northern state].' He says, 'How do you like it down here?' I said, 'I don't. People aren't friendly.' He says, 'I'm glad you said that. I'm an outsider, too.' He came from [another northern state]. He says, 'We'll never fit in down here.' And he's a young feller. I said to him I thought the war from the South and the North was over a long time ago. He says, 'We'll never fit in down here.' Oh, I never met such people in my life!

I was telling my daughter the other day when she called, we've got a neighbor here, a neighbor there, a neighbor there—really, I haven't seen them since July. They don't ask how you are, could they do anything for you.

I said to him the other day, I said, 'Now when I go up to my daughter's, I go across the street to the neighbors, they come across to our house. I have someone to talk to.' It takes my mind off my leg, you know. She seems to think it'll be better when I get up there."

AUTHENTICITY OF REPORTS

Did Mrs. Silvestri put her best foot forward to impress me, the director of the study of older women? Did I talk to her on a day when she was in unusually high spirits? By the same token, was Mrs. Farnsworth feeling unusually blue and going through a particularly bad patch when she recounted to me her numerous grievances? How much can we rely on the evidence of a few hours' conversation to reflect an older person's true feelings and to provide an accurate portrait of the conditions he or she is facing in old age?

The longitudinal design of this study enabled me to test the validity of the women's responses by comparing the open-ended interviews with the information from the two previous surveys. If a consistency was noted between these women's responses to the Temple University interview in 1987 and what they said to me nearly a year and a half later, there was strong support for accepting the authenticity of their self-reports. In fact, the overall tenor of the women's responses in November 1988 was consistent with their responses to the more structured questions in the 1987 survey.

Sense of Well-being

In 1987, as when I met her over a year and a half later, Mrs. Silvestri described herself, unambiguously, as a contented woman. Indeed, on every indicator of well-being on the 1987 survey—objective or subjective, environmental or attitudinal—Mrs. Silvestri indicated the highest level of personal satisfaction and sense of well-being (table 1.1). She answered, "Not at all, "to the question, "Do health problems stand in the way of your doing the things you want to do?" With Social Security her only source of income, she said, "I have enough to get along, and even a little extra." She characterized the space in her cottage as "just the right amount," rejecting the alternatives, "more than I need" and "too small." She said she "almost never" had time on her hands (that she didn't know what to do with), rather than "all the time," "quite often," or "just now and then." She described the neighborhood as "very convenient" (for shopping and getting the things you need), and said that, in her opinion, changes in the neighborhood had made it "a much better place to live," rather than "a somewhat better place," "a somewhat worse place," or "a much worse place."

Compared with Mrs. Silvestri's 1987 survey responses, Mrs. Farnsworth came across in the 1987 survey as a person deeply dissatisfied with her lot. Her responses then were markedly negative on almost all indicators of a sense well-being (table 1.1). At that time, she defined her health as poor (compared with others her age), and described herself as, "not very happy." She did not think of herself as having anyone to confide in about things that were important to her or as having friends or neighbors who would help out if she became ill. She said she had no relative(s) to whom she could turn for help in case she had major medical expenses. She answered in the affirmative to two negative statements about the effects of aging: "Do things keep getting worse as you get older?" and "Do you feel that as you get older you are less useful?" She replied, "All the time," to the question, "How often do you have time on your hands that you don't know what do with?" All told, her raw score of 6 points on this selection of indicators of a sense of well-being is less than half that of Mrs. Silvestri's score of 17 points.

BACKGROUND INFLUENCES

What accounts for Mrs. Farnsworth's deep sense of distress and Mrs. Silvestri's apparently unalloyed peace of mind? Has Mrs. Farnsworth

Table 1.1 INDICATORS OF A SENSE OF WELL-BEING, 1987 SURVEY:
MRS. SILVESTRI AND MRS. FARNSWORTH

	Mrs. Silvestri	Mrs. Farnsworth
Perceived Health (Compared to others in age group)		
4 Excellent		
3 Good	3	
2 Fair		
1 Poor		1
Level of Happiness		
3 Very happy	3	
2 Pretty happy		
1 Not too happy		1
Emotional Support (Someone you confide in?)		
2 Yes	2	
1 No		1
Instrumental Support (Friend/neighbor to help when sick?)		
2 Yes	2	
1 No		1
Time on Hands		
4 Almost never	4	
3 Just now and then		
2 Quite often		
1 All the time		1
Satisfaction with Neighborhood (Convenience for shopping and getting things needed)		
3 Very convenient	3	
2 Fairly convenient		
1 Not very convenient		1
Total score:	17	6

Notes: The highter the score, the higher the sense of well-being. The weighted scores for these items on the 1987 survey are discussed in chapter 6.

just been unlucky? Was she destined to taste the bitterness of misfortune? Or has the character of events that underlie her dissatisfaction been shaped partly by the manner in which she herself has approached problems as they have arisen? By the same token, did Mrs. Silvestri's level of satisfaction just happen? Is it the result of luck and random good fortune, in which she has played only a minor creative role?

The data obtained to answer these questions are, of course, incomplete. Only a partial picture emerges of these women and the events that have colored their life chances, as revealed in the three personal interviews—the two surveys in 1978 and 1987 and my conversation with them in November 1988. Already in 1978, both women were in their late 60s—that is, well into the time of life that American society defines as "old age." By the time we first talked to them in 1978, they had been negotiating the challenges of life for many years. Whether their different orientations toward aging flow from external events over which they have had little control, or whether the manner in which they have characteristically tended to cope with the world has somehow shaped the very nature of the events themselves is a moot point. To resolve this question would require a more experimental research design than the one here.

Nevertheless, this caveat does not exonerate us altogether from the important quest for explanations for differences in the ways women 77 to 87 years old in this sample experience aging. The longitudinal design and the recollections of the women themselves permitted me to examine the development of their feelings and the techniques they have used to cope with problems in the past. We know, for example, that Mrs. Silvestri's life has not been trouble-free. She lost her husband 12 years ago ("Sweetheart from 16 years up. No one else will take my husband's place"), she is certainly not rich (she lists her annual income from all sources as $4,000 to $5,000), and she has some health problems (she is being treated for cataracts and high blood pressure). Her contentment, rather than being due to an absence of trouble, appears to be a consequence of conscious effort on her part, the outcome of "a transactional process" (Hendricks 1984: 94) operating over the whole of her life course, in which she has applied substantial thought to developing a set of orientations and ways of coping that work for her. In her social contacts and management of daily affairs, Mrs. Silvestri's goal appears always to have been to act in such a way as to do whatever would make the most of the resources she has at hand. In my interview with her, she produced in explicit detail an arsenal of prescriptions for the successful management of aging, as follows.

Strategies for Aging Effectively: Mrs. Silvestri

Stay out of debt.
"I make every penny do. Pay my bill as it comes in. Check [Social Security] goes to the bank. That way you don't have to worry, see?"

Comply with medical advice, but ask your doctor questions.
"I take my medication. I never miss a day. Do what the doctor tells you. Don't skip and say, 'Today I'm not going to take.' Take the medicine the way the doctor tells you to do. If you don't understand what the doctor say, ask him to explain to you what it is. That's what you're going there for! I mean—why come out of his office and be in doubt! 'Oh, I wonder what he said,' or anything like that. No, it doesn't have to be that. That's why he's there—for you to ask questions. What you don't understand, say, 'Please explain it to me, you know, what you mean.'

"Now, the eye doctor has says to me, 'Now about once a week I want you to pour water in your eyes.' And I said to him, 'Now, doctor, will you please explain why I have to pour water in my eyes.' And he says to me, 'The reason for that is to keep your eyes moist. Cataract make your eyes dry.' I can see fine. He said, 'They're standing still, they're not moving.' So I says, well, I told him, 'Stay where you are!'"

Accept help, and return the favor.
[The bus driver asked Mrs. Silvestri if she could use a bag of peppers that he couldn't use because he had peppers in his garden.] "And I said to him, 'Mrs. Silvestri will take anything you don't want. I'll take, 'em.' So what I did—come home, chop 'em all up and put them in the freezer. Well, it's all these little things that keep you busy."

"Across the street that house is always for rent. So far we always have nice people. The reason for that is because you have to be nice yourself. Because those people are just as worried as you are to get nice neighbors, you know what I mean? I mean it works both ways."

"When I go and pick strawberries, maybe, I pick four quarts—one quart for the lady that picks me up for church. I think of her. And the other for someone else."

Do everything in moderation and use your common sense.
"Maybe twice a week I have a soft-boiled egg. I don't eat many because they do have cholesterol. You have to watch out for your cholesterol. Same with oil. Learn how to measure. Get a teaspoon, get a tablespoon. Don't just pour it on. In other words, you have to use

your common sense—in everything not only in cookin', in bakin', in dressin'—in everything."

Prepare ahead, don't wait for a crisis.
[What would you do in case you became suddenly ill?] "Like I say, I push my button [special emergency device] and the ambulance will be here. You have to do those things. You have to prepare. In other words, don't wait until something happens. Be prepared for it, that's it. In case something happens, you know what to do."

Get involved and don't feel sorry for yourself.
"I'm kept pretty busy. I tell you that is the best thing to do. When you live alone, you don't [can't] feel sorry for yourself. Get involved. Now, I made four telephone calls this morning. Tomorrow, we're going to receive our commodities on the bus, us people that do not drive. I call these people up and tell them the bus is going to bring them home, and they can get their commodities on the bus."

Do unto others.
[Do you have friends in this community?] "Yes, you make friends and you keep 'em. Be nice to them. Be a good listener. I have one lady, I hate to talk to her because she interrupts you right away. You can't end a conversation. I said, 'Helen, will you give me a chance to finish what I was talkin'.' She said, 'Oh, I thought you'd finished.' I'm not a fast talker. As you can see, I'm calm. I'm not an excitable person. So that's the thing that you have to do in this world. You have to live with people. You can't live by yourself, you know what I mean? Like, treat people like the way you like to be treated, see. So that's my motto, and it's worked out pretty well, believe me."

Loss of Control

So far as Mrs. Farnsworth is concerned, responses on the survey showed that, already in 1987, she was very unhappy, concerned about her health, and feeling isolated in the community. This was prior to her husband's stroke and presumably prior to the development of his more severe behavior eccentricities. It was also prior to the two recent hip replacements that Mrs. Farnsworth claimed were causing her so much difficulty. Thus, her discouragement at that time cannot be seen as just a fleeting phenomenon, or as caused wholly by her predicament then. Her helplessness seems more the result of what Rossi (1980) has termed "subjective assessment of the lifescript." In other words, whether or not events are experienced as stressful is related to one's expectations and modes of interpreting the meaning of what happens in one's life (for further discussion, see chapter 8).

Support for this view is suggested by the fact that, unlike Mrs. Silvestri, Mrs. Farnsworth could think of no suggestions for successfully managing aging. She was so involved in her own affairs that she could not see beyond her personal experience to universalize the process of aging. Moreover, she was falling back on flight and dependency as solutions to her dilemmas. These are secondary and indirect approaches, not the sorts of strategies calculated to produce a lasting practical solution that would meet her husband's needs as well as her own. In short, she wanted simply to abandon her husband to his own devices and escape to her daughter's home, care, and attention. She claims that her daughter supports her hopes for a permanent separation.

"I'm going up for the winter to see what happens—to live with my oldest daughter. She's a widow. She'll be 61 tomorrow. She doesn't want me to [go] back [after the winter]. They won't have him. . . .They don't think he used me right since we've been married. He's spent my money. . . .He don't like it up there—it's too cold, but even if he went up there, they aren't going to take care of him when he's got four children to care for him. I can't bring him up there and force him on them.

She's got my, what she calls, 'my room.' It's not very big, but it's big enough for me. I don't have nothin' to do. She does my laundry. I go out on the porch and sit, and I come back and the laundry's folded on my bed. Tell the truth, I want to stay—I don't want to come back. . . . What I'd like him to do is to sell this place and go live with his daughter. She's got room for him. She only weighs about 300 pounds. She sits in a chair all day reading and watching television. She's never worked a day in her life. Her husband gets along with him better than any of the others.

At least at my daughter's, I'll have somebody to talk to—somebody to know I'm all right. No more lugging groceries and wash."

Orientations toward Aging and Receptivity to Help

If we cannot unravel the causal web of subjective orientations and the nature and sequence of life events for these two women, we can at least look at the consequences of their very different attitudes toward the practical matter of seeking outside help when they are overwhelmed by problems. Understanding the dynamics of help-seeking among older people is a crucial prerequisite to developing policies to assist them to remain in charge of their affairs as long as possible.

Mrs. Silvestri's positive orientations toward neighborliness, reciprocity, and responsibility for her own physical and mental welfare make her an ideal candidate for using the substantial resources for older people available in her community. She recognizes the potential vulnerability of an older women living alone and takes advantage of the senior citizens club and the free bus for many of her needs: companionship; entertainment; food subsidies; transportation to shopping, doctor's appointments, and the beauty parlor; and, in general, keeping in touch with people and the outside world. She stated:

> "Senior Citizens Center is beautiful . . . very, very nice. Anybody that doesn't come, its not the club's fault. It's your fault, if you don't come—it's true. I go five days a week. Don't become a hermit! I don't drive so I depend on the bus. The bus is free. You have to take care of your meal, and that's understandable, you know what I mean?
>
> We have five sites. And everybody has food home, right? But you don't have companionship, you don't have people to talk to. And that is what this place is for—it's for you to get out of the house and get with the people and talk with them. And that will make your day. When you come back, your house looks nicer because you've been away for a couple of hours, and that's it."

Mrs. Farnsworth's negative orientations, on the other hand—toward the neighbors, her husband, and her own capacity to negotiate the system make her an extremely poor candidate for using community resources creatively in her own behalf. She sees the senior citizens club as an uncongenial in-group, the free bus as irrevelant to her needs, and the service providers in the community as unsympathetic and not in her camp:

> "They won't give me any help. They wouldn't give me any after he came home. They said, 'He's well enough to do things.' People don't pay any attention.
>
> Senior citizens [club members] are all right if you happen to be one of their people, that they like you. They aren't crazy over him because he's deaf—so that lets us out."
>
> Then they talk about your senior citizens [club members]—when he was in the hospital, nobody came. Not one of them sent him a card or anything."
>
> It's harder to use the bus because you have to—I can't carry the groceries.
>
> I thought that he should have went there [to a nursing home] when

he went home from the hospital. I asked her [the social worker],
'What do you think?' She said, 'We'll see.' She came in one day when
I was with him and said, 'We're going to send him home. He's fine.'
Didn't have a leg under him. She called a couple of days later and
said, 'I think the best thing to do would be for you *both* to go to a
nursing home.' I wouldn't go to a nursing home down in this place. I
told her, too. But she just ignored me. It was my job, I know, to take
care of him—that's what she thought. I can't do it. . . . She said,
'What kind of help do you want?' 'I'd like to get help with laundry
and to get to the store to get groceries.' And she said, 'Who's been
doing it?' 'I have.' 'Then you do it.' "

From the partial evidence that we have, it seems likely that Mrs.
Farnsworth may always have been a less confident, less competent
person than Mrs. Silvestri. Certainly when I met her, she did not
appear to be trying actively to resolve the real difficulties she faced.
A set of interrelated problems—physical pain, incapacitating functional disabilities, a sick husband, a loveless marriage, and being
away from the place she considers home—had caught her in a vise
of misery and helplessness from which she was finding it impossible
to extricate herself. She was obviously at the breaking point—unable
(or unwilling) to seek and accept help to ease the routine activities
of life, and unable to carry on as she is. She had chosen escape as
the only way out, and to assuage her guilt, rationalized that her
husband would actually be better off for her absence:

"He seems to be better on his own when I'm not around. When he
goes out with me he gets lost.

He's so cross, and he swears. The worst words you've ever heard in
your life. . . . I still think he'll probably be better off by himself. Then
he can swear and curse and nobody'll hear him.

It makes me feel kinda funny leaving him. But I feel, why shouldn't
I? I couldn't get help at night if I needed it. He wouldn't pay any attention to me. I've tried it. I'm all alone. If I couldn't get to that
phone, I'm done for.

The doctor says, 'He's fine.' I don't know whether it's me. It's time
for me to try something else."

This leaves Mr. Farnsworth to fend for himself, or place himself
at the mercy of his children, who, according to Mrs. Farnsworth,
have ignored him except to try to take advantage of his stroke to
commandeer his few belongings for themselves and keep him from
leaving his modest assets to his wife.

IMPLICATIONS OF NARRATIVES

What does this comparison of the attitudes and circumstances of two older women, of similar age and living in the same community, contribute to the study of successful aging?

Focus on Concrete Activities

The stories show that, in essence, aging successfully involves effective management of the ordinary activities of daily life: doing the shopping and housework, keeping up contacts with relatives and friends, getting out and about, attending social functions, going to doctors' appointments, and so forth. These stories thus highlight the point that an understanding of successful aging starts with a search for explanations of the differences in the ways women in their late 70s and 80s manage day-to-day transactions with people and events in their lives.

Diversity of Circumstances

These stories furthermore underscore the extraordinary diversity between women in this age group in outlook, resources, and prospects. The fact of this diversity is particularly compelling in terms of these two women, since they are of identical age, have experienced the same duration of widowhood from their first husbands, and live in the same community. These similarities accentuate the major differences between them and emphasize another significant point, that is, the role of factors other than chronological age. These are the so-called "extrinsic factors" (Rowe and Kahn 1987:143–49) associated with differences in the experience of aging, such as life-style, composition of social networks, and environmental factors including quality of housing and residential amenities. These factors are independent of age in years, yet are highly significant in shaping the aging process.

Issues in Research on Aging

A third contribution of these stories is that they illustrate a number of important themes in current research on older people and their social support. One of these, which is now beginning to receive considerable attention in the literature, is the complex relationship between family networks and the quality of support that people have available to them in late life. The spate of studies from the late 1960s through the early 1980s, which debunked the myth of abandonment of the elderly by their children, may have fostered still another myth, namely, that the availability of children ipso facto is an asset in later life. As Mrs. Farnsworth's story clearly suggests, not all family relations are supportive or good for older people; some may in fact have negative effects on the capacity for independent activity (Wellman and Hall 1986).

In Mrs. Farnsworth's story, we see two families squaring off in a contest over material belongings, economic assets, responsibility for care of the infirm, and even national origins and traditions. The two old people appear caught in the middle—neither, because of severe functional handicaps, capable of really defending his or her interests. The sense of obligation of stepchildren to stepparents is also at issue here, an emerging concern that is connected with the increasing incidence of divorce and remarriage (Symer and Hofland 1982:61–77). Mrs. Farnsworth's experience suggests that couples who remarry in their late 70s may not have sufficient time to "earn" close relationships with their step-relatives, raising the point I made in the preface that changing family patterns over the last two decades are forcing us to rethink our traditional views of kinship (Riley 1983).

And what of the comparative advantages of living alone versus living with a spouse for aging successfully? The conventional wisdom is that marriage is the ideal condition for aging gracefully, an important reason being that married couples run the least risk of having to go into an institution. But "A Tale of Two Women" suggests that quality of marital relations in late life is also an important consideration. For the elderly, as for persons of any age, can we say that a bad marriage is less undesirable than living alone or living in an institution? Or is spousal support, regardless of the personal costs and quality of relationships, to be encouraged because people who are very old need the full-time, hands-on care that a husband or wife generally provides?

This chapter has focused on subjective dimensions of well-being as indicators of "success" in managing the aging process. However, by extending the scope from the 2 women to the entire 589 in the study, I will look, as well, at a variety of background characteristics that may be associated with a sense of well-being among women in this sample, such as size of birthplace, parents' occupation, education, employment history, husband's occupation, family size, and experience of the Great Depression. Moreover, since social support is important to a sense of well-being, and involves an ongoing exchange between at least two people, the characteristics of the people with whom these women have close personal ties can add another key dimension to understanding the factors associated with successful aging.

Finally, these stories raise questions concerning the responsibility of communities (as well as of individuals and families) to improve the quality of life of older people. Should Mrs. Farnsworth's predicament be seen as primarily a private matter in which the wider community has no concern and can play no remedial role? Is the fact that a situation as intolerable as hers could exist over an extended period of time, without community knowledge or intervention of some kind, an indictment of the way our system treats the aged? And should we as Americans expect more community involvement—for our parents and ourselves—in helping to civilize the later years?

Note

1. To protect the confidentiality and privacy of the women in this study, all the names and places used in this book are fictitious.

Chapter Two

IN SEARCH OF SUCCESSFUL AGING

The ideas are heterogeneity of older adults, modifiability of aging processes, and choices regarding alternatives in constructing the future of aging.

—George L. Maddox, "Aging Differently"

The search for successful aging, like that for eternal youth, has intrigued people throughout the ages. Indeed, in his old age, Cicero developed a set of rules for elderly men, detailing how to maintain fitness and social standing in ancient Roman society. Only in the past two decades, however, have social scientists conducted much formal research in this area. The relative immaturity of systematic inquiry in this field makes the current study of older women both an intellectual challenge and a research adventure.

The stories in chapter 1 launched this volume's search for relevant concepts and innovative approaches, illustrating in fine detail how two older women manage the ordinary activities of daily living and illuminating many basic features about what it means to age effectively. Of particular note in these stories is what they reveal about the characteristics of psychological well-being and the significance to older people of three key areas: a sense of control, social relationships, and the nature of the environmental setting. Research in these areas has figured prominently in previous efforts to identify the characteristics of successful aging. A review of this research enhances appreciation of the scope and complexity of the quest to understand the aging process, in general, and of the importance of the capacity to age successfully, in particular.

This chapter therefore reviews these previous studies of approaches to successful aging. There are two good reasons to follow chapter 1's description of concrete lives with a more general literature review: one is to draw upon the substantial insights of previous scholars, in order to identify any emerging consensus about the markers of successful aging; and the other is to highlight the importance of "the communal character of science" (Merton 1949:316). To understand a global phenomenon like aging successfully, one must become familiar with the accumulated knowledge of people working at different times and in different disciplines. Development of a common foundation of knowledge is what makes the pursuit of scientific understanding a "cooperative and cumulative" enterprise. Nowhere is this more fundamental than in developing our knowledge about what matters in leading constructive and satisfying lives in old age. It is an issue in which all of us—as children, parents, and individuals who are aging ourselves—have a crucial stake.

AGING AND "SUCCESSFUL AGING"

Over the last three decades, a vast literature has accumulated on aging as a social process. Researchers have increasingly drawn attention to the intricacy of the process, and to the fact that the study of aging involves complex interconnections between phenomena in different fields—for instance, biology, psychology, and history (Riley, Abeles, and Teitelbaum 1982). One result of this expanding interdisciplinary focus is the availability of a rich and fascinating body of research on a wide variety of aspects of aging.[1]

Research on the narrower question of how to age successfully is much less abundant. In fact, applying the term *success* to the phenomenon of aging is a relatively recent convention. The idea of identifying the "markers of successful aging" as an important research goal was first widely popularized in the United States at the 1986 Annual Scientific Meeting of the Gerontological Society of America. Two major characteristics of the idea of *success* make the concept difficult to subject to scientific scrutiny: first, by its nature, *success* is highly subjective and colored by individual values and cultural prescriptions; and second, interest in *successful aging* implies concern with the applied aspects of research, as well as belief in the reform of the social process. Many social scientists have been slow to regard aging in these terms, but interest in these aspects is rapidly increasing.

Thus, in his 1987 presidential address, "Aging Differently," George Maddox challenged his colleagues in the Gerontological Society of

America not only to undertake the task of accounting for the marked differences between individuals in the older population but also to commit themselves to exploring how their research and training could influence the political process and lead to an improvement in quality of life for older people. According to Maddox, the diversity observed among older people provides both the key to understanding the aging process and the impetus for reallocating resources to shape a better future for the aged. "Heterogeneity," Maddox argued, "constitutes prime evidence of the modifiability of aging processes and hence the potential for intentional modification of these processes."

SUBJECTIVE DIMENSION OF "SUCCESS"

Another major shift in orientation toward the study of aging has involved the recognition of the importance of subjective attitudes. The dependence of the concept of *success* on individual and cultural values has meant that much of the research on successful aging has been concerned with "a sense of well-being." After ignoring for a long time the place of "subjective" data in sociological and epidemiological studies, researchers are now turning to such data to answer many questions about human health and well-being. A recent example is Leonard Sagan's provocative book, *The Health of Nations* (1987). An epidemiologist, Sagan is among a growing number of medical practitioners and researchers arguing that "health" should be regarded as something more than a "diagnosis by exclusion," that is, as more than simply the absence of disease. Also essential to health, Sagan concludes, is "a sense of subjective well-being, happiness, joy or exuberance." To emphasize this point, he has observed (1987:8): "Presumably judgments of 'well-being' are subjective judgments of the individuals themselves. If this is the case, how do we identify persons with good health other than by asking them?" Indeed, the rationale for beginning the search for successful aging with the testiments of individuals such as Mrs. Silvestri and Mrs. Farnsworth (see chapter 1) is that these accounts reveal important and authentic insights about aging as seen through the eyes of the persons most affected.[2]

HEALTH AND AGING SUCCESSFULLY

Of all the conditions studied in connection with aging successfully, human wellness, broadly defined, is the criterion most generally agreed upon. Many of the women in this study would concur. "There's no secret to it, as long as you keep healthy," said Mrs. Silvestri, and she described in detail how one should follow the doctor's orders fully, while making sure one understands the reasons for them. Although Mrs. Farnsworth dodged the question about successful aging, her story clearly shows that she, too, regarded good health as a fundamental condition to getting along in old age. Her ongoing battle with the disabling consequences of illness, both her own and her husband's, colored every aspect of her daily struggle to exist.

In 1958, the World Health Organization (WHO) defined health as "a state of complete physical, mental, and social wellbeing and not simply the absence of disease or infirmity" (WHO, 1958). This definition comes very close to the way many people might perceive successful aging. But as a guide to understanding effectiveness in later life, it stops short of suggesting how well-being is generated over the life course, or of indicating what personal and social conditions are associated with the notion of success. Besides, "wellness" is, itself, a complex phenomenon, and there are many different ideas about its chief components.

Mrs. Silvestri, for example, understands well that good health is only one—albeit a basic—building block of successful aging. Another block is having sufficient money (of course, Mrs. Silvestri's own satisfaction with a very modest income emphasizes that "sufficient money" is a subjective assessment, born of personal attitudes and behavior regarding money). She offers the prescription: "Never pray for money. If you are healthy you can always make money," and makes a point of saying that she has her Social Security check put directly into the bank—"That way you don't have to worry, see?" Still another building block, she stresses with reference to her own experience, is involving oneself with others, and not dwelling on one's aches and pains and fears about the morrow. In sharp contrast, Mrs. Farnsworth commenced our interview by cataloguing her health woes.

The remainder of this chapter describes landmark studies relating to the dynamics of successful aging. This review should enable us to go beyond traditional definitions of "wellness" to a view of the kindred, but quite distinct, phenomenon of aging effectively.

The studies discussed here are outlined in table 2.1. and are grouped under three main headings: (1) developmental perspectives and psychological well-being, (2) psychosocial factors contributing to health and longevity, and (3) environmental perspectives: physical and social setting. The three headings reflect different levels of focus—from a concern with individual development and well-being, to factors influencing the behavior of groups, to the consequences of the physical and social environment for achieving well-being. First, I describe the contributions of each of these main strands of thought to a theory of successful aging. Then, referring back to Mrs. Silvestri's and Mrs. Farnsworth's stories, I illustrate how these ideas apply to the women in this study. This highlighting of concepts by means of personal experience lays the groundwork for many of the key themes to be explored in this search for successful aging.

DEVELOPMENTAL PERSPECTIVES AND PSYCHOLOGICAL WELL-BEING

Two developmental psychologists, Erik Erikson and Abraham Maslow, made giant strides in increasing understanding of healthy human beings.[3] Each took as his central interest the development of the individual over the life course. Each explored the characteristics of strong, psychologically healthy people, rather than focusing on the ill and maladjusted. Each described the building of a strong personality in incremental terms, maintaining that what happens late in life is linked inextricably to individual development in the earlier stages. In their emphasis on how psychological strengths develop throughout life, Erikson and Maslow anticipated a number of prominent research interests in aging today: for example, the impact on aging of social structure and social change over the life course (Riley, Abeles, and Teitelbaum 1982), the focus of attention on fit as well as frail older people (Rowe and Kahn 1987), and the contribution of psychosocial factors to health and longevity (House, Landis, and Umberson 1988; Rodin 1986).

In *The Life Cycle Completed*, Erikson (1982) integrated his life's work on the major stages in psychosocial development. He began the discussion with his views on the desirable qualities associated with *old age*. Starting with the ultimate stage is appropriate, Erikson

Table 2.1 SELECTED APPROACHES TO SUCCESSFUL AGING: A REVIEW OF STUDIES IN CHAPTER 2

Category of Approach	Date of Cited Work	Desired Goals	Markers of Successful Aging
1. Developmental Perspectives and Psychological Well-being			
E. H. Erikson	1951 1982	Psychological strengths	Wisdom Generativity Integrity
A. H. Maslow	1962 1971	Self-actualization	Dedication Commitment Honesty Acceptance of self Trust in others Hardworking Concern for others Interest in self-growth Joy in life Capacity to universalize
J. L. Esposito	1987	Social respect High Status Productive place	Dignity Self-worth Sense of meaningful place
2. Psychosocial Factors Contributing to Health and Longevity			
G. L. Maddox	1987	Health and longevity Equitable access to social resources	Optimism about health Active social involvement More equitable life conditions for older people
J. W. Rowe and R. L. Kahn	1987	Health and longevity Extension of functional capacity	Management of daily activities Physical and mental well-being Independence
B.J. Langer and J. Rodin	1976 1986	Self-determination Control of important life events	Physical and mental well-being Life satisfaction Independence
J. S. House et al.	1988	Health and longevity Social support Supportive social relationships	Physical and mental well-being Friendship networks Social interaction, not social isolation

continued

Table 2.1 SELECTED APPROACHES TO SUCCESSFUL AGING: A REVIEW OF
STUDIES IN CHAPTER 2 (*continued*)

Category of Approach	Date of Cited Work	Desired Goals	Markers of Successful Aging
3. Environmental Perspectives: Physical and Social Setting			
S. Benet	1974	Social integration	Long life Psychological well-being
		Respect for the elderly	Continuity between roles over life course Trust
		Intergenerational cooperation	
M. P. Lawton and S. L. Hoover	1981	Match between needs and capacities	Health and longevity Life satisfaction
V. Regnier	1981		Independent management of daily activities
		Supportive person—environment service system	
		Access to community facilities	

claimed, because each of the eight stages he identified—1, "Infancy";
2, "Early Childhood"; 3, "Play Age"; 4, "School Age"; 5, "Adoles-
cence"; 6, "Young Adulthood"; 7, "Adulthood"; and, finally, 8, "Old
Age,"—is grounded in all the earlier ones. Thus, *wisdom*, the crowning quality of old age, and defined by Erikson as a kind of "informed
and detached concern with life itself in the face of death itself (p.
61)," depends for its achievement on the individual's capacity to
attain mature development in each of the other seven stages. Erikson
believed that the capacity to achieve *wisdom* is closely tied to the
capacity for "*generativity*", which he defined as the crowning quality
associated with the previous stage, "Adulthood." Interviews with
the women in this book's study (see chapter 8) confirmed the importance of achieving wisdom as described by Erikson.

Generativity also emerges in this volume's study as a significant
aspect of aging effectively. Erikson saw this quality as relating to
caring and caregiving, and defined it in broad terms such as "to be
care-ful," "to take care of," and "to care for." By stressing the capacity
to care for others, Erikson was one of the early writers to recognize

the importance to older people of interdependence and of maintaining close ties with family and friends. "For there can be little doubt," he explained (1982:63), "that today the discontinuity of family life as a result of dis-location contributes greatly to the lack in old age of that minimum of vital involvement that is necessary for staying really alive." Thus, Erikson saw a connection between individuals' ability to care for others and the quality of his or her family relationships. Family ties, in turn, he felt, were a crucial bridge between an older person and the outside world. The capacity to genuinely care for others was, therefore, seen as a key element in the development of *wisdom*, and that detachment about one's own mortality that Erikson believed was essential to dealing effectively with the transitions of later life.

Maslow emphasized a different, and yet somewhat similar, concept of "success"—the capacity to be "self-actualizing." He described self-actualization as a sense of infinite extension, of "individuality freed of isolation" (1971:xvi). His research is relevant to the themes of this book for three reasons: (1) he focused on the attributes of pscyhological success over the entire life cycle, (2) he reached many of the same conclusions about psychological well-being as does Erikson, and (3) he intimately examined the conditions that must be met to engender a profound sense of well-being.

For his study of "extension," Maslow wrote (1971:43) that he purposely selected "older people—people who had lived much of their lives out and were visibly successful." Like Erikson, Maslow viewed psychological well-being in terms of the individual developing and changing throughout life. Thus, he saw self-actualization as an incremental, ongoing process, not something achieved by grace, as it were, overnight, but a state that had to be earned. "Self-actualization," said Maslow (1971:45), "is a matter of degree, of little accessions accumulated one by one." And, life is "a process of choices, one after another." At each deciding point, there is the possibility of making a "progression choice" or a "regression choice." "To make the growth choice instead of the fear choice a dozen times a day is to move a dozen times a day toward self-actualization."

Affirmation of self is clearly a core characteristic of people with the capacity that Maslow defined as self-actualization:

> They listen to their own voices; they take responsibility; they are
> honest; and they work hard. They find out who they are and what
> they are, not only in terms of their mission in life, but also in terms
> of the way their feet hurt when they wear such and such a pair of
> shoes and whether they do or do not like eggplant or stay up all night

if they drink too much beer. All this is what the real self means. They find their own biological natures, their congenital natures, which are irreversible or difficult to change. (1971:50)

Maslow was sensitive to the fact that his selection of healthy individuals might expose his work to criticism of bias. When your research subjects are strong, creative people, he conceded (1971:43), "you get a different view of mankind." Nevertheless, his commitment to the study of wellness rather than pathology is advocated by researchers on aging today. Morever, in two other important respects, his work foreshadowed current research directions: he undertook to develop a typology to describe the characteristics of self-actualizing people, and he acknowledged the likelihood that there were differences between men and women in the pathways to psychological well-being.

Like other such typologies being compiled today, Maslow's set of preconditions for the self-actualizing person is a composite of biological, psychological, and social factors: "a) that he be sufficiently free of illness, b) that he be sufficiently gratified in his basic needs and c) that he be positively using his capacities, but also d) that he be motivated by some values which he strives for or gropes for and to which he is loyal" (1971:315).

Similar criteria—that is, good health, basic security, meaningful activity, and commitment to a larger cause—can be found in many current profiles of successful older people (Sagan 1987:187). Among these conditions, Maslow emphasized particularly the importance of the last, that is, the ability to see beyond the confines of one's own personal space. "In examining self-actualizing people directly," he observed (1971:315), "I find that in all cases, at least in our culture, they are dedicated people, devoted to some task 'outside themselves,' some vocation or duty or beloved job."

Lastly, of particular interest in a study of older women, is Maslow's contention that devotion to a task outside themselves holds true for women as well as men, "even though in a different sense." For women who are working full-time as wives and mothers, Maslow speculated that there may be more variety in the sorts of experiences that are self-actualizing. And, for those women who combine family and professional roles, self-actualization may be found in "a dedication to something perceived simultaneously, both as beloved and also as important and worthwhile doing."

In what seems almost a note of surprise, Maslow concluded (1971:316) that a woman may achieve self-actualization "even in having a baby, all by itself, at least for a time." But, he demurs,

"However, I should say that I feel less confident in speaking of self-actualization in women." In this aspect, he is more candid than many scholars who have based their conclusions about the behavior of young and old people primarily on observations of men.

Life-Course Approaches to Aging

Over the three decades since Erikson and Maslow first explored human development and well-being from youth to old age, the life-course approach has become a major framework in the study of aging. The spate of journal articles and books in the 1980s devoted to life-span development, in fact, may be seen as a virtual "reformulation" of ideas about the aging process (Henricks 1987:94). As part of this extensive reconstruction of methods of viewing social history, life-course theorists are integrating the perspectives of many disciplines. No longer is the study of life span an interest mainly of developmental psychologists. Instead, scholars from many disciplines, such as sociology, history, and economics, are recasting their work in life-course terms.

Philosophers, too, are adopting a developmental framework to study the existential status of old people. An interesting recent example is Joseph Esposito's, *The Obsolete Self: Philosophical Dimensions of Aging* (1987:216). "Most afflictions of aging," he wrote, "result from specific life circumstances—the lives individuals have led, their psychic temperament, working conditions, use of leisure time, interpersonal relations, etc." "Aging," he says, "even from a strictly biological point of view, does not happen automatically or inevitably but relates to the way organisms live from moment to moment."

Esposito traces the development of theories and perspectives that have shaped the ways American society views its burgeoning population of old people. In American attitudes toward death, he sees a cultural negation of old age itself: "Our notion of death as premature is not a medical notion but a psychological one. The young are said to die prematurely because they have so much left to do; the old die in their time because they have ceased to matter to society" (1987:50).

Erikson and Maslow almost certainly would have found this philosophical interpretation of "the obsolete self" congenial. As with Esposito, their ultimate concern was with how individuals develop psychological strengths that enable them to transcend the shocks of life to realize their identity and come to terms positively with "the afflictions of aging." Given the austerity and economic hardship that many old people face today (Dunbar 1988), an emphasis on wisdom and the capacity for self-actualization may seem altogether too metaphysical to be taken seriously as practical strategies for aging well. But for frail old people who live alone and confront each day the stark reality of a circumscribed and finite future, the capacity to transcend one's particular circumstances may well be one essential component of a sense of well-being.

In Esposito's view (1987:5), no less than such a transcendence (on the part of both the aged themselves and society as a whole) is necessary if we are to engender a new attitude about the "dignity of ageness" and provide an antidote to the "social extinction" and "obsolescence of self" that appear to be widespread among older Americans.

Life Stories and Psychological Well-being

Illustrations of the qualities of psychological strengths abound in the stories of Mrs. Silvestri and Mrs. Farnsworth. From Mrs. Silvestri's responses to the 1987 survey, I anticipated that she would answer Maslow's description of a healthy, creative, self-actualizing individual. In person she seemed, if anything, more remarkable than she appeared on paper: trustful, calm, intelligent, interested in people and things outside herself. Her small, crowded cottage bore witness to her many hobbies and enthusiasms. In everything she said, she indicated that she was a "yea-sayer" rather than a "nay-sayer," life-positive, rather than life-negative, "eager for life rather than nauseated or irritated by it" (Maslow 1971:281). Her anecdotes about all aspects of her life—diet, favorite recipes, exercise, family ties, friendships, relationships with doctors, club activities—reveal a capacity to universalize her experience and to put her intelligence to work to grow and develop as a human being. In short, her outlook and life-style fit precisely Maslow's description, just cited (1971:50), of the myriad small ways in which healthy people go about achieving self-actualization. She listens to her own voice. She wants to live in her own cottage in the country, and she knows that her diet should include one banana a day.

It would be too neat to say that Mrs. Farnsworth is a complete opposite of her neighbor—that she is as unrelievedly negative as Mrs. Silvestri is totally positive. In fact this is not so. Mrs. Farnsworth talks about her life in positive as well as negative terms. She is clearly very fond of her natural children and grandchildren, wanting above all to return to her home state where she can be near them. She invited me, a stranger, into her house, and confided her troubles to me with a sense of dignity, if with little joy. Her catalog of complaints do, however, reveal the ascendance of negative orientations in what Erikson (1951:232) termed the dominant antithesis in old age, "integrity versus despair." Unlike Mrs. Silvestri, she regards the past with a sense of regret and disgust, unable to accept, her "one and only life cycle," as Erikson prescribed, "as something that had to be and that by necessity permitted of no substitution (232)." In many respects, Mrs. Farnsworth's description of her feelings matches Erikson's devastating portrait of some of the older people who visited his clinic. They seemed, he observed, "to be mourning not only for time forfeited and space depleted but also. . . . for autonomy weakened, initiative lost, intimacy missed, generativity neglected—not to speak of identity potentials by-passed or, indeed, an all too limiting identity lived."

Finally, Mrs. Farnsworth's remarriage and move away from her family and roots to an unfamiliar community can clearly be seen to have contributed to her sense of "dis-location." By her own admission, she lacks that sense of vital involvement that Erikson maintained is "necessary for staying really alive." Mrs. Farnsworth's description of the lack of involvement in her life with Mr. Farnsworth echoes these feelings of "not staying really alive": "I'd lay there dead for a day or two before he'd come to. I can't live like that!" Her plan to flee to her daughter's home can, in fact, be seen as a life-affirming gesture, a strong will to survive and to not have her Self annihilated by social isolation and indifference to her pain.

PSYCHOSOCIAL FACTORS CONTRIBUTING TO HEALTH AND LONGEVITY

Issac Newton is said to have attributed his scientific vision to "standing on the shoulders of giants." In their contribution to understanding the bases of psychological well-being, Erikson and Maslow were such giants. But granting the importance of their research in this area, are we to assume that a sense of well-being, subjectively defined, is all that counts in the definition of successful aging, or should we aim for a broader perspective, one that includes the presence or absence of disease conditions, objectively defined, or, as Esposito's work suggests, one that also takes into account social attitudes as powerful influences on the context in which aging occurs? How do we move beyond aging as an individual process to encompass broader social issues? Why, for example, does one person get sick instead of another, or why are rates of disease higher in one group than in another (Syme 1988:9)?

These types of questions are being raised by physicians and public health professionals in their desire to understand the bases of successful aging, not just among individual older people but among different social groups and whole societies. This approach is crucial to our study of aging among older women, because it emphasizes that effective aging is shaped not just by individual attributes but also by the characteristics of the social and environmental setting in which people are born, grow up, raise families, work, and eventually retire.

In the 1980s, research in gerontology has produced a number of provocative new approaches. In terms of our study of older women, the most useful of these are the distinction between "usual" (or "normal") and successful aging, and the identification of control and social relationships as crucial influences on older people's physical and mental well-being.

Usual versus Successful Aging

In their seminal article, "Human Aging: Usual and Successful," Rowe and Kahn (1987), two physicians who challenged conventional approaches to aging, proposed a radical new way of looking at the older population. They argued that traditional perspectives have two significant flaws: first, they emphasize losses and ignore gains; and second, they focus on broad age groups (e.g., 65 years of age and older), ignoring the substantial differences between older people of approximately the same chronological age. According to Rowe and Kahn (1987), the outlooks on aging that are associated with both these flaws are by the same token defective. An emphasis on losses tends to attribute illness and frailty among older people to age-related causes, exaggerating the effects of the aging process itself and underrating the moderating effects of influences that are independent of age, such as diet, exercise, personal habits, and psychosocial factors. At the same time, focusing on differences between broad age groups, such as youth, middle age, young-old, and old-old, fosters a concentration on similarities rather than differences between older people, and leads to the implication that all individuals within these broad age categories tend to have the same characteristics.

The essence of Rowe and Kahn's plea for a new look is that traditional approaches have masked two significant aspects of aging:

first, the role of "extrinsic" or non-age-related factors in the quality of the aging experience; and, second, the substantial diversity among individuals of the same chronological age. The authors fear, moreover, that the impact of conventional approaches goes beyond encouraging a narrow, and quite possibly invalid, view of the reality of aging—which is bad enough. Scientific theory and policy interventions, they feel, are distorted as well. Thus, an emphasis on age-related conditions and homogeneity fosters stereotypes about what is "normal." The idea of normality implies harmlessness or lack of risk, and suggests that what is normal is somehow natural "and therefore is or should be beyond purposeful modification" (Rowe and Kahn 1987:143). In short, say these authors, "the emphasis on 'normal' aging focuses attention on learning what most older people do and do not do; what physiologic and psychologic states are typical. It tends to create the gerontology of the usual" (1987:143).

To place the field of gerontology on a more constructive footing, Rowe and Kahn (1987:148) urged researchers to pursue four major directions in the study of aging, including: (1) focusing on the diversity among older people and emphasizing the gains as well as the losses in the way people function in later life; (2) investigating factors that underlie major changes in the functioning of older people, especially those factors that result in improvement in physical and mental fitness; (3) studying factors that contribute to successful aging, in combination, not just as separate influences; and (4) emphasizing research that bridges different disciplines—for example, the mechanisms by which subjective perceptions of well-being are linked to physiological health and longevity.

"Control" as a Factor in Well-being

Rowe and Kahn's persuasive case for distinguishing between usual and successful aging is based to an important extent on research that examines the relation between psychosocial factors and stress and resistance to disease. Over the past two decades, research on two factors, in particular, control (or autonomy) and social support (or social connectedness), has profoundly influenced gerontologists' perceptions about the conditions that promote successful aging. Studies of control have gone under the guise of many different names. Some of the multiple clones of the control concept are: "mastery," "self-efficacy," "locus of control," "learned helplessness," "controllability," "predictability," "desire for control," "sense of control," "powerlessness," "hardiness," "competence," and so on (Syme 1988:5).

The concept of control has attracted the attention of dozens of scholars. For many, it seems to have great potential for bridging the findings of social science, medicine, and physiology. For example, Leonard Syme (1988:5), who now conducts epidemiological research on illness and longevity, started his professional career as a sociologist. He turned to psychosocial factors, such as autonomy and control, when he became interested in epidemiology in the hope of extending his understanding of the causes of disease: "I come to the study of concepts such as control and self-directedness not because I am interested in them per se but because I have been *driven* to them in order to explain disease patterns that are otherwise to me inexplicable."

Syme (1988:18) wrote that he found the concept of control particularly useful in integrating diverse findings from a large body of research—for example, the higher rates of disease found among people "who have poor social support, who have been mobile, who have had stressful life events, who are in jobs with little latitude and little room for discretion, who are in lower-economic positions and who exhibit Type A behavior."

To the layperson, the link between control and wellness may seem obvious. If people can have a meaningful influence on experiences in their lives such as moving residence or stressful job situations, one would expect that the likelihood of their becoming ill as a result of such potentially disruptive events would be lessened. In fact, research on relocation (Krantz and Schulz 1980; Langer and Rodin 1976; Syme 1988:6), for example, has shown that if older people can be involved in the decision making about when and where to move or about various aspects of their living arrangements, the disruptive consequences of changing residence in terms of illness and death are less pronounced.

However, the connections between a sense of control and health are not as clear-cut as they seem. Much research in this area has been cross-sectional and based on self-reports, thus opening the question of causal priority: Does a sense of control protect people from becoming ill? Or do people who are ill have less of a sense of control and reduced capacity to engage in decisions that affect their lives? Among a small number of researchers in the 1970s who tried to settle the question of causal sequence, Judith Rodin has pioneered in running controlled field experiments that studied the *prospective* effects of increasing the control that individuals exert over their daily lives. She designed controlled experiments in which groups of old people were placed in situations where they exercised different amounts of control over their care and living arrangements. Then the effects of the control factor were estimated by tracing changes in the morale and physical functioning of these groups over a period of months.

In one of the first of such experiments, Langer and Rodin (1976) conducted a study of old people in a nursing home in which residents were exposed to different levels of decision making and self-help: on one floor, staff gave a talk about decisions residents could and should make for themselves; on another floor, staff emphasized all the matters that residents should expect to have personnel do for them. Interviews conducted three weeks after the experiment showed that, according to their own reports, residents who were encouraged to make decisions for themselves said that they were happier and more active than did the control group. Nurses reported that the group who were encouraged to do things for themselves participated more actively in social activities and made more improvement than did those who were told everything would be done for them. These changes and the differences between the two groups persisted over an 18-month period.

Experiments in nursing homes and residential accommodations conducted subsequently (Rowe and Kahn 1987) have demonstrated that ("control-enhancing") approaches that encourage old people to take charge of their affairs tend to contribute to health improvement. In contrast, ("control-reducing") approaches that discourage discretion and self-help tend to result in a deterioration in well-being. Such studies suggest that direct assistance, which is the approach caregivers often take in responding to old people's needs, can be counterproductive and foster a downward cycle of learned helplessness, apathy, depression, and withdrawal. There are, however, exceptions. Some older people do better with firm guidance in decision making.[4]

Social Relationships and Health

Another strand of research on psychosocial factors has been concerned directly with the consequences of social support for health. Studies of social support, like those exploring the role of autonomy and control, have undergone exponential growth since the early 1970s. Among the many individuals who have conducted research on this topic, James House and his colleagues at the Institute for Social Research, University of Michigan, are particularly noted for developing the theory that social support contributes to the "quantity as well as to the quality of life." In other words, they believe that the support provided by human contact not only makes life more pleasant and rewarding, but it can also actually increase one's life expectation. In order to encompass the entire range of interpersonal relations that might affect health and well-being, House (1981) defined social support broadly as "the flow between people of emotional concern, instrumental aid, information, or appraisal."

Research on social relationships and health should not be confused with quite a different body of research on older people and their family support. For the last two decades, a large number of studies have examined the relations between the aged and their systems of social support.[5] This research has focused, in particular, on the characteristics of family networks in later life and the contribution family members make to the provision of care to frail older relatives. Concern about the implications of increased longevity for support of the very old has led to an interest in the changing relationships between adult children and aging parents. Such studies have contributed substantially to dispelling myths about the condition of older people in modern industrial societies, such as that the frail elderly are abandoned by their children and that a high proportion of the aged are locked away in nursing homes. However, research in this category has focused mainly on description and analysis of observed patterns of support, and has not concerned itself directly with the implications of social support for successful aging—that is, for the health or quality of life of older people.

Over the last decade, perspectives on social support and aging have undergone a major transformation. As exemplified by House's (1988) approach, the focus has shifted from an interest in "support," viewed in terms of the flow of care or exchange of moral and practical help between the elderly and their social networks, to the impact of social relationships as such (that is, as distinct from their supportive qualities) on the well-being of older people. Gerontologists and epidemiologists are trying to determine what actually happens to the functioning of older people when they are connected with others or, alternatively, deprived of social intercourse. In particular, the emphasis has been on how social relationships affect the experience of stress among people in different age groups and living in different social and environmental conditions.

In a recent article in *Science*, House and his research team (House et al. 1988) described changes in perspectives on social relationships and health that are as far-reaching in their implications for policy on aging as is the distinction between usual and successful aging (Rowe and Kahn 1987). House and colleagues wrote that, up to the

late 1970s, researchers mainly emphasized the role of social relationships "in moderating or buffering potentially deleterious health
effects of psychosocial stress or other health hazards." However,
since most studies at that time were cross-sectional and retrospective—as noted in the case of studies of autonomy and control—
scientists were concerned about how to interpret the causal priorities
and how to explain the observed associations. For example, what
accounts for the findings that—age for age—death rates are consistently higher among the unmarried than the married, or that unmarried and more socially isolated people have higher rates of
disorders, such as tuberculosis, accidents, and psychiatric disorders?
Are the effects of social relationships on health indirect, operating,
for example, through the promotion of habits, attitudes, or activities
that might lead to an improvement in health, such as proper sleep,
diet, exercise, moderate use of drugs, or seeking appropriate medical
care? Up to now, this has been thought to be the case. Or are the
effects direct, operating through some quality of interpersonal relationships or meaning to the individuals involved? This is the new
approach suggested by House.

Such questions have spurred two kinds of extensive research on
social relationships and health in the 1980s: prospective studies in
human populations; and laboratory and field experimental studies
of animals and humans. According to House et al. (1988:544), these
studies have now produced sufficient empirical evidence to enable
social scientists to state categorically that "social relationships have
a predictive, arguably causal, association with health in their own
right." In fact, they claim that the strength of the evidence on social
relationships and health approximates that adduced in the 1964 Surgeon General's report [U.S. Surgeon General's Advisory Committee
on Smoking and Health, Smoking and Health (U.S. Public Health
Service, Washington, DC, 1964)] establishing cigarette smoking as a
cause or risk factor for death and illness from a number of specific
diseases.

In short, the evidence is compelling that social relationships have
generally beneficial effects on health, not solely or even primarily,
attributable to the role they play in alleviating stress or in helping
older people to deal with their anxieties and fears.

If this remarkable conclusion is confirmed by subsequent research,
clearly the implications for the health and well-being of the aged are
enormous. What House has claimed in Science (1988) is that the
mere presence of, or sense of relatedness with, another individual
may have biological consequences that are beneficial to health and

that operate independently of supportive actions, such as, giving information about health services or encouraging behavior that is conducive to health. This claim underlines the key importance of social relationships to old people, and highlights many current concerns about demographic trends that may errode the sources of informal support in later life: the growing incidence of widowhood, the increasing number and proportion of very old women living alone, and the decline in family size, leading to a diminishing ratio of children to parents (Day 1985b).

Life Stories: Control and a Sense of Connectedness

Mrs. Silvestri's and Mrs. Farnsworth's stories present marked differences in terms of the qualities of control and a sense of connectedness. But again, as with psychological strengths, the contrast is not completely black and white. Mrs. Silvestri not only has a sense of being in full control of her life, but she revels in it. She says explicitly that she wants to maintain a separate residence to retain determination of her own affairs. She perceives herself as "controlling" the doctor, her children, her neighbors, and so forth, that is, she organizes her relationships to monitor the outcomes. At the same time, she has the wisdom and common sense to know that reciprocity (generativity) is essential to maintaining goodwill and good relationships: "It works both ways"; "Be a good listener"; "Treat people like the way you like to be treated"; "One quart [of strawberries] for the lady that picks me up for church." Although she resists her children's offers to come and live with them, she appreciates their concern and the knowledge that they are there as a source of help if she should need them. She keeps in close touch with them by telephone, makes annual visits, and provides advice whenever her opinion is solicited.

Mrs. Farnsworth, on the other hand, perceives herself as out of control in relation to her husband, her stepchildren, and the community workers with whom she comes into contact. The decision, when she was in her mid-70s, to marry Mr. Farnsworth set off a train of events over which she believes she has little mastery. A crucial event heightening her sense of impotence was the move away from her family and birthplace and relocation to a new and unfamiliar community. In that move, she feels she has lost the emotional and instrumental support of close family members. "My children and everything is all up there," she says. She herself sees this loss as damaging to both her mental and physical health.

The contrast with Mrs. Silvestri, however, is not as stark as it might be, for two reasons: first, as noted earlier, Mrs. Farnsworth has not totally abdicated her power to make decisions; that is, she has decided firmly that she will leave Mr. Farnsworth and return "home" to live with her daughter. Second, she still has the support of her family, albeit at some geographical remove. Thus, she is not totally isolated or lacking in a strong foundation of social relationships. Mrs. Farnsworth designated her daughter as the person most responsible for providing her with practical help and support. In an interview conducted in the 1987 survey with the daughter, as the person Mrs. Farnsworth designated as most responsible for her support (see chapter 3), it was clear that the daughter has a good relationship with her mother and would like to do what she can to alleviate her distress, including welcoming her to come live with her.

Although with only these data to go on, one cannot draw conclusions about the temporal priorities concerning the onset of Mrs. Farnsworth's poor health and her sense of loss of control, one can note that she believes, herself, that her pain will lessen when she is back in the healing ambit of family and neighborhood support: "It takes my mind off my leg, you know. She [the daughter] seems to think it'll be better when I get up there."

This association of a protective environment with improvement in health illustrates the point made earlier (Rodin 1986, see also note 4 to this chapter) that, in some cases, older people do better when they are relieved of responsibility for managing their own lives. They may choose not to exercise control, and opt for a certain amount of dependence on others in preference to unsupported autonomy and self-determination.

ENVIRONMENTAL PERSPECTIVES: PHYSICAL AND SOCIAL SETTING

In the wake of new evidence about the beneficial nature of social relationships for health, a new conviction is emerging that the well-being of the aged may hinge on modification of the broader social and environmental setting. If wellness and long life are to be seen as basic criteria of successful aging, a key question for social policy is how to build physical and social settings that reduce social isolation and foster supportive social relationships. Indeed, House and colleagues (1988:543) maintain that a vital area for future investigation will be "the means to lower the prevalence of relative social isolation in the population or to lessen its deleterious effects on health." We must assess, they say, the consequences for social support of the elderly of demographic and social trends, such as family breakup and reconstitution, increasing widowhood, long periods of living alone, and the reduction through low fertility of the numbers of children potentially available to care for older, dependent parents. Otherwise, these researchers warn, the positive effects for well-being of behavior beneficial to health, such as the decline in smoking and a rising concern for physical fitness, may be neutralized by the negative effects for health of increasing social isolation and diminishing opportunities for close interpersonal ties.

Anthropological Perspectives

The impact of the broad social environment on aging is illustrated by anthropologist Sula Benet's (1974) study of the long-lived Abkhasian people of the Caucasus. The focus there was on the social structure that contributes to producing an unusual number of centenarians, specifically, conditions that maximize continuity between the generations and the predictability of individual and group behavior (Benet 1974:103). Together these conditions encourage continuity in activities throughout the life cycle and the "integration of the aged into the extended family and community life as fully functioning members in work, decision making, and recreation."

Significantly, the traits Benet used to describe Abkhasian social structure conform closely to the psychosocial factors that epidemiologists cited earlier in this review identified as predictors of lower rates of illness and death. Among the most important of these are a low level of geographic mobility and continuity of experience between the generations, both of which minimize the loss of social ties over a person's lifetime. At the time of Benet's study, the Abkhasians had been shielded from the disrupting effects of rapid social change. Close bonds between the generations were maintained by sharing a common tradition of knowledge about the world, as well as common standards of ethics and morality. The sense of discontinuity over time was lessened by the gradual assumption of adult responsibilities and the avoidance of sudden transitions between the status of child and parent (Benet 1974:107).

Finally, according to Benet, Abkhasian society avoids "the obsolete self," the condition identified by Esposito (1987) as a prominent feature of older Americans. Social isolation of aged individuals among Abkhasians was apparently unknown. Older people had a respected position that guaranteed them a wide participation in family and social activities. The reports of travelers and foreign visitors, observed Benet, all noted the Abkhasians' high level of self-esteem, and, at the same time, respect for others. These are the very traits that Erikson (1982) and Maslow (1971) identified as instrumental in the development of successful older adults. If Benet, because she was an outsider and not a native speaker of the Abkhasian language, may have exaggerated the cohesiveness of Abkhasian society, at the least, her study presented a typology of the characteristics of social structure that may foster personal satisfaction and physical well-being over a long life span.

Environmental Psychology Perspectives

A final conceptual strand that has made major contributions to ideas about successful aging is subsumed in the so-called environmental psychology approach. The strength of this approach, in my view, is its down-to-earth treatment of older people's basic requirements for day-to-day survival. Studies of this sort generally use a model consisting of three elements: the older person's capabilities; the demands that are placed upon the older person in order to manage in a particular environmental setting; and the consequences, in terms of the older person's social integration and psychological well-being, of the match between individual capabilities and the demands of everyday living.

Another special feature of this approach is its use of a framework that incorporates quality of life considerations. Thus, M. Powell Lawton et al. (1982a:92) wrote that "any conception of the 'good life' for the aged should include four major sectors, each with multiple domains: behavioral competence, psychological well-being, perceived quality of life, and objective environment."[6] The latter includes the impact on older people of the physical environment in which they live: housing, residential settings, transportation, neighborhood qualities, and the configuration of local amenities. In the breadth of these domains, this approach comes as close as any recent study I have seen to investigating ways to lessen personal isolation by taking into account the impact of the physical and social setting in which older people reside. It reflects a perspective on successful aging that spans individual, social, and environmental levels.

The precepts and methods of environmental psychology were well illustrated in Regnier's (1981) study of neighborhood images and use of community services. There the neighborhood was seen as a mediator of the personal independence of older people and their satisfaction with their physical surroundings. The study examined the relationship between the convenience of the neighborhood to meeting older people's needs and three characteristics of the local community: (1) objective physical conditions, such as distance from the older residents' homes, (2) the older residents' images of the community, such as attitudes toward safety and ease of access to facilities, and (3) the use of neighborhood amenities, such as the frequency of visiting shops, small grocery stores, supermarkets, variety stores, and banks.

Such a study vividly demonstrates how social relationships and control come together in older people's management of day-to-day activities. The characteristics of the local community affect older people's access to human contact, and, in turn, human contacts enhance or reduce the control older people exercise in meeting their daily needs. Lawton describes this association between human ties and the mastery of space in what he terms, the "person-environment service system":

> Basic to our view of transactions between the older person and the environment is a package of services—human, organizational, and physical services. People most frequently compose an essential element of the link between the older person and the physical environment. Physical services are delivered by people; physical resources are allocated by individuals and organizations; linkages such as transportation require human intermediaries; and people are enabled to use and enjoy their homes, neighborhoods, and communities by the efforts of family, friends, and formal services. (1981:6)

Throughout this book, this concept of the "person–environment service system" plays a key role in illuminating the experience of older women in managing their daily activities.

Life Stories and the Environmental Context

Chapter 1 noted Mrs. Silvestri's and Mrs. Farnsworth's quite different perceptions of their physical and social environments. Their images of the neighborhood grow out of their particular backgrounds and life experiences, and affect, in turn, their use of the community resources available to them. Their stories show that the way they perceive the neighborhood affects not only their sense of control and satisfaction with life but also their access to the system of community services and the enhanced independence that such access can provide. "The person–environment service system" is useful here in illuminating the connections between many of the concepts discussed in this chapter: a sense of control, social relationships, access to community services, independence, and health.

Mrs. Silvestri's image of the neighborhood as caring and supportive opens up to her a wide range of community services and instrumental support. Neighbors give her rides to church; the bus driver gives her peppers; and the senior citizens club provides activity, companionship, and the opportunity to "do unto others." In contrast, Mrs. Farnsworth's intense mistrust of her neighbors and her feeling that nobody cares whether she lives or dies bars her access to sources of help. She is aware that driving a car probably exacerbates the pain in her legs. Yet, she persists in taking her car to do the shopping and laundry instead of relying on the bus service for older people in the community. Her view that the senior citizens club is a group of unfriendly insiders effectively bars her from that organization as a potential source of companionship and support. In short, Mrs. Farnsworth is involved in a cycle of deepening handicap: distancing herself from her neighbors, becoming increasingly alienated from potential sources of help, losing a sense of control, and undergoing intensifying physical disability and psychological distress.

THE SEARCH FOR SUCCESSFUL AGING— STATE OF THE ART

Anecdotal material such as that contained in the life stories just discussed can take one only so far, however. To advance understanding of "aging differently" (Maddox 1987), I next examined differences in the collective experiences of women in the study population as a whole. What lessons can be learned from the review of past work to guide one in this task?

First, it is clear that the concept of successful aging is seen as important both to extending knowledge about the aging process and to improving efforts to make the later years of life more vibrant and rewarding. Researchers and policymakers alike now agree that viewing chronological aging as a process inevitably associated with frailty, loss, and dependency is an obsolete and unconstructive perspective.

However, agreement about how to identify and measure successful aging has been slower to develop. Scholars have tended to define success in terms of the particular criteria of their discipline. For psychologists, the desired goal is psychological well-being; for epidemiologists, it is health and longevity; for economists, it is income adequacy and material security; and for those with interests in the physical environment, it is adequate housing and community amenities. Few have attempted to integrate these separate approaches into a single coherent framework to describe the requirements of successful aging. As a result, there is little agreement about what the key markers to successful aging are, or about how the factors that foster successful aging evolve over the life course.

Nevertheless, there are strong pressures for an integrated approach. The enormous increase in the numbers and proportion of people in their late 80s and older puts a premium on developing policies to promote their independence and a meaningful social position for them. At the same time, the lack of a cross-disciplinary approach to the factors shaping successful aging is an obstacle to the development of policies that have more than piecemeal and fragmented effects.

EMERGING CONSENSUS

Despite a slow start, the research cited in chapter 2 reflects the development of consensus on a number of significant points. First and foremost, there is recognition that older people are not all alike. Because of the accumulation of different life experiences, there is a tremendous diversity among people in later life. Related to this appreciation of diversity is a growing conviction that to understand aging well we must focus on the active, nondiseased older population, those elderly who sustain a high level of functional capacity well into their 80s and even 90s. The research task then becomes one of examining the differences between "successful agers" and old people who are experiencing a more rapid decline in their physical and social capabilities.

There is evidence from the literature review, as well, that agreement is emerging about a number of psychosocial factors related to older people's well-being. The following hypotheses, for example, are receiving widespread attention: that a sense of control can reduce the threat of illness and death stemming from stress, unpredictability, and "learned helplessness"; that social relationships promote well-being—directly, by creating ties between human beings, and indirectly, by bridging the gap between what older people can do and

what they need to do; and that when the health-promoting consequences of different kinds of support (e.g., emotional support, provision of information, or practical help with everyday activities) are
compared, practical help is found to be the most robust in predicting
a lower incidence of illness such as coronary heart disease (Syme
1988:7). This last relationship is particularly significant for programs
for the elderly. It suggests that, for older people, being able to count
on help with specific needs such as borrowing money, making household repairs, obtaining advice about financial matters, or getting
assistance to go outside beyond walking distance is an important
deterrent to the onset of physical decline.

Agreement is growing, also, regarding the traits that writers associate with psychological strength in old age (table 2.1). Among
these traits are a sense of joy in life, trust, empathy for others, and
a dedication to something outside one's immediate personal concerns. In the emphasis on the importance of older individuals to be
able to transcend the finiteness of their situation and find meaning
in devotion to people and things outside themselves, we see the
influence of developmental psychologists like Erikson and Maslow.

A Healthy Environment for Healthy Persons

Perhaps the most challenging theme to emerge from the literature is
the idea that strategies for successful aging should include an examination of the characteristics of the environmental setting in which
older people live. Past studies have conventionally looked at two
dimensions of wellness: good physical health (objectively defined
in terms of functional capacity or the absence of disease symptoms)
and psychological well-being (subjectively defined in terms of happiness or contentment as reported by individuals themselves). These
are person-oriented approaches; that is, they focus on the characteristics of the individual and his or her circumstances. In such
approaches, health or successful aging is seen as the dependent, or
outcome, variable. Accordingly, the research task has been to inves-
tigate a variety of sociobehavioral and psychological factors that shape
levels of well-being: health behaviors such as smoking, diet, exercise;
psychological attributes such as a sense of control, self-efficacy, or
directedness; and social characteristics such as "social connectedness" or the number and quality of social relationships.

An alternative theory now being advanced is that to understand
the great differences in the way people age, such approaches may
be too one-sided (House et al. 1988; Maddox 1987; Syme 1988). In

this view, social relationships, which typically have been viewed as factors that influence levels of stress or health conditions, might profitably be turned on their heads and seen, instead, as forces that themselves are determined by the nature of the broader social and cultural milieu. Rather than treating social relationships solely in terms of their consequences for well-being (e.g., reducing mortality and lengthening life), so the argument goes, we should be looking at the determinants of the quality of social relationships in particular social contexts. What kinds of community amenities, housing arrangements, norms about men's and women's roles, and national health policies, for example, foster or deter opportunities for building community ties? What is needed, say adherents of this view, is to supplement a focus on healthy individuals with a focus on healthy environments. We need to identify environments that facilitate rather than discourage access to independent living and social cohesion—the kind of approach favored by the environmental psychologists (Lawton et al. 1982a).

Gender and Aging

Finally, there is a firm consensus that women experience aging in markedly different ways from men. As Maslow noted in his study of self-actualization, the existence of such gender differences strongly suggests that the search for successful aging needs to take special account of the position of women in society, and of the consequences for aging that flow from women's social roles and activities over a lifetime. To take social relationships as an example, men appear to derive more direct health benefits from marriage and relationships with the opposite sex than do women (see Litwak and Messeri 1989, chapter 8). Although such differences are not easy to explain, they are hardly surprising. Men and women occupy different positions in society, positions that are distributed on the basis of social values and expectations about age, race, and social status in conjunction with gender. Given the tenacity of different social norms for men and women, one would expect the effects of position on social relationships to be quite different for the two sexes.

Relevant questions about the impact of gender on successful aging might include: Do women, because of their different access to the traditional markers of success (such as wealth, power, economic security, and social prestige), experience in the retirement years less of a sense of "social extinction" and obsolescence of self? Do they feel relatively less deprived in old age because these markers have not absorbed as large a part of their social worlds? Does this mean that women can more readily transcend "the afflictions of aging," or are there losses, such as partings from family members and friends, that constitute for women a particularly jolting discontinuity with the past? Are there life events associated with later life, such as leaving the family home, that are formidable obstacles to women's achieving positive outlooks in old age?

In a study based on a sample composed solely of women, the answers to these questions can only be tentative. Moreover, women's position in American society is not static. Central to considerations about gender differences in aging is the fact that men's and women's roles over the life course are changing. Another set of questions arises in relation to these changes. Will new factors shape the successful aging of women as successive cohorts attain higher pay and more prestigious positions in the labor force? How will the decision to have no children or to have only one child—which many young career women are making today—affect these women's sources of satisfaction and support in old age? And, since dramatic increases are forecast in the number of women living alone, what kinds of arrangements will American communities devise to integrate older women into the community and counteract the forces that contribute to a withdrawal from public activities and a retreat into a private world of obscurity and obsolescence?

Notes

1. Findings from these studies are available to interested laypersons in a number of edited collections, such as the periodically revised *Handbooks on Aging*. The earliest edition in the *Handbook* series was: Binstock and Shanas (1976). A 1990 edition is by Binstock and George.

2. Economics provides another example of the growing interest in subjective perspectives. In "Economic Aspects of an Aging Population and the Material Well-Being of Older Persons," for example, Espenshade and Braun (1983:48–49) concluded that "there is a need to expand traditional notions of what constitutes material well-being" by exploring the extent to which "older people's subjective attitudes toward their levels of living coincide with the assessment of their material circumstances by outside observers."

3. I have liberally used and cited Erikson's and Maslow's terminology for a number of reasons. First, their ideas are unique and they have taken pains to describe what they mean without resorting to jargon. Second, their perceptions are germane to the situation of older women in this book's study. And, third, respect for the words that people use is a cardinal principle of the qualitative method. It seems fitting that this

principle should apply as equally to those who have pioneered in exploring the concepts of successful aging as to the older women interviewed in this research.

4. In "Aging and Health: Effects of the Sense of Control," however, Rodin (1986:1271) flagged the risks of making *any* broad generalizations about old people and well-being. Because of the accumulation of different life experiences, she wrote, advancing age may increase the variability between individuals in preferences for discretion and autonomy. "Sometimes greater control over activities, circumstances or health has negative consequences including stress, worry and self-blame." In working with old people (or with young people, for that matter), the challenge is to provide the opportunities for self-direction without the coercion. For, observed Rodin, "the need for self-determination, it must be remembered, also calls for the opportunity to choose not to exercise control, especially since control has been shown to have negative psychological and physical effects in some cases."

5. Some examples of studies of older people and their social support included in the list of references are: Day 1985a, 1985b, 1989; Kendig 1986; Shanas 1979; Wellman and Hall 1986; Wolf and Soldo 1988.

6. M. Powell Lawton, director of behavioral research at the Philadelphia Geriatric Center since 1963, has pioneered developing methods that integrate data from the major life dimensions to assess the quality of life of older people. He and his colleagues constructed the Philadelphia Geriatric Center Multi-Level Assessment Instrument (PGC-MAI), which is designed to assess "behavioral competence in the domains of health, activities of daily living, cognition, time use, and social interaction and in the sectors of psychological wellbeing and perceived environmental quality" (Lawton et al. 1982a:1). The PGC-MAI was used as a guideline in constructing the 1987 survey in this study.

Chapter Three

COLLECTING INFORMATION FROM AND ABOUT OLDER WOMEN

Constantly, as one talked to the aged, one felt this struggle to say who they are, not just who and what they have been.

—Ronald Blythe, *The View in Winter: Reflections on Old Age*

A study based on empirical findings stands or falls on the quality of the data collected and on how well the available information advances the investigator's overall purposes. Data collection starts with a question that a researcher seeks to answer and, ideally, ends with a new set of ideas about further questions to raise and future directions to explore. The study design aims to incorporate approaches to collecting data that will elicit information to enable the investigator to address initial questions and formulate new ones. Broadly speaking, then, the study design includes every phase of the research process—from the criteria for selecting the sample, to the conduct of the fieldwork, to the presentation of key findings, and, finally, to the assessment of the significance of the information collected.

This chapter looks at the match between the purposes of this book's study and the conduct of research. Data collection is discussed, as well as the study design and the resulting characteristics of the study population. The chapter is organized into three sections. The first section considers four general ground rules that were adopted in this study to guide data collection. In adopting these ground rules, it should be emphasized that the study population comprised older women, a group of people who until recently have been largely invisible and with whom social researchers have had little previous experience. The reasons I present for using various approaches draw substantially on the recommendations for the study of aging reviewed in chapter 2.

The remaining two sections describe how specific components of the study implement these guidelines for collecting data on older women. Section two provides details about the 1978 and 1987 surveys and the qualitative interviews with a selection of the women in their homes. This is the research framework and the backbone of the study. Finally, section three looks at the characteristics of the study population and, in particular, at the tricky question of representativeness—to what extent does the study sample represent the larger population of American women 77 to 87 years of age?

The main research findings are presented in subsequent chapters. However, interspersed throughout this chapter are findings from this and other studies of aging. Although anticipating data described in later chapters in some ways jumps ahead of the story, it is important to substantiate the main points with research evidence, as well as to illustrate the kinds of information generated by different research approaches.

GROUND RULES FOR COLLECTING DATA

The guidelines applied to data collection in this study were anticipated in chapters 1 and 2, which pointed to the importance of incorporating four general approaches into the study of aging: (1) a look at the perspectives of older people themselves, (2) a focus on the contextual features of old age, (3) the disaggregation of statistics and attention to the particulars of individual lives, and (4) an examination of quality of life issues in various life domains.

Subjective Perspectives

A number of studies reviewed in chapter 2 stressed the subjective dimension of well-being and the need to listen to what older people say about their health and morale. As Sagan noted (1987:8), judgments about well-being are presumably subjective. That being the case, the best way to find out whether people are healthy and happy is to ask them.

That I was guided by this idea was demonstrated by my beginning the search for successful aging with the stories of two individuals. I wanted to explore the views of older women by talking to them, not just about them (Day 1985a; Knopf 1975: xxi). The women in this study, born seven to eight decades ago, acquired their attitudes in response to a different set of social and historical conditions.

I included a strong qualitative component in the research design because I felt that women their late 70s and 80s might have perspectives on successful aging quite different from those that I, in a younger age group, might anticipate. Open-ended, semi-structured interviews allowed respondents to tell their stories—on their own terms—without having their priorities and concerns predetermined by the investigator. Because these older women grew up in a very different world from the one we know today, the so-called "qualitative" approach is particularly important to learning their perspectives.

Contextual Features of Aging

A second ground rule stemming from the studies reviewed in chapter 2 involved studying older people's experience within a broad social and environmental context. Thus, a major aim of the research reported here was to examine how the expectations and orientations of older women interact within the context of change over time—change in their physical capabilities and in the physical and social environments in which they live.

Ideally, a concern with the contextual features of aging would draw upon the concepts of a number of different disciplines: psychology, epidemiology, sociology, anthropology. However, there are formidable obstacles to a multidisciplinary approach. In a cogent overview of the sociology of aging, Passuth and Bengston (1988:334) stressed that there is still substantial disagreement within the social science disciplines themselves as to the most appropriate areas for investigation. According to these authors, each of the major strands in contemporary sociological theory (for example, structural functionalism, exchange theory, symbolic interaction), or in contemporary psychology (for example, Freudianism, behavioralism, cognitive theory) would produce a radically different approach to aging. Nevertheless, Passuth and Bengston conclude "The most fruitful areas of analysis for social gerontology lie in a more thorough examination of the contextual features which surround the aging person. This includes historical, political, and economic features, as well as the ongoing social construction of everyday aging experiences" (1988:347).

The qualitative data in this study offer a particularly rich source of insights about "the social construction of everyday aging experiences." Becoming a widow, an event occurring to 55 percent of women in this study between the time of the first and second interview, is one such experience. The contextual approach explores the social and economic circumstances surrounding the meaning of this event (see chapter 8). How do women at this late stage in life, when their personal and social resources are wearing thin, come to terms with being deprived of the person with whom they have been intimate for half a century or more? All of the women in the study sample said that after sharing everyday experience for so long, one does not soon "get over" losing a husband. As one woman put it, "After 50 years, you get wrapped up in him." Although not in the sample, my mother, born in 1901, is a member of these cohorts. Widowed at age 84, five years ago, she confided recently, eyes welling with tears, that she still missed my father acutely: "He was just like a brother to me. I'd known him since he was 15."

The strategies women in these cohorts develop to meet the demands of everyday life reveal much about their enormous will to overcome major reversals—with their essential self intact. As described in chapter 8, some read, some garden, some attend their church or synagogue, some play bridge with their friends. My mother walks—a mile or so a day in clement weather.

The key to understanding the factors that ease pain and promote readjustment may be found in close attention to such small daily happenings. Indeed, in The Drowned and the Saved (1988), Primo Levi observed that it was the mundane routines involved in the daily struggle for existence that kept him going for a year in Auschwitz. "The aims of life," he said, "are the best defense against death and not only in the Lager." The detailed account of ordinary happenings at the death camp is what gives Levi's book a terrible immediacy. By the same token, a focus on the ordinary happenings that are the context of old age can illuminate how well or poorly women are managing the challenges of their 80s.

Disaggregation of Statistics

Concern with the context of daily life gives rise to a third ground rule for data collection on older women, that is, disaggregating large statistical categories and focusing on a more detailed description of individual lives. Much information about the very old has been concealed within broad categories of age, gender, race, and social class. Increasingly, researchers are urging that concentrating on more circumscribed studies of individuals and communities can enrich understandings based on aggregate statistics. Many latent aspects of aging are coming to light as researchers delve more deeply into the particulars of what older people think and do. The following are examples of studies that have challenged stereotypes by exposing the very old as "statistical ghosts."

GENDER AND STAGE IN THE LIFE COURSE

As noted in chapter 2, one legacy of disaggregation has been increased appreciation of the significance of gender and age as factors shaping the meaning of growing old (Riley 1987). Introducing a study of very old men and women, Longino (1987:1) wrote: "Basic research begins with description in areas where the nature of the phenomenon is unknown." Longino's concern was with the economic and social characteristics of the "over 85's," the oldest segment of the elderly population. Building a case for description on the distortion in image created by the paucity of data about very old men, he claimed that because these men make up only 31 percent of this age segment, they have been invisible in our image of this group. The stereotype is that the very old are financially insecure, physically frail, isolated, and at risk of being institutionalized. Yet, unlike their female counterparts—on average, very old men do not fit this picture: they have fairly comfortable incomes, remain married until death, and are much less likely than women to reside in nursing homes. "There is a sense," concluded Longino (1987:7), "in which the generalizations about the very old [have] a feminine bias. The hidden minority of men fit the stereotype of the very old less well than do the women."

AGE

In American society, there are many stereotypes about older women as well. Although women in their late 70s and 80s numerically dominate the very old population, they have also been largely invisible. The new information coming to light is partly the result of disaggregating the statistics on older people by age. Only recently have researchers begun to examine the characteristics of the elderly within a narrow age band, of say, 10 years, as in the study described in this book, rather than the much wider, open-ended range, "60 years and older."

Research on retirement, for example, has tended to emphasize the early post-retirement years and the withdrawal from paid employment. Writings on how to adjust to the post-retirement years have thus been less relevant to women now in their 80s, many of whom have not worked for pay since marriage, or have been retired for 20 years or more. The need for description of individual lives, therefore, is highly relevant to the situation of women in the very advanced years.

Notable revelations have resulted from decanting aggregate statistics on age. Torrey (1988:378) has described the very old as the "statistical ghosts." Addressing the conventional view that the main aim of older people is to save so that they can bequeath their wealth to their heirs, she examined, in detail, the ways in which the very old deploy their financial assets. She discovered that the economic behavior of the very old reflects a strong determination to retain control over their financial assets as a way of determining their own affairs. The high priority older women place on holding onto their assets is confirmed by data in this volume's study (chapter 6), showing that among women in the 1900 to 1910 cohorts, home ownership (and especially owning one's home in one's own name) is a significant component of a sense of well-being.

Testing Old Theories and Developing New Ones

Close observation of discrete categories and events is needed to test old theories and develop new ones. New research on the activities of people of different age and gender provides another example of the contribution of disaggregating statistics to new insights about aging.

One of the earliest and most influential theories of aging, "disengagement theory," argued that in old age the ties that hold people to society become looser (Cumming and Henry 1961). According to the theory, old age is characterized by a withdrawal from roles occupied in midlife and a weakening of social norms and prescriptions. The notion was that this "disengagement" is mutually beneficial— for society and for older individuals themselves. Not only was such a withdrawal seen as what actually happens, but "getting out of the way" and leaving the territory to younger generations was proclaimed as what old people really want (in Fontana 1977:10).

About the same time that disengagement theory was in vogue— in the late 1950s and early 1960s—proponents of "activity theory" were advancing an opposing view. The claim here was that maintaining a high level of activity and social involvement was the best way to achieve life satisfaction and to successfully adjust to old age (Passuth and Bengston 1988: 341).

New studies of the activities and life-styles of old people are reassessing these earlier theories. Again, the research approach involves disaggregating statistics by age and gender. Using data from a 1986 nationwide household survey of 3,617 adults aged 25 and older, Herzog and her colleagues (1989:S129) found that, contrary to the popular image, women and men spend about the same amount of time in "productive activities," that is, activities defined in the conventional economic sense as "behaviors that add to the stock and flow of valued goods and services." Not surprisingly, the researchers found that men and women differ in the kinds of activities they perform and in the hours they spend in different pursuits. Over the life course, women generally spend more time in unpaid work and less in paid employment. A less-expected finding, however, was that while the hours of "productive activity" (as just defined) declined in the post-retirement years, "people at virtually every age do some housework, and that the average hours they spend do not differ by age."

Data on the older women in this book confirm the continued involvement in housework. Over half of the women interviewed in the 1987 survey were still shopping and doing their own laundry and housework without help (see chapter 4). Contrary to disengagement theory, the role of "homemaker" is one from which many women do not withdraw even in very old age. As Herzog and colleagues (1989:S137) acknowledged, although unpaid housework is still not defined as a "productive activity," the capacity of older women to "do for themselves" greatly reduces the costs to American taxpayers of providing subsidized home maintenance services.

The 1987 survey reported on here revealed other types of day-to-day activities that belie the idea that the elderly withdraw from social involvement. A substantial proportion of women in these late ages were not only helping themselves but were trying to keep up their contributions to people outside the circle of their immediate relatives. Nearly 3 in 10 women (27 percent) in 1987 were doing volunteer work and nearly half (47 percent) were attending their church or synagogue as often as once a week or more.

The study results could not unequivocally confirm or deny the disengagement and activity theories. One reason for this inconclusiveness was the tremendous diversity in the sample in terms of the nature and level of activity. Some women said that passive home-centered pursuits, such as watching television, eating, and sleeping were favorite pastimes. Others mentioned physical exercise or working with people (chapter 4). The sheer variety within the group argues persuasively against the simple view that women in these ages universally want to or do withdraw from active social roles. Indeed, nearly 6 in 10 women (56 percent) said they had no time on their hands, implying that their lives were full of activities that were meaningful to them.

In short, collecting detailed information about what people in the upper ages actually do exposes critical shortcomings in previous theories of aging. Such theories fail to account for the diversity in life-styles and preferences among the elderly, themselves. Some withdraw and become comtemplative, others see activity as a key to successful aging. Disengagement theory, moreover, treats old people as though they were passive agents, stepping aside to prepare for death, rather than actively shaping, as well as passively responding to, social values and relationships (Dannefer 1988; Passuth and Bengston 1988:336).

THE SEARCH FOR ANOMALIES

Examination of social phenomena in "complex and particularistic detail" (Kunitz, 1989:1) has been heralded from yet another perspective. In a paper presented to an international workshop on health transitions, Stephen Kunitz (1989), a physician conducting research on the causes of illness and death among Navajo Indians and Australian aborigines, has argued that knowledge about individual experience can provide a basis for discovering anomalies and, thereby, can strengthen the grounds for building generalizations. Applying this principle to his particular interest, the study of mortality, said Kunitz, means that one must understand deeply what statistics on death truly signify in each instance. This can only be accomplished by "immersion in the lives of the people whose deaths we are seeking to explain" (1989:21).

Anomalies and their explanation are essential to understanding the experiences of older women in this study. The satisfaction with life that many of these women express seems out of kilter with the accumulation of personal losses, declining stamina, and reduced opportunities for social integration they have collectively experienced (chapters 4 and 8). The intense desire of women in these ages to live on their own and to manage their affairs independently also seems inconsistent with their longing for close contact with their adult children (chapter 5). On the one hand, when asked why they would choose not to live with a child or relative, many in this sample gave as a reason, "I do not want to be a burden" or "I do not want to get in the way" (chapter 4). On the other hand, when asked what they would really like to be doing in a couple of years, a substantial proportion said that they wanted most to continue to be involved and not to have their lives circumscribed by health restrictions. A number said that, above all, they wanted to continue to be able to do their own housework. The meaning of housework to women in this sample (chapter 4) provides clues to this apparent anomaly—

the tension between self-effacement and the desire for autonomy, between withdrawing and hanging on.

Quality of Life Issues

Finally, the studies reviewed in chapter 2 point to a fourth guideline for collecting data on older women—the desirability of incorporating quality of life issues. Only by seeking to understand what contributes to older people's well-being can we learn about the conditions conducive to successful aging.

Psychological well-being provides one example. A number of studies in chapter 2 posited continued personal development as a major condition of effective aging. How does one sustain in one's 80s the quest for continued personal growth? Canadian sociologist Mark Novak (1986) described this process as the search to "discover a good age." The question regarding women in these cohorts is: What does discovering "a good age" entail, when one is alone, physically slowed down, and, in the eyes of society, "nonproductive,"—even, as philosopher Esposito would have it, "obsolete"?

To examine this issue, I included questions about interests and favorite pastimes. The purpose was to see to what extent women in the sample were doing things that enabled them to use their skills and keep up with the activities they had enjoyed in the past. Questions were asked about the sorts of occupations that might give a woman scope to exercise her particular interests and abilities, such as doing paid jobs, hobbies, volunteer work, and participating in clubs and religious organizations (chapter 4). I assumed that, although a high level of activity was not necessarily a prescription for happiness, and might not be to everyone's taste, having a favorite pastime and at least a minimum level of social intercourse would contribute to the quality of life in old age (Ringen 1987).

The findings are reported in chapter 4. However, the point I wish to make here is that nearly half of the sample attended religious services. It was clear from what they said that, for these women, keeping an active involvement in the church contributed to "a good age." Apart from whatever spiritual sustenance religious activities may provide, regular attendance at services offers an opportunity for socializing and for informal exchanges of assistance, such as rides to church. It is likely, moreover, given the hypothesis that social relationships have direct effects on health (House et al. 1988) that regular church attendance may be beneficial to the quantity as well as to the quality of life of older people. Indeed, as shown in chapter

6, attendance at religious services was found in this study to be significantly associated with measures of successful aging.

The remainder of this chapter demonstrates how this study's research design implements these four data collection guidelines. The presentation has two over-arching aims: to show how the study blended information collected by quantitative and qualitative methods, and to illustrate the fit between the research design and the study of successful aging.

DESIGN AND CONDUCT OF RESEARCH

This section addresses, first, the purposes and design of the 1978 and 1987 surveys. I describe the research instruments used to collect the bulk of quantitative information about women in the follow-up sample and compare selected characteristics of the 1978 and 1987 survey populations. Then I look at the purposes and conduct of the smaller qualitative study, and outline the characteristics of the 20 women I talked to informally in private dwellings and residential homes for the elderly.

1978 Survey: Factors Underlying Low Fertility

Women born during the period 1900–1910 experienced what had been up to that time the lowest recorded fertility in United States history. In their young adulthood, women in these cohorts produced a distinctive pattern of childbearing, something of a "Quiet Revolution" (Dawson et al. 1980), with average family size limited to unprecedentedly low levels. The average number of children borne by these cohorts was smaller than that of either previous or subsequent generations: 2.3 as compared to 3.5 for their mothers and 3.2 for their daughters.

How and why did women born during the years 1900–1910 produce a historically unprecedented low level of fertility? This was the main research question prompting the 1978 survey. To address this question, the National Institute for Child Health and Human Development (NICHD) funded Jeanne Clare Ridley, professor of demography, Georgetown University, Washington, D.C., to develop a survey to explore the factors underlying rigorous family limitation. The study population consisted of a nationally representative sample of 1,049 white ever-married women aged 66 to 77. The criteria of eligibility were white race, married at least once, born in the years 1900–1910, and having resided in the United States for at least 30 years prior to the 1978 interview. Over 27,000 households were screened to locate women with the requisite characteristics.

Personal interviews were conducted with the 1,049 sampled individuals, addressing, in particular, questions concerning marriage and family building, reproductive behavior, and contraceptive practices.[2] A major interest was in the impact of socioeconomic conditions on the desire for children during the Great Depression, when women in these ages started their families. As a group, they responded to economic uncertainty and hardship by postponing childbearing at a time when modern means of contraception were not so readily available as they are today.

In seeking to understand the forces shaping low fertility, the 1978 survey collected a wealth of information on the background characteristics of the sample, including parental background, size of community when growing up, level of schooling completed, religion, timing of marriage, demographic characteristics of spouse, employment histories, and the impact of economic conditions on life-style, continuity of work, and attitudes toward their family's future. Questions were also included about functional capacities and sources of help with particular tasks. In chapter 6, these background characteristics are used to examine the kinds of factors that differentiate women who are aging well from those whose circumstances spell dependence and insecurity.

Findings from the 1978 Survey

FAMILY SIZE

Data from the 1978 survey showed that the unusually low completed family size among these cohorts actually masked a wide range of family sizes—from no children to five or more. True, the proportion of women who had no children or only one child was substantial. The research team reported (Dawson et al. 1980:77): "By age 50, approximately 42 percent of the white women belonging to these cohorts had had fewer than two children: 20 percent were childless, and 22 percent had had only one child."

However, 26 percent of the women in the sample had four or more children, and 31 women had nine or more. Diversity of family size among the initial sample was of more than academic interest to the 1987 follow-up research. In fact, as shown in chapter 6, having had four or more children is one of the background factors associated with aging less well. Women who had families in the smaller size range were, typically, among the more successful agers.

CONTRACEPTIVE USE

So far as the likelihood of practicing contraception is concerned, the 1978 data showed that those who were less likely to use a method of birth control had the following characteristics: they were older—that is, they were born between 1901 and 1905, and had thus reached their peak reproductive years somewhat prior to the depths of the depression. Compared to contraceptive users, on average, they were women who had had fewer than two live births, who had less than a college education, lived outside large urban centers, whose husbands had blue-collar rather than white-collar occupations, and who were members of the Roman Catholic religion (Dawson et al. 1980: 76).

1987 Survey: Factors Shaping Social Support

Quite a different set of interests prompted the 1987 survey. Here the emphasis was on the characteristics and availability of social support. Questions were directed to understanding the consequences of small family size, rather than to factors motivating unprecedentedly low levels of childbearing. The low fertility of the 1901 to 1910 cohorts has meant that in late life they have had fewer adult children with whom to share companionship, emotional support, and practical help. This raises an important question concerning social support: Has the fact that these women had small numbers of children been a liability to them, or have they formed relationships of other kinds to substitute for those they might have had with children of their own?

Children and Social Support

There is ample evidence from past work that, indeed, people with no (or very few) offspring may be comparatively disadvantaged in older age. Starting in the late 1960s, a large body of research has indicated that adult children are the main source of help to enable older people to remain living in their own homes. Even in the largest metropolitan areas, once believed to be especially isolating for the aged, studies have found that strong family ties and patterns of support existed between generations (Bengston, Burton, and Manger,

1981; Cantor 1979, 1980; Cantor and Little 1984; Horowitz and Dobrof 1984; Shanas and Townsend 1968). The implication of such findings was that having fewer children available to help might lead to
the greater likelihood of isolation or institutionalization. As evidence
of the protective role of children, data were cited to show that a
higher proportion of old people in institutions were childless. One
study found that although four out of five persons 65 and older had
at least one surviving adult child, almost half (46 percent) of the
institutionalized elderly were childless (Shanas and Maddox 1976:16).
     Nevertheless, evidence as to whether children are "the ultimate
resource" in old age is still ambiguous. A new survey conducted
through the Hebrew Rehabilitation Center for the National Bureau
of Economic Research (NBER) Aged-Child Survey characterized the
prevailing pattern of contact and assistance among the elderly and
their children as "bi-modal." The researchers, Kotlikoff and Morris
(1987), claimed that although many old people appear to be quite
well served by their children, a substantial minority of the poorest
and most vulnerable "either have no children or have no children
who provide significant time or care." Their survey found that "over
one-fifth of the elderly have no children, over one half do not have
a daughter, or do not have a daughter who lives within one hour of
them." Moreover, even among old people who are very poor, reported
these authors, it is rare to find children who are providing financial
support, except in the form of shared housing.
     The dwindling ratio of children to elderly parents has led re-
searchers in many western industrial countries to ask: Who will care
for the elderly in the future (Day 1985b)? In a recent paper, Canadian
demographers Nicole Marcil-Gratton and Jacques Légaré (1988) raised
just this question in relation to today's low fertility adults in Canada:
"Have they jeopardized the very source of support they will need in
their old age?" From data on people 65 years and older in the General
Social Survey (1985) conducted by Statistics Canada, these Canadian
researchers concluded that small family size does not necessarily
predict isolation in old age. Among Canada's cohorts aged 65 to 74,
they found that when children are not available, "collaterals" (spouse,
siblings, friends, other kin, neighbors) fill in. Chapter 5 presents
evidence suggesting that a similar practice prevails among women
in this sample.
     In a comparison of "kinship sets" for people in different age groups
in preindustrial 18th- and 20th-century England, British social demographer Peter Laslett (1984:388), concluded that "our superior
capacity to survive" compensates, demographically, for shrinking

family size by making more (and more diverse) kinship relationships available to persons in old age." The question remains, however: Will more distant kin be able and willing to provide the amount of assistance that adult children have been seen to provide in the recent past (Day 1989:183–207)?

Using the rich database from the 1978 survey as a resource on background characteristics, the 1987 survey sought to explore patterns of social support in relation to a number of life domains—such as living arrangements, family composition, capacity to perform specified tasks, involvement in community activities, and financial resources.

Analysis of Major Transitions

A key recommendation for research on human aging proposed in chapter 2 is to direct attention to the major transitions in later life. The 1987 survey incorporated this focus. The 10 years preceding one's late 80s are crucial in terms of their implications for financial security, physical fitness, and the availability of family members to help in case of need. A prime concern, therefore, was to describe major transitions among women as they moved from their eighth into their ninth decade, and to examine the impact of these transitions on four key conditions underlying women's life chances in later life: primary mode of support, living arrangements, institutionalization, and survivorship. A main reason for following up the 1978 survey was thus to have a representative sample and a longitudinal design to trace the outcomes of these four conditions in the lives of the 1,049 women who took part in the earlier survey.

From Social Support to Successful Aging

The initial purpose of the 1987 survey was to examine patterns of social support in the context of these major life transitions. As work progressed and information began to come in, I became increasingly interested in the conditions contributing to successful aging. Several studies, such as those reviewed in chapter 2 (Maddox 1987; Rowe and Kahn 1987), convinced me that asking why some older women do well and others do poorly was a fruitful approach to understanding the situation of women in these age groups. This was a case of what I referred to at the beginning of this chapter: the initial questions giving way to new ideas about the directions of the research.

From an interest in social support to an interest in successful aging is but a short step conceptually, for, as discussed in chapter 2, the two are closely linked. Indeed, supportive social relationships have been found to be strongly associated with two of the most widely accepted markers of successful aging—good health and long life. As noted earlier, new research on older people (e.g., House et al. 1988) suggests that social relationships and the support they provide—both direct and indirect—contribute to physical health and longevity, as well as to happiness and a sense of well-being.

Assets of 1987 Research Design for Study of Successful Aging

A number of features of the 1987 survey design make it particularly well suited to an examination of successful aging. For one thing, the questions incorporated a substantial subjective component. In drafting the 1987 survey instruments, I was concerned, for example, not only with what had happened to women in the study over the decade since the first interview but also with how they felt about their current circumstances in the light of the changes they had experienced over those years.

There are other design assets of a more structural nature, as well—the characteristics of the 1978 sample, the longitudinal design, and the use of multiple sources of information. The contribution of these to the study of successful aging is discussed in Appendix 3-A. Two other components of the 1987 survey deserve special mention here: the format of the survey instruments and the conduct of the interviews with the older women.

FORMAT OF SURVEY INSTRUMENTS

The women located in the follow-up study represented several quite distinct categories (see table 3.1). Eight out of 10 of those contacted in 1987 were living in private households, but 9 percent lived in retirement buildings or nursing homes. A third of the original sample (N = 307) were deceased. A fourth category consisted of the persons designated by the older women as the main providers of informal support (see table 3.2).

Four separate questionnaires were constructed to obtain information about these categories—that is, one for each of the following: (1) women living in private households, (2) women living in institutions, (3) people informed about the circumstances of the deceased, and (4) primary caregivers (PCGs). The strength of this approach for a study of successful aging lies in the fact that the 1987 study design took full account of the diversity of circumstances of women in the

Table 3.1 DISPOSITION OF SAMPLE: 1987 SURVEY

	Number	Percentage Total Sample (N = 1049)	Percentage Known Survivors (N = 712)
Total, 1978 survey	1049	100	NA[a]
1987 survey:			
Located, survivorship status known	1019	97	100
Alive:	712	68	100
Living in private households:			
Complete/partial interview	568	54	80
No interview	82	8	12
Living in institutions:			
Complete/partial interview	62	6	9
Deceased:	307	29	NA
Interview with AIP[b]	290	28	NA
No interview with AIP	17	2	NA
Not located, survivorship status not			
known	30	3	NA
Total	1049	100	NA

a. NA, not applicable.
b. AIP, any informed person.

follow-up study. Having a separate questionnaire for each of the four categories left plenty of scope in the primary respondent schedule for attention to a variety of life domains.

Life Domains and Social Support. So far as content was concerned, I deliberately chose to spread a wide net, including multiple measures of the women's personal and social circumstances, rather than concentrating on any one area, such as functional capacity or illness symptoms. In line with the fourth ground rule for collecting data on older women, a concern for quality of life issues, I wanted to include indicators of the "good life" in a broad spectrum of domains.[3]

The main headings of the 1987 primary respondent questionnaire (table 3.3) show the breadth of life domains about which information was collected. The domains included interests and activities; help contributed and help received; health and capacity to manage; major transitions, such as loss of a spouse or child or moving one's residence; psychological orientations toward life; and attitudes toward the future. Adopting such a variety of topics may jeopardize a depth of understanding about a few key relationships, but a broad perspective seemed important to understanding the many facets shaping these women's journey through aging.

Table 3.2 DISPOSITION OF INTERVIEWS WITH PRIMARY RESPONDENTS AND
CAREGIVERS, 1987 SURVEY

	Number	Percentage Known Survivors (N = 712)
Total known survivors, 1987 survey	712	100
Primary respondents:	630	88
Living in private household	**568**	**80**
Complete interviews with PR[a] and CG[b]	502	71
Complete interviews with PR/incomplete with CG	46	6
Incomplete interviews with PR/complete with CG	17	2
Partial interviews PR/no CG	3	—
Living in institutions	**62**	**9**
Complete interviews with PR and CG	34	5
Complete interviews with PR/incomplete with CG	2	—
Incomplete interviews with PR/complete with CG	26	4
No response	**82**	**12**
PR refused	77	11
Other (ill, incompetent, out of town)	5	1

a. PR, primary respondent.
b. CG, caregiver.

Table 3.3 PRIMARY RESPONDENT QUESTIONNAIRE—MAIN HEADINGS

a. Living Arrangements/Care of Older Relatives
b. Family and Household Composition
c. Transitions
d. Interests and Activities
e. Help Respondent Provides
f. Health, Capacity to Manage and Helpers
g. Health Care Financing
h. Accommodation and Housing
i. Attitudes and Expectations
j. Income and Assets
k. Interviewer Observations

Pursuing breadth of focus, I adopted a broad definition also of social support. The concept included both emotional support (e.g., talking about personal problems, sharing common activities, providing companionship) and practical help (e.g., shopping, doing housework, providing transportation, helping to manage money). It encompassed unpaid help from family members, friends, and neighbors, and "formal" paid (and volunteer help) from service providers, such as nurses, social workers, clergy, and bankers. Appendix 3-B describes the methods used to record these different kinds of supports.

Positive Life Events. Change in social support in these later years is usually seen in terms of depletion of networks and losses in close ties through death and drifting apart. Such negative events are seen to be the inevitable lot of the very old. The survey collected an inventory of such losses. However, attempting to comply with Rowe and Kahn's (1987) precept that "psychosocial factors should be studied in their full range, not only in their negative aspects," I included questions, as well, addressed to any increments to the older women's circle of family and friends over the decade—new friendships, new family ties (with grandchildren, for example), and social and recreational activities that might widen the women's access to intimate relationships. One can hypothesize that such events would have a positive impact on a key indicator of successful aging (see Sagan 1987, chapter 2)—a sense of psychological well-being. The significance of these different types of life events for successful aging is considered in chapter 6.

CONDUCT OF INTERVIEWS

Those with experience interviewing the very old (Gibson and Aitkenhead 1983; Job 1983; Schmidt 1975) agree that good survey instruments are short, varied, and clear. "They leave the respondent with a sense of accomplishment rather than a reaffirmation of failure" (Schmidt 1975: 544). Thus, fostering success should be built into the very fabric of the survey design (for discussion, see Appendix 3-C). Every effort was made to employ these criteria—that is, to develop survey schedules that not only were short, interesting, and comprehensible but that also could be answered without threatening the women with a sense of failure.

Since the sample included a collection of very diverse individuals, reactions to the interview varied a great deal—some women liked it and responded willingly and fully; others were put off and were indifferent or even curt. Such varied reactions are attributable, however, not just to differences among the women themselves but also to the fact that the highly structured survey format limited the opportunity for individual expression (Appendix 3-C).

On a study such as this one, which touches on topics that are profoundly threatening to many people, the attitudes of interviewers can intervene in the collection of information. The questionnaire raised many issues—for example, the onset of illness and dependency, death and family breakdown, the possibility of having to go to a nursing home—that could well have made some interviewers, themselves outsiders to the world of the very old, feel distressed and uncomfortable. If conveyed to the older women, these feelings might have formed a barrier and inhibited candid replies. Interviewer comments written in the margins of the 1987 survey schedules reveal that some interviewers were, indeed, distressed by the conditions in which they found some of the women living. This was particularly true in the case of older women who seemed "confused" and disoriented (for example, Mrs. Sergio, chapter 8).

The interview schedules, however, show the other side just as often. They contain numerous spontaneous marginal notations by interviewers who were tremendously elated by the energy and spirit of women coming to terms with—what seem to younger people— extraordinarily taxing circumstances: "This is really an incredible woman!" or "Mrs. Smith is a very intelligent, independent person! I loved talking to her." Moreover, in nearly 6 out of 10 cases (58 percent) in 1987, the interviewer characterized the respondent as "friendly and eager" (see section titled, "Unmeasured Qualities of Successful Aging," chapter 6).

Tracing Results

The results of tracing the 1,049 women who participated in the 1978 sample are a remarkable feature of this study. Only 30 women from the original survey disappeared without a trace—that is, their whereabouts could not be determined, and no one could be found who knew anything about them. Since the 1978 survey was based on a national sample, the follow-up study in 1987 had to locate the women all over the continental United States.[4] Finding these women and obtaining their permission to be interviewed a second time had all the suspense of a detective adventure.[5] The interviewers, in fact, were trained in the techniques of locating missing persons. To the credit of the fieldwork team at the Institute for Survey Research, all but 3 percent of the original sample were located. A breakdown of the results is presented in table 3.1.

All told, the tracing yielded 712 known survivors and 307 known deceased (table 3.1). Among the surviving women, 62 were living in institutions. Twenty-four of the women who had moved to institutions refused to be interviewed or were too ill to speak to the interviewers. On the basis of comments made by interviewers after consultation with nursing home staff, 16 to 18 of these appear to have been suffering from dementia.

Altogether 551 women living in private households and 38 living in institutions were interviewed in the 1987 survey. This was 83 percent of the known survivors, that is, those located and known not to be deceased. Counting interviews with people familiar with the circumstances of the deceased prior to death, results were obtained for some 89 percent of the 1978 sample. This is a remarkable return for people in any age group, and it represents a response rate substantially higher than rates reported in most panel studies of people 60 years of age and older living in private households (Ridley and Gruber 1989:5).[6]

In addition to information collected from the survivors, interviews were conducted with 581 caregivers, yielding 536 completed interviews with matched pairs of older women and their designated primary caregiver (table 3.2).

These caregiver interviews supplement the older women's perspectives on the help they need and are receiving. The caregivers' response to the question about how providing support to the older women has affected their lives introduces another dimension on successful aging—the perspective of the provider on the exchange of support (see chapter 8, Mrs. Peters and Mrs. Sergio).

Sociodemographic Characteristics of Study Populations

How do the characteristics of the women traced and reinterviewed after nearly 10 years compare with those of the entire sample of 1,049 who participated in 1978? Data in table 3.4 tell the story. To assess these comparisons, it is important to know how the figures in the two distributions were derived. The 1978 sample was assigned weights to permit comparisons to be made with the general population. The weights were designed to correct for sampling bias in factors such as age, survivorship, geographic distribution, size of community, and so forth (Ridley and Gruber 1989). No such weights correcting for differential survivorship, failure to locate, or nonresponse were computed, however, for the 1987 follow-up population. Hence, the two distributions are not strictly comparable. Moreover, because the 1987 data are not corrected, statistical inferences to the population of 1900–1910 cohorts at large cannot be drawn from the characteristics of the 1987 sample.

What, then, is the point of the comparison? The answer is that placing these two distributions side by side enables us to obtain an approximate picture of the impact of change on 1,049 American women aged 66 to 77, traced and reinterviewed after an interval of 10 years. The data in table 3.4 show what the two study populations actually looked like at the two times the women were interviewed. Although the actual numbers would alter somewhat if correction weights were assigned to the 1987 data, the underlying trends driving

Table 3.4 SOCIODEMOGRAPHIC CHARACTERISTICS OF EVER-MARRIED WHITE WOMEN BORN IN 1900–1910: 1978 SAMPLE AND SURVIVORS INTERVIEWED IN 1987

Respondent Characteristics	1978[a] (%) (N = 1049)	1987 (%) (N = 589)	
Age (century month of birth)			
1901–1905	48.5	42.1	
1906–1910	51.5	57.9	
Total	100.0	100.0	
Highest year of schooling completed			
<8	21.0	16.3	
8–11	45.4	43.9	
12	16.5	22.7	
>12	17.2	17.1	
Total	100.0	100.0	
Marital status			
Married	44.4	24.1	
Widowed	51.2	72.0	
Divorced/separated	4.2	3.9	
Total	100.0	100.0	
Number of living children			
0	17.3	11.9	
1	21.1	24.1	
2	27.0	28.9	
3–4	23.3	24.3	
5+	11.4	10.7	
Total	100.0	100.0	
Living arrangements			
Alone	41.1	47.9[b]	54.8[c]
Husband only	39.5	19.0	21.8
Husband and others	4.5	1.7	2.0
Adult child and others	11.4	14.3	16.3
Sibling and others	2.5	3.0	3.4
Nonkin	1.0	1.4	1.6
Institutional resident	—	9.8	
Total	100.0	100.0	

continued

Table 3.4 SOCIODEMOGRAPHIC CHARACTERISTICS OF EVER-MARRIED WHITE
WOMEN BORN IN 1900–1910: 1978 SAMPLE AND SURVIVORS
INTERVIEWED IN 1987 (continued)

Respondent Characteristics	1978[a] (%) (N = 1049)	1987 (%) (N = 589)
Perceived health status (compared to others in age group)		
Excellent	22.2	20.8
Good	36.6	38.5
Fair	28.3	27.2
Poor	11.8	12.7
Not ascertained	1.1	.1
Total	100.0	100.0

a. Data for 1978 are from a nationally representative sample of 1,049 ever-married white women in a survey directed by Jeanne Clare Ridley, professor of demography, Georgetown University, Washington, D.C.
b. N is 630, which includes completed interviews with 551 women in private households, 38 with residents in institutions, and 41 incomplete interviews with located respondents.
c. N is 551, representing respondents interviewed in 1987 living in private households.

the major changes revealed in table 3.4. would still remain. There would still be substantial increases in widowhood and in the proportion of women living alone, for example.

Given these caveats, the distributions in table 3.4 highlight the following points of change. (Note: Percentages from table 3.4 in the next several paragraphs have been rounded off to their nearest whole numbers.)

Age (century month of respondent's birth). As measured by century month of birth (1 = January 1900, 2 = February 1900, and so on), there was an increase in the proportion of younger to older women between the two interviews. The drop of from 49 percent to 42 percent among those born in the earlier half of the decade (1900–1905) and the rise of from 52 percent to 58 percent among those born in the later half (1906–10) partly reflects the greater depletion of older women owing to their higher mortality in the interim between the two interviews. The drop in the proportion of older women may also be due to a greater nonresponse rate among them in the follow-up study, as a consequence of their higher incidence of illness and disability (see later subsection on "Population of 'Elites'?"; also Maddox 1987).

Highest year of schooling completed. Those who were interviewed a second time had, on average, completed slightly more years of schooling. A somewhat larger proportion among those interviewed in 1987 had completed 12 years of schooling (23 percent as compared to 17 percent), and a somewhat smaller proportion had completed less than 8 years of schooling (16 percent as compared to 21 percent). It is worth noting that, among women born at the turn of the century, fewer than one in four finished high school, and less that one in five (17 percent) had any formal education beyond high school.

Marital status. Of all the characteristics listed in table 3.4, marital status underwent the greatest change. The proportion of currently married women was almost halved, going from 44 percent of the sample in 1978 to 24 percent in 1987. The increase in the proportion of widowed women was correspondingly large. As will be discussed in chapter 4, the magnitude of change in marital status over the period had a major impact on the living arrangements and sources of support of the survivors interviewed in 1987.

Living arrangements. Because women living in institutions were omitted in the 1978 sample, changes in the living arrangements of these women are best seen by comparing those living in private households only (table 3.4, "Living arrangements," right-hand column). Table 3.4 also shows the distribution of living arrangements when women living in institutions are included in the denominator (column 3).

The impact of these changes on the lives of women in these cohorts is discussed in chapter 4. However, the following main changes are noted here: a one-third increase in the proportion living alone, a decline of nearly one-half in the proportion living only with their husbands, and an increase of one-fifth in the proportion living with others. In addition, almost 6 percent of those interviewed in 1978 and traced in 1987 had moved from private households into institutions.

Number of living children. Data in table 3.4 show that women interviewed in the follow-up study had, on average, somewhat higher proportions of living children. The proportion with no children declined 5 percentage points—from 17 percent in 1978 to 12 percent in 1987, whereas the proportions with one, two, and three to four children slightly increased. The proportion with five or more remained virtually the same. This apparent anomaly, that is, of a group of women, 66 to 77 years of age, with slightly higher proportions of living children 10 years after the initial interview, may be accounted for partly by the fact that 44 women remarried over the interval, resulting in the addition of stepchildren to their family networks.

Other possible explanations, such as that children contribute to survival, or that women with, say, three to four children, were easier to locate in the follow-up study than those with no children or only one, are of a highly speculative nature.

Perceived health status (compared to others in age group). The distributions on perceived health compared to others ["Compared to other people your age would you say, that your health is: excellent, good, fair or poor?"] for the two interviews were markedly similar. In both years, nearly 6 out of 10 (59 percent) defined their health as good to excellent. Results from other questions in the 1987 survey show, however, that the view of one's health compared to others is an unreliable indicator of one's actual capacity to perform specific tasks (see chapter 4).

Additional Attributes of 1987 Study Population

Moving to another set of indicators, table 3.5 presents data on the 1987 sample: capacity to manage daily tasks, priorities about living

Table 3.5 SELECTED CHARACTERISTICS OF EVER-MARRIED WHITE WOMEN
          BORN 1900 to 1910: 1987 SAMPLE

Respondent Characteristics	Percentage Distribution (N = 589)
Age in years	
76–79	43.5
80–83	42.7
84–87	13.8
Total	100.0
Household size	
1 person	58.4
2 persons	34.1
3 + persons	13.8
Total	100.0
Functional capacity	
ADLs[a] (1 or more)	
Without help	86.9
With some help	8.8
Unable to do without help	4.2
Total	100.0
IADLs[b]	
Without help	53.3
With some help	23.9
Unable to do without help	22.2
DK/NA[c]	2.0
Total	100.0

continued

Table 3.5 SELECTED CHARACTERISTICS OF EVER-MARRIED WHITE WOMEN
BORN 1900 to 1910: 1987 SAMPLE (continued)

Respondent Characteristics	Percentage Distribution (N = 589)	
Financial Management		
Without help	77.9[d]	91.8[e]
With some help	13.4	5.1
Unable to do without help	7.5	1.9
DK/NA	1.2	1.1
Total	100.0	100.0
Preferred living arrangements		
Stay at home with outside help	67.2	
Move in with relatives	7.0	
Move to a retirement home	16.6	
Move to a nursing home	7.5	
DK/NA	1.7	
Total	100.0	
Person designated PCG		
Husband	16.8[f]	10.8[g]
Son	17.8	16.2
Daughter	29.3	37.8
Other relatives	21.6	10.8
Nonkin	11.1	5.4
No one	3.0	5.4
DK/NA	4.0	8.1
Total	100.0	100.0
Income		
<7,000	37.7	
7,000–9,999	16.3	
10,000–24,999	22.8	
25,000+	8.7	
Refused	6.3	
DK/NA	8.5	
Total	100.0	

a. ADLs, Activities of Daily Living.
b. IADLs, Instrumental Activities of Daily Living. Includes: Shopping, housework, laundry, meals preparation, and financial management.
c. DK/NA, Don't know; No answer.
d. N is 589, which includes women living in private households and women living in institutions.
e. Capacity to handle financial matters, 1978 ("With difficulty," "With some difficulty," "Unable to do without help").
f. Women living in private households (N = 551).
g. Women living in institutions (N = 38).

arrangements, and designation of the person (primary caregiver, PCG) with main responsibility for providing practical help and support.

Comparable data on most of these characteristics were not collected in 1978.

Particularly noteworthy here is the fact that over half (53 percent) reported that they can do all the housekeeping tasks (Instrumental Activities of Daily Living, IADLs) without help. Only 9 percent of those needing at least some help with housekeeping (47 percent) said that they needed some help with personal grooming and mobility inside the house (Activities of Daily Living, ADLs).[7]

A further striking characteristic of these women is shown by the high proportion who said that their preferred living arrangement was to "Stay at home with outside help." Nearly 7 out of 10 (67 percent) preferred this arrangement, and a mere 7 percent said that they would like to move in with a son, daughter, or other relative. This was so even though the question was phrased with a significant condition: "Which arrangement would you prefer—if you could no longer manage on your own?"[8] These responses highlight a major theme of this book—the high priority of women in this study to stay in control to the end.

Another notable feature about women in this study is revealed in the distribution of persons designated as primary caregiver. Among women living in private households, adding together the categories, "Other relatives" and "Nonkin," a total of 3 out of 10 (33 percent) selected a person other than a member of the nuclear family (a husband, son, or daughter). Some of these were widows with no children. But others designated people other than their immediate family, even when they were sharing a household with a husband, son, or daughter. The significance of these findings to understanding successful aging is explored more fully in chapter 5.

The Qualitative Interviews

Finally in this discussion of data collection, I return to the key importance of "immersion in the lives" of the people whose values and behavior we are seeking to understand (Kunitz 1989). In one way or another, the four ground rules described earlier all point to finding out from older women themselves what they do in their daily lives and how they feel about it. In this study, implementation of this approach rested primarily on the qualitative interviews.[9]

The taped conversations I conducted with 20 women from the 1987 survey are a crucial component of the research design and greatly enhance the study of successful aging. They permitted women in the sample to speak at leisure and at a pace they chose themselves. I visited them for these semistructured, open-ended talks in October and November 1988, some 16 months after they had been interviewed in the 1987 survey.

Purposes

Qualitative interviews have a number of purposes: to provide "apt illustrations" of observed behavior, to aid in the development of alternative hypotheses, to refine social indicators, and to monitor the validity of data collected in more structured approaches (Becker and Beer 1957; Katz et al. 1983; Mitchell 1983).

My purposes included all of these. By the time I selected the 20 women for personal contact, I was committed to a focus on successful aging. I was in accord with Sagan's view (1987, see chapter 2) that the best way to find out whether old people are happy and feel well is to ask them themselves. I wanted to meet the women where they lived, to see how they were coming to terms with aging in their own homes, and to hear them describe in their own words what successful aging meant to them.

In addition to exploring quality of life issues firsthand, I wanted to develop alternative hypotheses concerning the bases of activity and satisfaction in old age. I felt that by supplementing the two previous interviews with a third open-ended contact, I might discover new clues about the links between various life domains—such as that between psychological well-being and social activities, or between functional capacity and attitudes toward help.

Further, I hoped that a third, more informal, meeting would help assess the usefulness of the 1987 questionnaire items as indicators of successful aging. Were women who seemed in control of their lives in 1987 managing well 16 months later? Were they finding ways to compensate for declines in their physical capacities, weathering changes in family relationships, keeping up with their friends, and emphasizing the positive in their skills and personal resources? These are the sorts of measures of successful aging available in the 1987 survey. My question was: Would I find some degree of consistency over time in the women's behavior and attitudes with respect to these indicators? Using the 1987 survey schedules as a basis for comparison, did the same women 16 months later seem to be staying the distance, and were the same ones seemingly falling behind?[10]

Finally, I felt that conducting the qualitative interviews addressed the challenge proposed by George Maddox in his 1987 presidential address to the Gerontological Association of America—that is, to use one's research on the elderly to reform social systems and make social institutions respond more humanely to "the rhythms of aging." Giving older people the chance to speak for themselves provides essential insights into "the rhythms of aging" and affirms the elderly's control over decisions that affect their lives. The United Nations World Assembly on Aging (1982) was the first of a growing number of national and international forums to advocate the participation of older people in defining the parameters of their own well-being. In the qualitative interviews, a small selection of women from the larger survey were given the opportunity to speak about what successful aging meant to them, and about how aspects of the social system in the United States today affect the quality of their lives.

Fieldwork Procedures

To select women for the qualitative interviews, I identified three sampling areas within a day's drive of my base at The Urban Institute in Washington, D.C. (The names of the three states are withheld to protect confidentiality.) Together these areas contained a sufficiently large number of women from the 1987 survey to construct a solid core of qualitative interviews and still allow for refusals and failure to contact. The main fieldwork procedures, response rates, and conduct of the qualitative interviews are outlined in Appendix 3-C.

From the outset, I had not intended to draw a sociodemographically representative sample from the 1987 survey population. In a national study, where the respondents lived throughout the continental United States, choosing a representative sample would have involved many more people than I could interview myself, and would have been prohibitively costly in terms of time and travel. Instead, I mailed letters requesting an interview (Appendix 3-D) to a total of 47 women, that is, all of those living in the three sampling areas. Taking each area in turn, I followed up the letter with a telephone call requesting a personal visit, and, on three separate field trips, tried to reach as many women living in those areas as I could.

"Guided Conversations"

The interviews were in the nature of "guided conversations" (Job 1984) and covered many of the same topics as those in the 1987 survey. Generally, I opened the conversation by asking the women about their interests and activities, and then moved on to discussing how well they were managing daily household tasks, their feelings about health, changes in their physical capabilities over the last 16 months, family relationships, and ties with friends and neighbors. I prepared an outline of these major topics (Appendix 3-D—"Guide for Qualitative Interviews"), but used this only as a guide, not as a rigid format.

A good interview, wrote Bertraux (1981:39)—and even more so a good life story—is one in which "the interviewee *takes over the control of the interview situation* and talks freely" [italics in original]. So it was with the qualitative interviews with the 20 older women. Each woman had a particular set of concerns and priorities, which became the core of what we talked about. As the guide indicates, however, I did raise the issue of successful aging directly, asking each woman at some point how she herself would define the meaning of successful aging. Only one woman, Mrs. Farnsworth (see chapter 1), balked at trying to formulate an answer.

Shortcomings of 1987 Survey

To increase confidence in one's research and establish the validity of using multiple methods, a researcher seeks to identify the shortcomings of relying on a single approach. In the course of conducting the qualitative interviews, I detected two general types of shortcomings for collecting information about elderly women that were associated with the 1987 survey method. The first was that the structured survey format tended to suppress the reasons underlying patterns of behavior, and the second was that the pressure of time tended to foster incomplete reporting.

These shortcomings can arise in using survey techniques to collect data on any age group, but, in an exploratory study of successful aging, the suppression of information about older individuals and their social activities and relationships is more potentially limiting. This is true because older women and their worlds have been largely invisible. There is much to learn and few precedents to go by. At the same time, women born at the turn of the century tend to be modest and self-effacing. Many have been involved in "home duties" all their adult lives. When I called to arrange an interview, it was difficult for me to persuade some women why I should want to talk to them—they said that they were "just an ordinary person" and had little of value to contribute. This perspective reflects both societal attitudes toward people who are outside the work force, and hence not seen to be engaged in "productive activities," and also the fact that many older women are largely, and partly involuntarily, confined to their homes. They assume that as a visitor from the world of the productively employed, I, too, will define housebound experience as inconsequential.

Two examples—attitudes toward help-seeking and the enumeration of social networks—illustrate the kind of information that can be lost when research on older women relies wholly on the structured survey approach (for illustrations from the qualitative interviews, see Appendix 3-E).

CONCEALMENT OF UNDERLYING MOTIVATION

Concerning help-seeking behavior, it became clear in the qualitative interviews that women in these ages are aware that their intense desire for autonomy may be counterproductive. That is, they know that in refusing to seek help in the short run, they may be compromising their quality of life in the longer run. Said Mrs. Smart, for example, "It's good to be independent, but I know I overdo it."

This ambivalence suggests an explanation for the overwhelming preference of older women for "intimacy, but at a distance" (Rosenmayr and Kockeis 1968)—a relationship that allows them to have close affectionate ties with their adult children and yet maintain separate living arrangements. The reason for this is older people's reluctance to expose themselves to being helped too much. Three women who were particularly articulate about this issue (Appendix 3-E) were aware that being helped is a "two-edged sword," having the potential to harm as well as to aid the elderly recipient (Karuza, Rabinowitz, and Zevon 1986:373).

There are implications here for needs-based policy. The findings highlight the difficulty of identifying the presence of need when women in these ages—out of pride and reluctance to accept what they see as charity—suppress requests for assistance that would improve their lot (see Day 1985a; Day and Harley 1985). At the same time, the existence of such awareness argues strongly for the desirability of enlisting the cooperation of older women themselves in making decisions about arrangements that crucially bear upon their autonomy.

UNDERREPORTING OF COMPLEX RELATIONSHIPS

A second discovery from the qualitative interviews is that the structured survey probably results in the underreporting of social relationships, particularly those involving friends. The speed with which interviewers are obliged (even, instructed) to work in order to maximize the cost effectiveness of large-scale surveys tends to curtail older women's responses to questions about complex events. An example in the 1987 survey is the question about whether these women had developed any new, mutually supportive relationships over the last two or three years. This is a major area in which I found discrepancies between the information reported in the survey and what women told me when they had time to talk informally. The bonds and social activities they described, especially those with friends and neighbors, appeared to be more extensive than those recorded by interviewers 16 months earlier (Appendix 3-E).

Here, again, there are policy implications. The finding that friendship relationships may be more important to older women's wellbeing than survey data might have led us to believe argues for local communities to make more intensive efforts to build opportunities for older women to share activities with their peers (see Binstock 1985; also chapter 9, this volume).

Characteristics of Women in Qualitative Interviews

Women in the qualitative interviews comprised a collectivity, as well as being individuals with unique life histories. To convey a picture of their features as a group, selected characteristics are presented in table 3.6. Bearing in mind that the 20 women were not intended to be a representative sample, it is still instructive to see the extent to which they embody the diverse circumstances found among the larger study population.

Age. The age distribution spanned the full range found among women in the 1987 survey—from the youngest, Mrs. Carlton, aged 78, to the oldest, Mrs. Hoffman, aged 88.

Marital status. Their marital statuses were also diverse. Thirteen were widowed, seven were married, and four had been married more than once.

Income. The spread in incomes, too, encompassed almost all categories represented in the 1987 survey. Although there were no women in the lowest income, category A (under $3,999), the incomes ranged from Mrs. Silvestri with between $4,000 and $5,000 to three women (Mrs. Hoffman, Mrs. Eisenstein, and Mrs. Hammerstein) each with incomes of $35,000 or more.

Education. In years of schooling, again the 20 women spanned a

Table 3.6 SELECTED ATTRIBUTES OF 20 WOMEN IN FIELDWORK STUDY, 1988

Living Arrangement and Name	Age in 1988	Marital Status 1988[a]	Income after Tax[b]	Years of Schooling	Perceived Level of Health[c,d]	Housing Tenure	Psychological Well-being Score[e]
Living alone							
Mrs Silvestri	79	W	B	4	G (2)	Own	41
Mrs. Smart	82	W	D	12	E (2)	Own	41
Mrs. Esherman	82	W (2×)*	E	10	G (1)	Rent	34
Mrs. Fleischmann	80	W	E	12	F (3)	Own	27
Mrs. Tyler	79	W	F	12	E (2)	Own	25
Mrs. Hoffman	88	W	H	8	F (1)	Rent	33
Mrs. King	81	W	DK[f]	14	G (2)	Own	36
Living with husband							
Mrs. Dewitt	80	M (2×)*	D	16	E (2)	Own	37
Mrs. Porter	79	M	D	7	F (3)	Own	41
Mrs. Farnsworth	79	M (2×)	E	9	P (2)	Own	24
Mrs. Worth	85	M	E	15	G (2)	Rent	36
Mrs. Crawford	86	M	F	14	G (1)	Own	43
Mrs. Eisenstein	81	M	H	12	G (2)	Rent	34
Others living with respondent							
Mrs. Danburger	79	M	D	7	F (1)	Own	35
Mrs. Carlton	78	W	E	11	G (2)	Own	32
Mrs. Carter	83	W	E	17	G (2)	Own	36
Mrs. Hammerstein	80	W (2×)	H	20	E (2)	Rent	34

continued

Table 3.6 SELECTED ATTRIBUTES OF 20 WOMEN IN FIELDWORK STUDY, 1988 (continued)

Living Arrangement and Name	Age in 1988	Marital Status 1988[a]	Income after Tax[b]	Years of Schooling	Perceived Level of Health[c, d]	Housing Tenure	Psychological Well-being Score[e]
Living in a retirement home							
Mrs. Grainger	78	W	E	6	F (3)	Rent	37
Mrs. Wright	82	W	E	8	G (3)	Rent	29
Mrs. Farmer	87	W*	E	16	G (3)	Rent	31

a. In this column: W, widowed; M, married; (2×), two times; asterisk (*), childless.

b. A, under $3,999
   B, $4,000–4,999
   C, $5,000–6,999
   D, $7,000–9,999
   E, $10,000–14,999
   F, $15,000–24,999
   G, $25,000–34,999
   H, $35,000 and over.

c. Perceived health compared to others in age group: E, Excellent; G, Good; F, Fair; P, Poor.

d. Perceived health now compared to what it was three years ago: (1), Better; (2), Same; (3), Not as good.

e. The well-being score was computed from 14 affect-balance items in "Section I: Attitudes and Expectations" of the 1987 survey questionnaire. The range in scores was 14 to 43 points, with 43 representing 100 percent, that is, the highest possible score indicating a sense of psychological well-being on all 14 items.

f. DK, Don't know.

Source: The data on the living arrangements, age, marital status, and housing tenure were collected from the 20 women I interviewed in their homes 16 months after the 1987 survey was conducted. The characteristics on income, years of schooling, and well-being were collected in the 1978 and 1987 surveys.

Note: To ensure confidentiality for respondents and their families, all names are fictitious. To further protect anonymity, I have avoided referring to the location of resident.

wide range, with Mrs. Silvestri having less than a full primary school education and Mrs. Hammerstein with university and postgraduate training to her credit. Among the 7 women who continued their formal schooling after high school, 1 went to business college, 2 were paraprofessionals, and 4 were teachers.

Perception of health. The way these 20 women defined their health compared to others in their age group again includes the full spread of possibilities: 4 still defined their health as excellent, 10 ranked their health as good, 5 said fair, and, finally, Mrs. Farnsworth said her health was poor. Interestingly, the distribution of psychological well-being scores among the 20 provides no support for the expectation that a sense of well-being might be positively related to level of schooling and income. If anything, the relationship is in a slightly reverse direction.

Functional capacity and social support. Another important characteristic of these women is the extent to which they can manage daily activities on their own, and the people whom they rely upon to provide support. Among the many measures of capacity for self-help and availability of social supports collected in the 1987 survey, six are listed in table 3.7. Three of the six indicators are subjective: How much do health problems stand in your way? Can you do the shopping? and How often do you have time on your hands? The other three are quantitative measures of social relationships: number of children, number on the support roster, and relationship of the person designated as primary caregiver. These indicators are discussed briefly next.

In terms of assertion of independence, the data reveal a number of striking things. First, attitudes toward health problems, activity levels, and capacity for self-help confirm yet again the great value that women in this study attach to independence. Although 14 admitted that health problems stand in their way "a little," 17 out of the 20 said that, even so, they can handle the shopping without help, and 3 out of 4 said they almost never have time on their hands. Only the most severely disabled, Mrs. Crawford, who is confined to a wheelchair, and Mrs. Danburger and Mrs. Grainger, both with serious heart conditions, said that they depend on others to do the shopping for groceries. Even Mrs. Farnsworth, the only woman among these 20 who defined her health as "poor," and said that health problems stand in her way "a great deal," insisted that she could manage the shopping without help.

Regarding attitude toward use of time, this selection of women also presented themselves as people who were fully occupied—they

Table 3.7 SELECTED INDICATORS OF CAPACITY FOR SELF-HELP AND SOCIAL
SUPPORT—20 WOMEN IN FIELDWORK STUDY, 1988

Living Arrangement and Name	Health Stands in Way[a]	Can Do Shopping[b]	Number of Children	Number on Roster	Primary Care-giver[c]	Time on Hands
Living alone						
Mrs. Silvestri	2	1	3	9	Friend	4
Mrs. Smart	1	1	1	7	Daughter	4
Mrs. Esherman	1	1	0	2	Friend	3
Mrs. Fleischmann	2	1	2	10	Daughter	3
Mrs. Tyler	2	1	2	8	Friend	4
Mrs. Hoffman	2	1	3	5	Neighbor	2
Mrs. King	2	1	1	4	Daughter	4
Living with husband						
Mrs. Dewitt	1	1	0	9	Niece	4
Mrs. Porter	2	1	0	13	Husband	4
Mrs. Farnsworth	3	1	8	12	Daughter	1
Mrs. Worth	2	1	1	15 +	Husband	4
Mrs. Crawford	1	2	1	9	Husband	4
Mrs. Eisenstein	2	1	2	5	Husband	4
Others living with respondent						
Mrs. Danburger	3	3	2	7	Sister	1
Mrs. Carlton	2	1	2	5	Daughter	4
Mrs. Carter	2	1	2	8	Neighbor	4
Mrs. Hammerstein	2	1	1	7	No one	4
Living in a retirement home						
Mrs. Grainger	3	2	3	10	Son	4
Mrs. Wright	3	1	8	13	Daughter	4
Mrs. Farmer	2	1	0	4	Niece	4

Sources: All data are from the 1987 survey—not from the qualitative interviews.
Note: To ensure confidentiality for respondents and their families, all names are
fictitious. To protect anonymity, I have avoided referring to the location of residence.
a. Do your health problems stand in the way of your doing the things you want to do:
   1, Not at all
   2, A little, or
   3, A great deal?
b. Can you do the shopping for groceries:
   1, Without help
   2, With some help, or
   3, Are you completely unable to do the shopping?
c. Of all the people in your life which *one* would you say is *most* responsible for
giving you practical help and support?
d. How often do you have time on your hands you don't know what to do with:
   1, All the time
   2, Quite often
   3, Just now and then, or
   4, Almost never?

saw time as a precious commodity, not a tedious burden. The exceptions were four women (Mrs. Hoffman, Mrs. Fleishmann, Mrs. Farnsworth, and Mrs. Danburger) who defined their health as "fair" or "poor," and Mrs. Esherman, twice widowed with no children, and with only two persons listed on the support roster (but see Appendix 3-E for another view of Mrs. Esherman obtained from the qualitative interviews).

It is worth noting that among these 20 women, those perceiving their lives to be full and active come from all social categories, including formal schooling, income level, and living arrangements: from four years of primary school through graduate school; with incomes ranging from under $5,000 to $35,000 and over; from living alone to living with a husband, as well as three women living in a residential accommodation for the frail and ill elderly.

In terms of children and social relationships, table 3.7 shows a contrast between the small number of children and small range of family size, and the considerably larger range in number of persons listed on the support roster. With the exception of the two women with eight children (four of Mrs. Farnsworth's eight children were stepchildren from her second marriage), average family size was quite small. Three women had no children, five had one only and six had two. In contrast, the range in numbers of persons on the support roster was much larger—from Mrs. Esherman with only 2 to Mrs. Worth with over 15. In addition to husband and children, people on the support roster included siblings, more distant kin, and friends and neighbors with whom these women said they had close personal ties. The data show that children by no means have a monopoly on the intimate relationships of their mothers in their 80s.

Regarding the primary caregiver indicator, nearly half of the 20 women designated as their primary caregiver someone other than a member of the nuclear family—that is, someone other than a husband or adult son or daughter. In some cases, this was because they had no such relative, but in others, they chose a friend or neighbor over a family member. The reasons are discussed in chapter 5. The point to emphasize here is that these women illustrate the diversity of social relationships found among women in the 1987 sample. As with the larger sample (table 3.5), their choice of primary caregiver indicates their reliance on people other than close family members to provide practical help and emotional support.

Women in Qualitative Fieldwork Compared with 1987 Survey Population

How can one summarize the outstanding differences and commonalities between the women who participated in the qualitative interviews and the larger sample of women from which they were drawn? A few key characteristics are presented here as a general basis for comparison; these are summarized in table 3.8.

In considering the comparison, note, first, that the size of the two populations is widely discrepant (that is, 589 in the 1987 survey population and 20 in the 1988 fieldwork study). Second, as already mentioned, the subsample was not intended to be representative of the larger group. The comparison is included to show the characteristics of the women interviewed in the qualitative study side-by-side with those of the larger follow-up sample. As in the case of the 1978 and 1987 study populations (table 3.4), the smaller group followed up for the qualitative interviews is not—in a statistical sense—representative of the larger.

SOCIALLY ADVANTAGED "ELITES"

On the strength of almost every indicator in table 3.7, the women in the qualitative interviews are what might be called more "socially advantaged." They had higher proportional scores than those in the 1987 sample as a whole in all of the following categories: married and living with husband; post–high school training; able to do the shopping without help; almost never have time on hands; perceive health as good; psychological well-being in the upper range of scores. In addition, a higher proportion than in the full 1987 sample are better off financially, and a lower proportion fall near or below the poverty threshold (category A, incomes below $7,000). Also, proportionately more women in the qualitative interviews have no children or one child only, and fewer have four or more children. As pointed out earlier, having had a family in the smaller size range may also reflect advantages for women in this study that accumulate over the life course (see chapter 6).

In short, women in the qualitative interviews have more of the characteristics one might associate with successful aging. Nevertheless, they illustrate bad times as well as good. There are individuals among them who are grieving, physically dependent, feeling isolated, and unprotected by a firm backlog of social support.

Table 3.8 SELECTED CHARACTERISTICS OF 1987 SURVEY POPULATION AND
WOMEN INTERVIEWED IN QUALITATIVE STUDY, 1988

Respondent Characteristics	1987 Survey Population (N = 589)	1988 Fieldwork Study (N = 20)
Age (year of birth)		
77–79	43	50
80–83	43	30
84–87	14	20
Total	100	100
Living arrangements		
Living alone	48	35
Living with husband only	19	30
Living with others	a	—
Others live with respondent		20
Living in an institution	10	15
Total	100	100
Marital status		
Married	24	35
Widowed	72	65
Divorced/separated	4	—
Total	100	100
Highest grade completed		
<8 years	16	20
8–11 years	44	25
12 years	23	20
Over 12 years	17	35
Total	100	100
Number of living children		
0	12	20
1	24	25
2	29	30
3–4	24	15
5	11	10
Total	100	100
Can you do the shopping for groceries?		
Without help	65	85
With some help	19	10
Unable to do without help	15	5
No answer	1	—
Total	100	100

continued

Table 3.8 SELECTED CHARACTERISTICS OF 1987 SURVEY POPULATION AND
WOMEN INTERVIEWED IN QUALITATIVE STUDY, 1988 (continued)

Respondent Characteristics	1987 Survey Population (N = 589)	1988 Fieldwork Study (N = 20)
Perceived health compared to others in age group		
Excellent	21	20
Good	38	50
Fair	27	25
Poor	13	5
Not ascertained	1	—
Total	100	100
Time on hands		
Almost never	56	75
Just now and then	27	10
Quite often	10	5
All the time	6	10
Total	100	100
Income		
<$6,999	38	5
$7,000–9,999	16	20
10,000–24,999	23	50
25,000 and over	9	10
Refused	6	—
Not reported/DK[b]	8	5
Total	100	100
Psychological well-being score		
43–40	14	20
39–32	47	60
31–25	26	15
24—14	9	5
Not ascertained	4	—
Total	100	100

a. The distinction between "living with others" and "others live with respondent"
was not made in the coding for the 1987 sample as a whole.
b. DK, Don't know.

Inconstancy of Life Circumstances

A final observation underlines the value of the qualitative interviews
in the search for successful aging. Not only do these interviews enrich
the meaning of findings from the 1987 survey, but they provide a
third point of reference from which to observe the transitions ac-
companying aging.

Tables 3.6 and 3.7 outline the characteristics of the 20 women on the basis of the interviews in fall 1988. However, this snapshot view conceals the story of the profound changes that occurred in many of these women's lives in the 16-month interval between the two contacts. Seeing these changes and the women's responses to them sharpened the image of successful aging as an ongoing process of adjusting to life events over the whole life course. Following are two case examples.

Mrs. Grainger and Mrs. Crawford:
Changes in Life Circumstances over 16 Months

Mrs. Grainger, who, in June 1987, was married and living with her husband in a home they then owned, was widowed and renting a unit in a home for the disabled and frail aged when I talked to her the following November. She said she missed her husband and old life intensely. Multiple health problems slowed her down, but she was making friends and adjusting cheerfully to a life of comparative confinement.

Mrs. Crawford, who, in 1987, described her health as better than it had been three years earlier, was, when I met her, immobilized in a wheelchair, and dependent on her husband for all personal care and help with household tasks. She had fallen down the steep flight of steps from the second floor of the house that she and her husband had built themselves as a young married couple. In 1987, with 43 points, she had the highest raw score on psychological well-being, and, in 1988, despite extensive dependency, she was still outwardly one of the most cheerful of the 20 women I met.

The intensive effort required to recruit 20 women from among the initial 47 also reveals much about the impact of the passing years on the lives of women in this study. In some cases, letters were returned "Address Unknown," and telephones had been disconnected. For those who had stayed fit; still lived where they had been in 1987; if married in 1987, still had their husbands; and, if they had children, those children and their children had suffered no unforeseen calamity—life over the 16 months had been marked by stability and continuity. However, for those who had experienced any of these events, it had been a time of great flux. Some had changed living arrangements or moved to a different state; some had gone into nursing homes; and some I could not locate at all, either by telephone or by inquiring in their local communities (see Appendix 3-C for a breakdown of tracing results). At one address I visited when my telephone calls remained unanswered, I found a vacated house and a few pieces of furniture abandoned in the empty rooms. When I telephoned the person recorded on the 1987 survey as the primary caregiver, a daughter, she said her mother had Alzheimer's disease and had at first been living at home with paid help. Over the past year, however, her condition had worsened, and she had gone to a nursing home. Her house was up for sale.

"I don't need more help—at the moment." This phrase, which I found so characteristic of old people in Sydney, Australia (Day 1985a), aptly describes the cutting edge for these 20 American women, as well. Changes in functional capacity were marked. The qualitative interviews support many studies showing that physical deterioration accelerates as one moves into the ninth decade. A number of the 20 women said they had gone downhill over the last 16 months. Mrs. Dewitt, Mrs. Hoffman and Mrs. Eisenstein specifically mentioned the onset of new illness symptoms, and Mrs. Farnsworth, as seen in chapter 1, said her hips were giving her a lot more trouble. There were others (Mrs. Carter, Mrs. Carlton, Mrs. Hammerstein) who mentioned failing eyesight and feared that poor vision was becoming a major factor limiting their capacity to stay in their own homes.

REPRESENTATIVENESS OF WOMEN IN 1987 STUDY

I come now to a closer look at the issue of representativeness. To what extent can one say that the findings of this study reflect the circumstances and views of older American women born at the turn of the century? This question has both statistical and sociological dimensions, which, although related, also involve different kinds of considerations. I first briefly examine some issues regarding statistical representativeness, and then outline from a sociological perspective the main features of the 1987 follow-up sample that limit the scope of its generalizability to the population of older American women at large.

Drawing Statistical Inferences

For a follow-up study of the kind described here, estimation of statistical representativeness is complex and technical. It involves developing methods to compensate for selective participation and dropout, and techniques for comparing sample statistics with statistics for the larger population. As noted earlier, the 1978 sample included the assignment of weights to permit such a comparison with the general population. The 1987 follow-up study did not. Hence, all of the findings from this study should be treated as "representative" only of the 1987 sample itself. The 1987 data describe the characteristics of the particular group of women who were located and reinterviewed: they are not in the strict sense "representative" of the 1900–1910 cohorts.

Comparison of 1987 Sample and Current Population Survey

Table 3.9 shows the differences in proportions in selected sociodemographic characteristics between women followed up in 1987 and ever-married, white women born during 1900–10 in the general population. The data compare the 551 women living in private households in the unweighted 1987 sample with the 4,258,970 older American women in the March 1987 Current Population Survey (CPS).[11] The table reveals a number of statistically significant differences between the two distributions. On the whole, higher proportions of women in the 1987 sample were younger, were living in the Midwest rather than the Northeast, were renting their homes, and had completed less than 12 years of schooling. A markedly larger proportion of women in the 1987 sample also fell into the lowest income category, that is, under $10,000.[12]

Statistical Representativeness and Study Goals

In the face of these differences and the limited capacity to draw statistical inferences, it is important to recall the basic goal of this study—that is, to trace and reinterview the participants in a large, nationally representative survey. As noted earlier, the tracing results were unusually good. Information was available for nearly 9 out of 10 of the women followed up. In addition, the response rate of 83 percent among women known to be alive in 1987 is impressive. The strength of this study, therefore, lies in its opportunity to examine with a longitudinal design three largely unexplored aspects of older women's worlds: changes in their lives as they move into their late 70s and 80s, the meaning of life events over this period to the experience of aging, and the factors contributing to how well or how poorly these women are managing the major transitions of the later years. In the narrow statistical sense, inferences from the sample to

Table 3.9 COMPARISON OF SAMPLE OF 1901–1910 BIRTH COHORTS AND
MARCH 1987 CURRENT POPULATION SURVEY

Respondent Characteristics[a]	1987 Household Sample	Current Population Survey, March 1987[b]
Region		
Northeast	20.7	24.7
Midwest[c]	34.9	27.3
South	30.1	32.4
West	14.3	15.6
Total	100.0	100.0
Housing tenure[d]		
Owner	62.3	71.5
Renter	26.3	26.1
Other[e]	11.4	2.3
Total	100.0	100.0
Household size[f]		
One	54.8	54.0
Two	34.1	34.3
Three and over	11.1	11.7
Total	100.0	100.0
Age[g]		
76	4.2	2.9
77	15.2	14.1
78	12.5	10.6
79	11.6	11.3
80	12.2	9.9
81	11.1	9.5
82	10.5	10.8
83	8.9	9.8
84	6.0	8.8
85	4.5	7.0
86	3.3	5.3
Total	100.0	100.0
Marital status[h]		
Married	25.0	26.6
Widowed	70.8	70.1
Divorced	4.0	2.9
Separated	0.2	0.4
Total	100.00	100.0
Highest grade completed		
1–7 years	16.3	16.2
8–11 years	43.9	38.3
12 years	22.7	27.2
Over 12 years	17.1	18.3
Total	100.0	100.0

continued

Table 3.9 COMPARISON OF SAMPLE OF 1901–1910 BIRTH COHORTS AND
MARCH 1987 CURRENT POPULATION SURVEY (continued)

Respondent Characteristics[a]	1987 Household Sample	Current Population Survey, March 1987[b]
Household income[i]		
Under $10,000	62.7	44.7
10,000–14,999	13.2	16.9
15,000–24,999	14.0	17.7
25,000–34,999	6.0	8.4
35,000 and over	4.1	12.4
Not reported	12.0	—
Total	100.0	100.0
Number of women	551	4,258,970.0

Source: Data in the table were prepared by Jeanne Clare Ridley in May 1988.
a. Differences between 1987 sample and the Current Population Survey (CPS) are significant at the $p \leq .05$ level ($x^2 = 15.10$, $df = 3$).
b. The estimates are from the Public Use Sample (PUS), Current Population Survey (CPS), March 1987, for white ever-married women between 76 and 87 years of age.
c. The U.S. Bureau of the Census renamed the North Central region as the Midwest in 1984.
d. Differences between 1987 sample and CPS are significant at the $p \leq .05$ level ($x^2 = 206.46$, $df = 2$).
e. "Other" refers to respondents who lived with others and paid no rent.
f. Differences are not significant at the $p \leq .05$ level ($x^2 = 0.258$, $df = 2$).
g. Differences are significant at the $p \leq .05$ level ($x^2 = 24.36$, $df = 10$).
h. Differences are not significant at the $p \leq .05$ level ($x^2 = 3.46$, $df = 3$).
i. Differences are not significant at the $p \leq .05$ level ($x^2 = 9.14$, $df = 3$).
j. Differences are not significant at the $p \leq .05$ level ($x^2 = 72.90$, $df = 4$). Income was not ascertained for 66 cases in the 1987 survey and thus was excluded for the chi-square analysis. All missing income data are allocated in the CPS.

the population of women born at the turn of the century are beyond the power of this study. However, the 1987 sample contains important lessons about older women's lives that can be applied to the larger population.

Sociological Implications of 1987 Sample Characteristics

Turning from representativeness in a narrow statistical sense to the broader sociological issues, the eligibility criteria of the 1978 sample excluded three large categories of women from the 1987 sample: black women, women who never married, and women too frail or ill in 1978 to live at home or participate in a long interview about their backgrounds, reproductive practices, and methods of contraception (see note 2).

Given the fact that white, ever-married women constitute some four-fifths of the population of women aged 77 to 87 years old, what are the implications of excluding the fifth who are nonwhite, have never married, or were not sufficiently fit to undergo an interview in 1978? The import for successful aging of omitting each of these categories is considered next.

RACE

Over the past decade, research on the black aged has had a poor showing. This study is no exception. James S. Jackson, professor of psychology at University of Michigan and a researcher on black aging, has observed that theories about aging are "white" theories. In 1985 blacks made up only about 8 percent of persons 65 and older. This means, says Jackson, that in large studies of the general population, the numbers of blacks have often been too small to make statistical comparisons that would throw light on the aging process in different subcategories (e.g., by sex, age, level of schooling, occupation, marital status).

Studies of the elderly that have included data by race suggest that the health status, kinship structure, and modes of support of the black elderly are markedly different from those of the white elderly. Although patterns of aged care among the races are becoming more similar over time, in the past, for example, black old people were substantially underrepresented among residents in nursing homes (Day 1987a). The reasons for racial differences in long-term care have yet to be thoroughly explored, but a new book, Black Aged (Harel, McKinney, and Williams 1990) addresses this and other questions concerning the impact of racism and economic limitations on service needs and uses. Cultural values about care of the aged at home, income, rules regarding medical entitlements, and discrimination against blacks and persons of low income in admission to nursing homes have been cited as possible contributory factors to racial differences in aged care (Day 1987a; Hing 1987).

The convention has been to assume that black families rely more on the extended family to divide responsibility for the care of their older dependent kin. However, another explanation that emphasizes the similarities rather than the differences between the races may be equally valid. Low income among older blacks and their families may preclude the option of maintaining separate households, just as it does among whites. The low proportion of home owners among elderly blacks living in large metropolitan areas would also contribute to observed racial differences in the distribution of extended households among the very old. Tracking changes in these factors over time by means of panel studies would contribute immeasurably to understanding current racial differences in living arrangements among the aged, and what future demographic trends portend.

So far as this study is concerned, the absence of nonwhite women means that this sample represents a group of women who, on average, are better educated and have higher incomes than the general population of older American women. As the proportion of nonwhites in the aged population increases, the numbers of very old nonwhite women living in large metropolitan areas can be expected to rise, correspondingly. Ensuring that these women have decent housing and adequate systems of support will require special vigilance. However, until systematic research is conducted comparing the particulars of aging among older women from different racial backgrounds, judgments about the impact of race on successful aging can at best be speculative. With the information now at hand, for example, we cannot say that older white women, typically, have a greater sense of psychological well-being than older nonwhite women, or that, age for age, white women in these cohorts are more likely to be able to manage daily activities with less difficulty than nonwhites.

MARITAL STATUS

Among women in these cohorts, marriage was overwhelmingly the norm. Some 95 percent of women born in the first decade of the 20th century were married at least once. Together, never-married men and women constitute about 5 percent to 10 percent of the cohorts 84 years and older (Longino 1987:4). The backgrounds, social networks, and aging experiences of people who have never married are quite different from those of the married. A higher proportion of never-married old women, for example, are employed outside the home, remain at home to care for elderly parents, live in households with people other than their blood relatives, and become institutionalized when they can no longer look after themselves.

Because of such differences in life experience, the conditions of successful aging among never-married women are also likely to be somewhat different. Marcil-Gratton and Légaré (1988:9) noted, on the basis of Canadian data, for example, that only half of the never-married live alone, whereas 8 out of 10 of the childless widowed or divorced do so. They accounted for this apparent anomaly by the fact that the never-married (who constitute 59 percent of the childless population aged 65 years and older in Canada) "have had a long time to develop other living arrangements."

Since the factors underlying low fertility were the main focus of the 1978 study, it made sense to restrict the 1978 sample to ever-married women. However, for research on successful aging, the exclusion of never-married women masks an important element of diversity that could illuminate the conditions underlying well-being in old age. A study based on Australian data found, for example, that never-married older people are self-sufficient individuals who enjoy spending time alone, and are living without the complications often associated with long-term commitment to one partner (Neyland and Shadbolt 1987). Never-married people in Neyland and Shadbolt's study, who were physically and mentally able and living outside institutions, were no more likely to suffer from depression, dissatisfaction, or loneliness than their married peers. In a similar result, using a random sample of individuals over 60 years of age from the Manitoba Health Services Commission, Chappell and Badger (1989) concluded that it is the type of relationship (such as having a confidant or a companion), not marital status or living arrangements, as such, that is related to a sense of well-being in later life.

The exclusion of never-married women constitutes an additional shortcoming in limiting the applicability of the results with respect to future cohorts of older women. If current trends continue, the proportion of never-married women may well be higher than it is today. Comparison of successful aging among married and never-married women, therefore, should make a fascinating and worthwhile topic for future research.

However, so far as successful aging is concerned, unless we assume a higher risk of being institutionalized as being the main criterion of less-successful aging—as with race, we cannot assume that never-married women are necessarily worse off in old age than married women or, consequently, that their absence from this research necessarily implies that the sample represents a more successful group of women than would otherwise be the case. There is no evidence to suggest that never-married women are less happy or less capable of managing independently than are their more numerous married counterparts.

POPULATION OF "ELITES?"

Earlier I pointed out that the 1978 sample was selected at random from women living in private households. A minimum level of frailty was not a criterion of eligibility,[13] and women residing in institutions were excluded. Does this mean that the women in this study are "an elite among older adults?" Because all respondents in the 1978 sam-

ple were living in "community settings," is one to assume that the
frail and the seriously ill were already underrepresented in the first
survey?

On one level, the answer is undoubtedly yes. Maddox wrote in
1987 that his early work with the Duke University panel study convinced him that, indeed, the study populations of most research on
older people have been biased in the direction of those who are
relatively fit, mentally and physically. The selective participation
and dropout involved in the collection of survey samples, he concluded, tends to ensure relatively elite samples: "In a sense, survivors
in later life who appear as participants in social surveys are, by
definition, elites of one sort or another" (Maddox 1987:558). However, in Maddox's view, the significant fact about the older people
in the Duke study was not their similarity but their extraordinary
heterogeneity. Despite the survey's bias toward "successful" individuals, he found a rich mix of health statuses and social circumstances. As noted in chapter 2, accounting for the fact of marked
differences even in an older population biased toward healthy individuals became, for Maddox, the prime issue in gerontological
research.

Heterogeneity is a marked feature of women in this book's study
also. Although the exclusion of race, the never married, and the
profoundly ill limits the breadth of generalizability, on most characteristics other than these, women in this sample (as is true of the
older population, generally) were highly diverse: some grew up on
farms, others in large urban centers; some had only a primary school
education, whereas others were college graduates; some married in
their teens, whereas others postponed marriage until their late 20s
and early 30s; some had no children, whereas others had five or
more; some had never worked, whereas others had been employed
since leaving school. When followed up in 1987, some were living
with husbands, whereas others were on their own or had moved in
with a son or daughter; some were fit and actively involved in the
community, whereas others were disabled and confined to home;
some had a large circle of close family and friends, whereas others
had only one or two people with whom they felt intimately connected.

In summary, accounting for diversity in the experience of aging is
a central research theme of this study. Including nonwhite, never-
married, and less fit women in the 1978 survey would have made
the 1987 findings more diverse and more generally applicable. But
so far as the consequences of excluding them for the findings on

successful aging are concerned, any conclusions must be considered highly speculative.

Women in the Qualitative Interviews: Spokespersons for Their Cohorts?

Women in the qualitative interviews were selected to enrich the survey findings and to explore a variety of research interests, not to represent the 1987 study population. All 20 women lived in the northeastern corridor of the United States—there were none from the Deep South, Middle West, or Far West. Moreover, the comparison with the full 1987 sample (table 3.7) showed that a higher proportion among women in the qualitative interviews had 12 years or more of schooling, moderate to high incomes, and the capacity to manage daily activities without help. In other words, the women interviewed in depth had a number of personal and social advantages. However, since they are not a representative sample of the 1987 follow-up population, any appearance of successful aging among them cannot be taken as a signal for complacency about the general population of women in their late 70s and 80s. Rather, the qualitative interviews are meant to provide concrete illustrations of aspects of older women's daily lives that facilitate or deter a satisfying experience of aging.

The "Family Filter"

A further observation about the qualitative study raises another question about representativeness in surveys of older women. In both this and the comparable qualitative study I conducted in Sydney, Australia (Day 1985a), I found it difficult to make contact with older women living in a household belonging to an adult child. I call this the "family filter" effect. I found that adult children with an older mother living in their home were often reluctant to have her talk to me. The distribution of living arrangements shown in table 3.6 illustrates this point. Four types of living arrangements are represented: seven women lived alone, six with their husband, four in their own house with someone other than a husband and, three in homes for the elderly. Conspicuously absent is the type of living arrangement in which a woman lives in a household belonging to someone else.

Although the proportion of women in this study living with a daughter or son is small (14 percent in the 1987 sample, see table 4.3), among the pool of 47 from whom I selected the women in the qualitative study, there were a number living in the homes of adult children. However, I was unable to reach them. The son or daughter with whom they were living tended to answer the telephone or door and claim that their mother did not care to be interviewed (Appendix 3-C).

There are good reasons why a "family filter" may operate. A substantial literature documents that among older people in urban societies, living in another person's household is associated with social and economic disadvantages: lower income, poorer health, and greater dependence for help with daily activities (see Wolf and Soldo 1988:389). In other words, an older women living in a daughter's or son's home is more likely to be unwell, and perhaps not up to talking to a stranger.

However, another factor may account for this apparent screening—that is, overprotection of the parent by the child. In this connection, the threat of loss of autonomy seems indeed to underlie the preference stated by over 6 in 10 women in this study for "staying at home with outside help" (table 3.5). The fact that only 5 percent said they would prefer to live with an adult child suggests that, barring moving to an institution, sharing a house with a child is the arrangement of last resort.

HOME OWNERSHIP AND AUTONOMY

Ownership of the home, not the presence of a child per se, makes the crucial difference. Four women in the qualitative interviews had others living in their home. Divorced daughters and sons, and grandchildren from broken marriages, were typical lodgers. Mrs. Danburger, for example, was in poor health and living in very modest circumstances. A divorced son lived with her and her husband. But he had no say in whom Mrs. Danburger spoke to or invited into her house. As she saw it, he was a guest in her home.

This observation about home ownership and autonomy, although based on anecdotal evidence, highlights an important condition of successful aging. There is a distinction between having to quit your home to move in with someone else and having someone move in with you. The experience of women in this study suggests that the consequences of the former are the relinquishment of autonomy and having to comply with someone else's rules; and that the consequences of the latter are the retaining of control and having others respond to your wishes. Chapter 6 presents quantitative data bearing out the insights from these qualitative perspectives.

LIFE-COURSE PERSPECTIVES AND
MAJOR LIFE TRANSITIONS

Life-course perspectives played an important part in framing the 1987 follow-up study, and they foreshadow the topic of the chapter following. A number of researchers cited in chapter 2 argued that aging must be seen as "a lifelong process of growing up and growing old" (Riley 1979). Not only does aging take place over the entire life course, but it is also in constant interplay with society—both shaped by and reshaping social institutions, technology, and values. Seen in this light, the transitions of women in this study are both affected by social conditions and historical events and, in turn, have implications for the social context in which future cohorts of women grow up and grow old.

Successful aging as a special case is subject to the same sociological principles. It is an outcome of lifelong personal experience, acquired within a particular social and historical setting. All the women in this study were born before the Great War and all endured the Great Depression at a time when they were getting married and making decisions about having children. As a consequence, they share certain common features that distinguish them both from people in other age groups and from people in past and future cohorts in the same age group. Therefore, in assessing how these women have fared in terms of successful aging, we need to know something about the major life events that have colored their aging experience.

I have called women in these cohorts "remarkable survivors," for two reasons. One is the nature of the social and historical setting in which these women have grown up, have married, borne children, and accumulated the skills and resources with which they now face the challenges of aging. The other is the nature of events they have experienced over the last 10 years, data which form the core of the 1987 survey. Hence, chapter 4 focuses primarily on what happened to these women during the decade from 1978 through 1987 and how they felt about it. The evidence presented supports the claim that women in this study are a courageous and resilient group of survivors.

Notes

1. For a description of the individuals involved in designing and conducting the 1978 and 1987 studies, see the Acknowledgments.

2. On the basis of letters that Koray Tanfer, research director at the Institute for Survey Research, Temple University, and fieldwork director for the surveys, received from respondents, as well as my own conversations with women in the field, it is clear that some women found the topic of the 1978 survey offensive. Several I spoke with remarked that the questions about sex and birth control techniques were really no one's business but their own. Nevertheless, the overall impression of interviewers in the 1978 survey was very favorable: they ranked the respondent's cooperation as "very good" in 69 percent of cases, and, in 53 percent of cases, they recorded the respondent's attitudes in answering questions about contraceptive practices and pregnancy history as "very comfortable."

3. As noted in chapter 2, in making this choice, I was particularly influenced by M. Powell Lawton and his colleagues at the Philadelphia Geriatric Center, who designed "the MAI" (Multi-Level Assessment Instrument). Lawton and his colleagues have argued (1982a:92) that to assess the "good life" for older people, data are needed on four major sectors, each with multiple dimensions: (1) functional capacity, (2) psychological well-being, (3) perceived quality of life, and (4) objective environmental conditions. Of these domains, Lawton believes that the last is probably the least well developed and that, therefore, one of the most pressing needs in research on the aged is to explore the way older people evaluate their environment—housing, neighborhoods, social amenities, transport, and so forth.

4. I personally interviewed the one woman from the 1978 survey who was living overseas in 1987. Born in Finland, but migrating to the United States as a young wife some 50 years ago, this respondent said she had returned "home" following her husband's death. The event, she said, that had affected her life the most in the last 10 years was not, however, her husband's death, but being able to speak once more in her native tongue—a striking example of the tenacity of language and of national origins in shaping people's feelings about identity and belonging.

5. A two-tiered system of searching was used. First, efforts to establish contact were made from the Institute for Survey Research (ISR), Temple University, through two mailings and telephone inquiries to persons (such as relatives, friends, pastors) whom women in the 1978 survey had designated as contacts who might know about their future whereabouts. When all attempts from the ISR office had been exhausted, extensive tracing in the field was carried out by interviewers who had been coached in techniques of locating missing persons.

6. If it is assumed that the 30 women not located were alive and residing in households in 1987 (a conservative assumption) the response rate for those eligible for an interview among those residing in households would be 81.3. If all the nursing home residents are included among eligible women, the total response rate for the 1987 follow-up sample would be reduced to 79 percent (589 interviewed, 742 eligible) (Ridley and Gruber 1989:5). In a recent attitudinal survey of urban Australians, for example, Kelley, Evans, and Headey (1989:8) described a response rate of 58 percent as a satisfactory figure for a long survey in modern Australian conditions and as "similar to most comparable recent surveys in other Western societies."

7. Women who said they could do all of their housekeeping without help were not asked whether they could do the less physically demanding tasks associated with grooming and mobility.

8. The question was phrased, "When older people can no longer manage on their own, what do you think most want to do: stay at home with outside help, move in with children, move in with other relative(s), move to a retirement home, or move to a nursing home? A second question asked, "Which one of these arrangements would you prefer? Would you prefer to:" and repeated the options just listed.

9. Fieldwork for the qualitative interviews was funded, in part, by a National Institute

of Health Biomedical Research Support Grant (BRSG), and, in part, by The Urban Institute's general administrative funds.

10. Although it is certainly true that grafting a small fieldwork component onto two social surveys can provide an experimental design that is rudimentary at best, the insights generated by the more in-depth communication made it seem worthwhile to undertake the qualitative interviews.

11. For further details about the representativeness of the 1987 sample see Ridley and Gruber (1989).

12. The income differential may be accounted for by the fact that fully 12 percent of women in the 1987 survey sample refused to state their income, whereas in the Current Population Survey (CPS) data, such missing data were redistributed (Ridley and Gruber 1989). The high proportion in the category, "Other," under housing tenure in the 1987 sample, may also be a function of different methods of collecting and processing the information.

13. For a discussion of the biases in studies of the burden on family caregivers (usually wives helping husbands and daughters helping elderly parents), introduced by selecting samples of older people from social service organizations, see Matthews (1985).

ASSETS OF 1987 STUDY DESIGN FOR STUDY OF SUCCESSFUL AGING

CHARACTERISTICS OF THE 1978 SAMPLE

Women participating in the 1978 survey were drawn at random from residents living in private households; those in institutions were excluded. The 1987 survey traced the original 1,049 respondents, tracking them, where possible, into institutions as well. Thus, the 1987 survey included women who are fit and healthy as well as those who are frail and ill, women living at home as well as those residing in institutions, the independent as well as the dependent.

Many American studies of people in this "very old" age group (e.g., National Long-Term Care Survey 1982; Informal Caregivers Survey 1983; McKinlay and Tennstedt 1987) have deliberately selected their samples to represent at least a minimum level of dependency, their samples being drawn from the clients of social agencies catering to the needs of frail older people and their helpers. In contrast, this study included many individuals who are managing well on their own and have had no need for formal care. In drawing upon women who are fully functional, the design of this study satisfies a criterion recommended by several researchers in chapter 2 (e.g., Maddox 1987; Rowe and Kahn 1987)—that studies of aging should include the full range of diverse elderly, rather than just the frail or ill, or dependent.

LONGITUDINAL DESIGN

Another study asset was the longitudinal design. Spacing the two surveys a decade apart yielded insights into the lives of these women as they moved into their 80s. This is a time when capacity to manage independently tends to decline sharply, along with increased losses of family and friends. It is also a time when the threat of dependency, and the need to make decisions relating to more comprehensive care, become increasingly prominent (see chapter 4). The heightened risk of drastic changes in life-style and in capacity for independent activity makes the study of successful aging among these cohorts particularly compelling.

MULTIPLE SOURCES OF INFORMATION

A third asset was the variety of source information. The 1978 survey interviewed only older women living in private households. The 1987 survey conducted interviews with three other sources: 1978 sample members who had moved into institutions; people, usually relatives, familiar with the circumstances of women who died in the 10-year interval; and "primary caregivers," designated by the older respondents as most responsible for providing help and support.

The interviews with the primary caregivers made available a linked sample of older women and caregivers (usually a husband, son, or daughter). This not only enabled study of reciprocity in the caregiving unit, but filled a gap in current research by providing information about caregivers in the general population of older people, rather than in one characterized by disability or institutionalization.

Research on successful aging often meets with skepticism, hardly surprising in this day of emphasis on "hard data" and "quasi-experimental" designs. Not only does the idea of success in old age seem contradictory, but, as described in chapter 2, previous approaches have used diverse definitions and an assortment of disciplinary frameworks. British researchers Nigel and Jane Fielding (1987:25) have pointed out that in social research, multiple sources of information can help to increase the researcher's confidence about the findings and lessen the need to resort to "the assertion of privileged insight." I can be confident about the research results, for example, because in addition to having data from a large structured survey, I have personally talked at length with a selection of women from the sample, in their own homes and on their own terms.

The Fieldings (1987:25) cited another role for multiple methods in social research: stimulating awareness that there is no one "truth" even in relation to events that seem "specific, discrete, and limited." This book's study makes it clear that different approaches and different sources produce different perspectives on "the truth" about aging among older women.

1987 FOLLOW-UP SURVEY: FORMAT OF SURVEY INSTRUMENTS AND CONDUCT OF INTERVIEWS

QUESTIONNAIRE CATEGORIES

The primary respondent questionnaire, addressed to women living in private households, provided the bulk of information about the survivors from the 1978 survey who agreed to participate in the follow-up survey. The instrument used for women living in institutions was virtually the same,[1] the only difference between it and the primary respondent questionnaire being the deletion of a few questions that clearly were not applicable to women living in group residential settings—for example, those relating to who provides help with the cooking, cleaning, and laundry were omitted on the grounds that in institutions, these tasks are performed by paid employees, whereas the intent of the questions was to find out about help provided informally in the home environment ("Who helps with housekeeping tasks?").

Spokespersons for the Deceased (N = 290)

A short questionnaire was designed to obtain information about the circumstances of members of the earlier sample who were deceased. Questions focused on the main outcomes of interest in this study, that is: mode of support, living arrangements, and institutionalization. Telephone interviews were conducted from the Institute for Survey Research office with a person informed about the deceased, preferably a close family member such as a son or daughter, or person with whom the deceased had been living prior to death. Interviews were obtained with spokespersons for 94 percent of the known deceased.

METHOD OF RECORDING SUPPORT PROVIDERS

Interviewers kept an inventory throughout the interview of the persons with whom respondents said they shared various kinds of informal support. For each of these "people who matter" (see chapter 5), the older women were asked to give a short description, including age, family characteristics, where and how far away they lived, and how often they had contact with that person (Appendix 5-A).

SUBJECTIVE PERCEPTIONS: ATTITUDE AND OPEN-ENDED QUESTIONS

I intended the survey to measure not just behavioral aspects of social support but also the subjective perspectives of the older women concerning the quality of their social support. Questions were included, therefore, not only to gauge general psychological well-being but also to determine levels of satisfaction with social relationships and with various community amenities such as safety, neighborhood facilities, and public transportation. The survey also incorporated a number of open-ended questions to explore the reasons why women in the sample had behaved in a certain way and held certain kinds of attitudes, such as why they had changed their residence in the interval between the two surveys or why some may have preferred living alone to sharing a household with an adult child or other relative.

CONTRIBUTION OF SURVEY INSTRUMENTS TO SUCCESSFUL AGING

The features of the 1987 instruments just described made it possible to build a broadly based model of successful aging. Chapter 6 integrates items on life domains and social support, gains and losses, and subjective orientations into scales of psychological well-being, capacity for self-help, and private reserves of social support.

CONDUCT OF INTERVIEWS

The interviewers were scheduled to run just under one hour, although, on the whole, interviewers found they took somewhat longer. Pilot interviews suggested that women in this age group would object to any hint that they were expected to be frail and dependent. Hence, questions about interests and activities were placed ahead of those dealing with illness symptoms and needs for help. Questions were included that, undoubtedly, left some women feeling sad, such as who among their family and close friends had died since 1978. But the interview also gave the women the chance to talk about their expectations and hopes for the future, and at the end they were asked to say what event in their lives over the past decade had affected their life the most.

Note

1. On the advice of Joy Spalding, former director of research for the National Citizens Coalition for Nursing Home Reform, Washington, D.C., I used virtually the same questionnaire for the nursing home residents as for women living in private homes.

QUALITATIVE INTERVIEWS: FIELDWORK PROCEDURES AND RESPONSE RATE

SELECTION OF PARTICIPANTS

Three criteria were used to select the areas in which to conduct the qualitative interviews: (1) proximity to Washington, D.C., (2) diversity of region within the radius of a day's drive of the nation's capital, and (3) degree of concentration of respondents around sampling points used in the 1987 survey. The initial selection of 47 women was thus determined by geographic location rather than by social criteria. Social factors, however, such as health and living arrangements, operated subsequently in narrowing the selection to 20 women (see description following).

RESPONSE RATE

The breakdown of outcomes from the 47 letters was as follows: 20 interviews, 10 refusals, 8 no contact (e.g., letter returned, no such person at that address, telephone disconnected), 2 moved to a nursing home, 6 unable to follow up (e.g., respondent was out of town or temporarily unable to be interviewed), 1 moved from previous address, but sent a letter saying that she would like to be interviewed.

There is evidence both from the Sydney, Australia, survey of people over 60 (Day 1985b) and this study of older American women that the elderly living with a family member have a considerable likelihood of being excluded from surveys in the screening phase by refusals at the door from family members responsible for their care. Among the 10 refusals in the fieldwork study (out of a total of 47 people contacted by letter), there were 4 instances where a relative with whom the older person was living refused for her. One of these, a son, said he saw "no benefit in it for her. If there was a benefit, she wouldn't mind doing it." He also said, "She is worse than last year." In the other 6 refusals, the respondents pleaded too busy, not interested, or ill health as their reasons for not wanting "to go through all that again." Such refusals fall into a catch-all category, "just don't want to be bothered."

RESPONDENT REACTIONS

In the 20 less-structured interviews I conducted myself, not one woman was curt or restless, although I took at least twice as long as did the interviewers on the 1987 survey. None became fatigued, and several said, "Come again, any time." I found the same difference in reactions to survey and fieldwork approaches among the old men and women I interviewed in Sydney, Australia (Day 1985b:16). Following the survey interviews, some of the old Australian men and women seemed let down, almost bewildered when the session was over. After the 80 minutes or so of highly structured questions, some even asked: "Is that all?"

This difference in reactions may be explained by an observation of British social historian Ronald Blythe (1979:15): "Constantly, as one talked to the aged, one felt this struggle to say who they are, not just who and what they have been." The structured format and pressures of time of the survey approach discourage older women from revealing what is on their minds. In contrast, the people who participated in the qualitative interviews were open and forthright because they had control over what was said and were able to determine for themselves what was significant.

Unlike the 1987 survey questionnaire where the questions were designed to apply to a typical woman aged 77 to 87, the flexible fieldwork format enabled the women I met to present themselves as unique individuals with idiosyncratic histories and particular concerns. Engaging in a life review of their own design permitted them "to say who they **are**, not just who and what they [had] been." This interpretation is also compatible with research reviewed in chapter 2 (e.g., Rodin 1986; Syme 1988), which suggests that older people tend to do better when they feel in control of a situation.

RESEARCH INSTRUMENTS

Letter Requesting Qualitative Interview

THE URBAN INSTITUTE

2100 M STREET, N.W. / WASHINGTON, D.C. 20037 / (202) 833-7200

PROJECT ON WOMEN BORN IN 1900-1910

October 31, 1988

Mrs. <name>

Dear Mrs. <sal>:

You may remember that we interviewed you in the Spring of 1987 in our study of women born in 1900-1910. You were generous enough then to contribute your time, and we appreciate your help very much. As Director of the project, I have gone over the information very carefully that you and the 600 other women in the study gave us. I am certain that your contribution will be very useful in the continuing effort to develop policies in the United States that will enable people in retirement to live comfortable, active lives.

The purpose of this letter is to ask your permission to come back to talk to you again. I am an older woman myself, and I have a mother 87 years old. The earlier study answered many questions about older women and their families, but it raised many others. I am particularly interested in things that you have found helpful in meeting the challenges of aging, what you do that you enjoy, and your views about things that would make it easier for you to live as you choose.

This interview will be more informal than the earlier one, and I will do all the interviews myself. I am planning to make a special trip from my home in Washington, D.C. to your area early in November. I will contact you to arrange a time we can get together at your convenience. I can answer any questions you might have then.

I hope I can count again on your interest and support. It means a lot. I look forward to talking with you.

Sincerely yours,

Dr. Alice T. Day
Project Director

Guide for Qualitative Interviews

Project on Women Born in 1900 to 1910

THE URBAN INSTITUTE

2100 M Street N.W., Washington, D.C. 20037

INTERVIEW GUIDE

INTRODUCTORY COMMENTS

I am the director of the study of women born in 1900 to 1910 in which you have been kind enough to participate twice before.

I think that women of your age are a special group of people. Your experiences have something to tell us about the times you have lived through and what it means to grow older in the world of today.

I wanted to meet some of you who were in those two earlier studies, and to talk to you myself about your life and the things that are important to you now.

I will guide you through the questions I am interested in—but mainly I am interested in YOUR ideas and what YOU think is important.

....

Of course, the interview will be entirely confidential, and you do not have to talk about anything you would prefer not to discuss.

....

MAJOR TOPICS

  A. ACTIVITIES

    What do you enjoy doing the most? Pastimes, hobbies? Social activities?

    Are you able to be as active as you were a year ago?

    Can you go up and down stairs? If not—who helps?

    Can you do the shopping? If not—who helps?

    Can you go outside walking distance? How do you go? Do you need help? If so—who helps?

    If you had more transportation, would you do anything you don't do now?

    Are there services in this community to help people get around? What are they? Are they sufficient?

Do you take trips/go visiting out of town?

B. FOOD

Is food important to your health and well-being?
What did you have for breakfast?
What are your favorite foods? fresh fruits, vegetables?
Have your eating habits changed over the past few years? How?
Do you do the cooking?

C. ENVIRONMENT/PHYSICAL SETTING

Safety—Do you feel safe: inside/outside–daytime/nighttime?
Amenities—Physical (shops/transport/parks/public spaces) Social (neighbors/groups/age distribution)
Housing—are you satisfied with your housing? Is there any way it might be improved? What about housing for older people in general—any ideas about that?
Police and other social services in neighborhood

D. SOCIAL SUPPORT

If the time came that you needed help of approximately 5 hours a week with eating, dressing, and getting around the house— who would you turn to for help? Family/Friends/Paid Help/ Community Services?
Are there services here that you could turn to? What are their names?
Plans for future care:
If you should need even more help than 5 hours with eating, dressing, and getting around inside the house, what arrangement would you prefer: stay at home with outside help, move in with children, move to a nursing home? How would you feel about going to a nursing home?
Have you made any plans/talked to anyone about what you would do? What did they think you should do?

E. CHANGES IN "ADAPTIVE DEMANDS" OVER THE PAST 5 YEARS
* **Physical fitness/capacity to get around/pace**
Serious illness or accident in past year?
Do you tire more easily? What do you do about it? Have you changed your routines to cope with feeling "slowed down"?

* **Role demands**
  Has what you do for others changed? Do you spend LESS time doing things for your friends/children? Do you spend MORE time helping anyone whom you are close to?
* **Daily routines**
  Are there any marked differences in your daily routines? Any activities you do more/any you do less?
* **Social networks**
  Have you lost anyone close to you over the last year? Who? How?
  Have you become close to anyone in the last year? Who? How?
  Have there been any major events in your family that are important to you—that may have changed your life in important respects?
  Do you see less of your friends/family than you used to? Why?
* **Financial affairs**
  Is your income adequate to your needs/to what you want to do? Has your financial situation changed over the past 5 years? Is it harder to make ends meet?

F. COPING STRATEGIES
  What experiences have you had that have given you strength?
  How do you usually go about solving problems that come up in your life?
  Do you have someone you usually talk to?
  Do you try to think things through on your own?
  Do you seek spiritual guidance (through prayer, for example)?

G. PAST EXPERIENCES THAT HAVE SHAPED COPING STRATEGIES
* Childhood: sibling relations/parental relations/illness, accident, disability/school—peers, teacher(s); hobbies; accomplishments/disappointments
* Young adulthood: work; marriage/childbearing; sport; accomplishments/disappointments
* Mature adulthood: empty nest; work experience; volunteer work; religious affiliation; accomplishments/disappointments

H. ORIENTATION TOWARD LIFE
  What would you say is the *best* thing that has happened to you in the past year?

What would you say is the *worst* thing that has happened to you in the past year?

What would you like most to happen in the next year? Dreams, hopes for the future?

All things considered, would you say your life is going: very well/fairly well/not so well/or not well at all? WHY DO YOU SAY THAT?

PARTING SUMMATION

WHAT DO YOU THINK IS THE SECRET OF A SUCCESSFUL LATER LIFE?

IS THERE ANYTHING WE HAVEN'T TALKED ABOUT THAT YOU THINK IS IMPORTANT TO YOU?

RATIONALE FOR CONDUCTING QUALITATIVE INTERVIEWS: SHORTCOMINGS OF SURVEY METHOD FOR COLLECTING INFORMATION ABOUT OLDER WOMEN

SUPPRESSION OF REASONS UNDERLYING BEHAVIOR: HELP-SEEKING

In suppressing much information about the reasons why older women act and feel as they do, the survey method can obscure key motivations underlying patterns of behavior characteristic of women in these cohorts.

Three women, for example, Mrs. Smart, Mrs. Carlton, and Mrs. King (see table 3-6)—all living alone and looking after themselves, but all beginning to experience a sense of physical vulnerability and of "slowing down"—swore they would not ask their children for help. At the same time, they themselves saw this insistence on independence as rigid and potentially threatening to their interests. With each, the issue arose when I introduced the question of "successful aging." "Is being independent important to success?" I asked. For all three, the answer was a qualified, yes and no. This response, perhaps, reveals an important aspect of successful aging, that is, a level of awareness that might be described as "perceptual muscle."

Each of these women was aware of encroaching dependence, and each understood the inherent weakness in rigid resistence to seeking help. Yet each saw asking for assistance and receiving help as a two-edged sword. Assistance might prolong their tenure in their house, for example. But a caregiver might also challenge their right to decide things for themselves.

UNDERREPORTING: ENUMERATION OF SOCIAL NETWORKS AND RELATIONSHIPS

The 1987 survey included a question asking whether, in the last two to three years, the women had formed a new supportive relationship.

It also asked about people with whom the respondents shared confidences and interests and activities. On the basis of responses in the qualitative interviews, my impression is that data in the 1987 survey understated the number and importance of these social relationships. It may be that the pressure for quick responses on the survey discouraged the women from taking the time to think carefully about the numbers of people with whom they enjoyed close relationships. However, the reporting of close personal ties may also be affected by a respondent's personal style.

An example is Mrs. Esherman who, although recorded in the 1987 survey as having only two persons on the support roster (table 3-6), described to me an active social life, lunching and doing craft work with old friends from school days and new friends she had met through church work. Her only living kin was a nephew.

A widow living alone in a comfortable, but somberly appointed two-bedroom apartment, Mrs. Esherman was a quiet, rather reserved person, very serious-minded, and not easy to draw out about herself or her private life. Given time, she began to talk about her interests and friends with quiet enthusiasm. Toward the end of our two hours together, she told me that she had remained childless to care for many years for an ailing mother, who lived with her and her first husband until death. She missed her second husband, she said, but her social life with her nephew and circle of friends was busy and very satisfying.

With over 15 persons on the support roster, Mrs. Worth presented quite a contrast. From the moment I entered her light, cheerful apartment and settled onto her bright flower-patterned chintz sofa, she launched into a spirited autobiography, enumerating her many friends and social activities and frequently lapsing into gales of laughter, while 90-year-old Mr. Worth looked on approvingly. Their one child, a son, was divorced and lived some hours away. But their lives were full of club and community events and they still enjoyed throwing an occasional large party. When I finally rose to leave, the Worths insisted that I have a ride on their electric chair, newly installed to ease Mr. Worth's climb to their third-floor apartment.

Thus, differences in personal styles may affect not only the number and quality of one's social relationships but also the ease with which they are recorded in a survey interview. This, in turn, influences an outsider's view of successful aging.

Chapter Four

MAJOR TRANSITIONS, MAJOR DILEMMAS

*The things that I can't change are the things
that bother me most . . .
my money and not being able to see.
Sometimes it gets tough.*

—Mrs. Peres, age 80

What kinds of events have women in this sample shared in common over the past decade? Chapter 3 called attention to the great diversity of backgrounds and circumstances found among the women in this research. This chapter examines whether any common patterns distinguish the aging process of this diverse group. The aim is to trace events in these women's lives from the time they were interviewed in 1978 to their follow-up interviews in 1987. What happened to their activities, their living arrangements, their families, and their capacity to manage day-to-day routines?

TWO PERSPECTIVES ON CHANGE

On the objective side of the story are demographic and social changes that shape the choices these women have in later life. On the subjective side are the older women's attitudes and feelings toward these changes, and the impact of events on their expectations and prospects for the future.

I start with the distribution of major changes among the sample as a whole. Because these changes involve the passage from one status or stage to another, I call them "transitions." Examples of such status changes are: married woman to widow, living with a partner to living alone, mother of one child to mother who has lost a child, person able to do her own housework to person dependent on help from others. These sorts of changes have significant implications for a woman's life-style and for her potential for independent living. Then, to highlight subjective reactions, I look at the attitudes and feelings of the women toward these passages. Together, the quantitative and qualitative perspectives provide a multidimensional view of the meaning of major alterations in these women's lives in the decade leading up to their late 70s and 80s.

QUANTITATIVE INDICATORS OF CHANGE

Table 4.1 presents a picture of changes in the sample's experience in quantitative terms. The data show the proportions of women in the 1987 sample who actually experienced alterations in at least one of six major domains—in marital status, living arrangements, functional capacity, perceived health status, network composition, and duration of residence.

Two ways of portraying these collective transitions are illustrated here. One is to look at the proportion of the 1987 survivors who underwent a particular kind of transition between the first and second interviews. For example, 21 percent of those whose status was "unmarried" in 1987 were "married" in 1978, while 7 percent of those whose status was "married" in 1987 were "unmarried" in 1978. Similarly, 10 percent of those who were living with someone (spouse or other person or in a nonprivate household) in 1987 had been living alone in 1978, and 14 percent of those describing their health in 1987, as "good," "fair," or "poor" described it in 1978 as "excellent."

The other way to look at life event transitions is to focus on women whose circumstances in 1978 placed them at risk of undergoing a status change. For example, 55 percent of those who had the status "married" in 1978 had entered the status "unmarried" by 1987. Similarly, 60 percent of those who were living with their husbands in 1978 were either living alone or with someone other than their husband nine years later.

This kind of longitudinal research has a limited capacity to measure the full complexity of change. Both approaches presented in table 4.1 record only net movement over the period. The actual number of transitions that have occurred may be somewhat greater. For example, a woman who was living alone in 1978 may be living in a nursing home in 1987, but in the intervening years, she might have

Table 4.1 MAJOR STATUS TRANSITIONS IN SELECTED LIFE DOMAINS, 1978–87: 1987 SAMPLE OF EVER-MARRIED WHITE WOMEN, BORN 1900–1910

Life Domains			Percentage of 1987 Sample (N = 589)	Percentage Net Change, 1978–87	Percentage of 1987 Population at Risk, 1978
Status 1978		Status 1987			
1. Marital Status					
Married	to	Unmarried	21		55
Unmarried	to	Married	7		11
2. Living arrangements					
Living alone	to	With spouse or with others or in institutions[a]	10		26
Living with spouse (only or with spouse and others)	to	Alone or with others or in institutions	38		60
Living with others (kin or nonkin)	to	Alone or in institutions	5		36
3. Functional capacity					
Status decline:					
No difficulty	to	Needs some help or cannot do without help	22		35
Some difficulty	to	Cannot do without help	9		33
Status rise:					
No difficulty	to	Can do without help	10		36
Unable to do without help	to	Needs some help or can do without help	2		3

continued

Table 4.1 MAJOR STATUS TRANSITIONS IN SELECTED LIFE DOMAINS, 1978–87: 1987 SAMPLE OF EVER-MARRIED WHITE WOMEN, BORN 1900–1910 (continued)

Life Domains			Percentage of 1987 Sample (N = 589)	Percentage Net Change, 1978–87	Percentage of 1987 Population at Risk, 1978
4. Perceived health status					
Status decline:					
Excellent	to	Good, fair, or poor	14		52
Good	to	Fair or poor	12		32
Fair	to	Poor	5		19
Status rise:					
Good	to	Excellent	6		23
Fair	to	Good or excellent	12		41
Poor	to	Excellent, good, or fair	3		45
5. Network relationships					
Network loss from death:					
Husband			21		55
Child			7		NA[b]
Son			5		
Daughter			2		
Grandchild			2		
Grandson			2		
Granddaughter			0		

continued

Table 4.1 MAJOR STATUS TRANSITIONS IN SELECTED LIFE DOMAINS, 1978–87: 1987 SAMPLE OF EVER-MARRIED WHITE WOMEN, BORN 1900–1910 (continued)

Life Domains	Percentage of 1987 Sample (N = 589)	Percentage Net Change, 1978–87	Percentage of 1987 Population at Risk, 1978
Sibling	39		
Brother	21		
Sister	18		
In-law	8		
Brother-in-law	5		
Sister-in-law	3		
Friend or neighbor	31		
Network loss from death of kin (other than husband):			
None	31		NA
1 or more	68		
2 or more	38		
3 or more	20		
4 or more	10		
Network gain:			
Husband	7		11
Child	8		NA
Close personal tie ("someone you can confide in")	34		

continued

Table 4.1 MAJOR STATUS TRANSITIONS IN SELECTED LIFE DOMAINS, 1978–87: 1987 SAMPLE OF EVER-MARRIED WHITE WOMEN, BORN 1900–1910 (continued)

Life Domains	Percentage of 1987 Sample (N = 589)	Percentage of 1987 Population at Risk, 1978	Percentage Net Change, 1978–87
6. Mobility status (years lived in current home, 1987)			
Stayers:			
20 years or more	46		
11 to 19 years	22		
Movers:			
6 to 10 years	13		
2 to 5 years	14		
Less than 2 years	9		

a. "Institutions" (or nonprivate households) covers all types of accommodation (e.g., homes for the aged, retirement homes, nursing homes) other than private households. Six percent of the 1987 sample lived in nonprivate households, a net change of 9 percent since 1978.

b. NA, not applicable. Population at risk not available from 1978 data, or at-risk category not applicable (e.g., 100 percent of the 1987 sample, including those in nursing homes in 1987, were in a position in 1978 to add a new relationship to their social network).

moved in with an adult daughter or son. Over the 10 years, she would thus actually have relocated twice, but only one change was recorded. We would have lost sight of the intervening move by having only two points of contact over the decade.

Change measured over a 10-year period can also overestimate the relative frequency of certain categories of moves. In the example just cited, the transition recorded is a move from living alone to living in an institution, when, actually, the more proximate type of relocation was from living with kin to living in a long-term care setting. The same sorts of abbreviated inventories of events are encountered in migration studies or in research into any kind of movement between two time periods—such as changes in household structure or in occupational status.

COMPARISON OF TRANSITIONS: WHOLE SAMPLE AND CATEGORIES "AT RISK"

Bearing this in mind, the data in table 4.1 show that the proportions in the "at risk" category are substantially larger because the denominators in these categories are smaller. For example, 1 in 5 (21 percent) of the women followed up in 1987 had become a widow over the decade, but among the 222 of those surviving to 1987 who were still married in 1978, more than half (55 percent) had experienced the death of a husband.

Another example is the change in the proportions who had no difficulty doing a number of tasks of daily living over the period under study. One in five (22 percent) of the whole sample moved from a position of being able to do all tasks with no difficulty to one of needing at least some help. However, among those who had experienced no difficulty in 1978, over one in three (35 percent) had undergone at least some decline in independent activity by 1987. By the same token, decline in the perception of health from excellent to something less than excellent, although only 14 percent among the sample at large, was fully one in two (52 percent) among those who in 1978 said their health was "excellent."

Negative and Positive Events

The transitions in table 4.1 reflect both losses and gains. Evidence of upheaval is implicit in several kinds of events: the number of deaths occurring to close family members, the net changes in living arrangements affecting nearly 40 percent of the sample, and the suggestion of a marked deterioration in functional capacity among a sizable proportion. Studies (see Maddox 1987) have reported that the way older people perceive their health is generally a reliable measure of their physical condition and capacity to manage. Hence, the sharp decline in the proportions thinking their health is "excellent" is indicative of the increasing sense of limitations many women in this sample experienced as they moved into their late 70s and 80s.

However, improvements as well as setbacks are seen in these transitions—in the capacity of these women to help themselves, in their perception of health, and in the 3 in 10 women (34 percent) who said that over the past two years they had formed a new supportive relationship. These findings show that not all passages at this late stage in women's lives are negative; rather, we need to think in terms of "the many faces of aging." The pages following look more closely at these major transitions and their significance for the outlooks and prospects of women at these ages.

LIVING ARRANGEMENTS AND SOCIAL SUPPORT

Household Composition and Quality of Care

The composition of an older person's household is a major determinant of the amount and type of social support potentially available.[1] Whether an older individual lives alone, with a spouse, or with an adult child, or in a nursing home both reflects and influences a variety of economic and social factors that in turn affect the character of caregiving relationships. Living with a spouse, for example, maximizes the opportunity for provision of substantial long-term care. Living alone, in contrast, requires a minimum capacity for self-help, with any assistance having to come from outside the household, thus incurring the risk of only casual outside attention to well-being, of delays in the receipt of needed help, and of inconvenience to the caregiver(s). Living with an adult child permits close monitoring and immediate reaction to need, but it involves intergenerational relations at close quarters, and the potential stress associated with dependency of the older person, role reversal between parent and child, and, for the primary caregiver, the possibility of competing loyalties and demands between husband and children and older parent (Parker 1988). Living in a nursing home or other protective environment offers security and comprehensive care, but challenges the individual's identity and autonomy.

General Population Trends

The close tie between living arrangements and characteristics of care underlines the potential significance for successful aging of trends over the past two decades in the household composition of older women in the United States.[2] "Numerically, the most important change in women's living arrangements is [the] large increase in independent living among older women" (Bianchi and Spain 1986:95). Because of their longer expectation of life, living alone in old age has been a much more prominent feature of women's life chances than of men's.

To account for the large increase in the propensity of older women to live alone, researchers have looked for major changes in income, in kin structures, and in general levels of health. In the context of such structural changes, scholars have speculated that there also may have been shifts in the norms, tastes, and preferences of the elderly and the people with whom they are most likely to share a household—their adult children. One explanation, for example, is that the desire for privacy among members of the nuclear family may have increased, leading to a shift away from the inclusion of grandparents in the core family household (Kobrin 1981:370–77). Researchers concur, however, that such changes in preferences cannot be seen in a vacuum; they are linked to changes in the capacity of younger and older generations to afford to live apart (Beresford and Rivlin 1966). A number of studies have purported to show that the propensity to live alone rises as income rises.

Wolf's research (1983, 1984) challenged this simple economic explanation. Extending analysis of the relationship between living arrangements and income to include a third variable, "kin availability," he argued that by reducing the "supply" of children, declining family size has introduced an important constraint on choices of living arrangements. This view conforms to earlier findings showing that although the probability of living with kin declined sharply between 1962 and 1975, the presence of at least one living child lowers the probability of an elderly person's living alone (Bachrach 1980:627–36; Wolf 1983).

For the purposes here, it is important to note that the relationship between income and living arrangements is a two-way affair. Not only is income an important influence on older people's choice of living arrangements, but living arrangements, in turn, have a profound impact on income security. Dramatic increases in the probability that older women will live alone are associated with a growing concentration of women among the elderly poor. Three decades ago (in 1959), women living alone or with nonkin constituted less than a third (29 percent) of all elderly poor; by 1984, this proportion had increased to over half (52 percent) (Holden 1988). Moon (1986:4) wrote that, contrary to what we might expect, poverty does not rise dramatically with age. "Rather, poverty among elderly women is almost exclusively associated with being unmarried." The fact that, among all women in each age group, poverty rates do go up is a function not of chronological age but of the rising rate of widowhood over women's life course.

Subjective Dimensions of Living Arrangements

Given these trends among the general population, what can the particular experiences of older women in this study tell us about the impact of changes in living arrangements on the preferences and lifestyles of women in these ages?

The data here show that for women participating in the 1987 survey, living arrangements were highly tinged with feelings about independence and support. Like people in the same age group interviewed in Sydney, Australia (Day, 1985a), these 77- to 87-year-old women clearly place great store in maintaining control over their decisions and activities. They see keeping a separate household both as the norm for people in their age group and as the situation they most prefer for themselves (see chapter 3). Altogether 530 (90 percent) of the 1987 sample said that, if they could no longer manage on their own, they would prefer an arrangement other than moving in with a son or daughter or other relative(s). Asked in an open-ended question why this was so, women in this sample gave two main reasons: (1) wanting to be independent and to control their own affairs, and (2) not wanting to be a burden or to interfere in the lives of others (table 4.2). Four in 10 (44 percent) spoke of wanting "to do things my own way," "to be my own boss." Nearly a third (32 percent) claimed, "it would be inconvenient for my children to have me," and that "children have their own lives." A total of 54 women (10 percent) specifically mentioned the dangers of generating bad feelings that can result when different generations share a household. One woman stated tersely: "I don't think there is a house big

Table 4.2 REASONS GIVEN FOR PREFERRING NOT TO MOVE IN WITH AN
ADULT CHILD OR RELATIVE: WOMEN BORN 1900–1910, 1987
SURVEY

	Number (N = 530)[a]	Percentage
Independence/control "To be independent." "To control my own life."/"Be my own boss."	231	44
Don't want to be a burden; inconvenient for children "Children have their own lives." "Living with others creates family conflict."	222 168 54	42 32 10
Accommodation not appropriate; better to live here "Not enough room."/"Too cold." "None of my friends live there."	27	5
No other choice "No children."/"No one to live with." "No one has asked me."	22	4
Miscellaneous reasons "Would like to live in a group house." "Too sick to live with family."	15	3
Don't know/no answer	13	2
Total	530	100

Source: 1987 survey question H22: "Why would you want to do that?" ["Stay home
with outside help, Move to a retirement/nursing home instead of moving in with one
of your children or other relative(s)"].
a. Excludes the 59 women (10 percent of respondents) who said that they would
prefer to move in with a child or other relative, or were already living with a child
or other relative.

enough for two women." The number and proximity of children
does not appear to affect these sentiments. They are shared alike by
those with large families and the childless. Witness the following
comments from the study sample:

Number of Children and the Desire for Independence

"I like my independence—I want to come and go when I please. I
wouldn't want anyone to feel they have to take care of me. It is very
convenient here . . . . help is just a few minutes away."
[Widow, age 82, living in a nursing home; two sons, one daughter]

"I think it's disruptive for children. I wouldn't have any independence at all."
[Widow, age 83, living alone in her own home; two daughters]

"It's better to be with strangers instead of relatives—no use in burden [sic] them."

[Widow, age 77, living alone in her own home; two sons, two daughters]

"Because it's mine [her home]. I don't have to listen to a lot of crap. I like to be independent."

[Married, age 80, living with husband in a home they own; no children. A niece, whom they are very fond of, has invited them to live with her.]

"INTIMACY, BUT AT A DISTANCE"

On the other hand, when asked which of the events in their lives over the last 10 years had affected them most, many mentioned the pain of losing touch with sons and daughters—through illness, premature death of children, family breakup or moving residence. These responses, considered in association with the preceding statements, support once again the well-documented desire of older people for "intimacy, but at a distance" (Cherlin and Furstenberg 1986; Rosenmayr and Kockeis 1968).

The ambivalence between wanting to live alone for independence' sake, and wanting the security and companionship of living with others is reflected in responses to, "Do you now live alone?" A number of women described their living arrangements as they might wish them to be, not as an outside observer might classify them. Some women, who had been staying with family members for six months or more, said they lived alone; others who had a family member living with them on a very intermittent basis said they did not live alone; some referred to a friend living in a same building, but a different apartment, as "a roommate"; others claimed they were living alone when actually they had a live-in "partner"; and some living with a son or daughter claimed they were on their own to shield the household from the interviewer.

The strong element of subjectivity in the way women in the 1987 survey defined their living arrangements underlines two important points: first, that the concept of *household* means different things to different people; and second, that older women themselves fully recognize the dual significance of *household* as a context for social support—that is, they recognize the potential both for opportunities for help and for constraints on control in different types of living arrangements.

ATTITUDES TOWARD LIVING ALONE

The findings in this research strongly reinforce previous studies showing that, given a choice, a majority of older women prefer to live apart from their children or other relatives. However, content analysis of the responses to open-ended questions also makes clear that this widely held preference does not simply reflect a desire to live alone. Rather, maintaining a separate household is seen by women in this sample as the price they must pay for safeguarding three other highly valued priorities. The first priority is keeping their pride in tact. As family sociologists Cherlin and Furstenberg (1986) found in their study of American grandparents, many women in these ages are still extending a helping hand to their children and grandchildren on a regular basis, and particularly at times of family crisis. They see any shift from the active roles of being a helper and a counselor to the passive roles of being dependent and of being monitored as a blow to their pride and sense of self. The desire not to become a burden reflects the difficulty of changing that role.

A second priority they seek to safeguard is that of retaining their independence—that is, keeping control over their decisions and social activities: daily routines, diet, health maintenance, interests, and conduct of outside events. And a third priority is remaining in familiar surroundings—that is, not having to move away from the place that they see as holding the key to their identity, continuity, and power to determine the rules and "how things should be done."

Illuminating these three underlying priorities within the more general category, "preference for maintaining a separate household," is important to understanding both the strategies women develop in their later years to protect their vital interests, as well as their resistance to pressures from family members and service providers to move from living alone into alternative living arrangements that typically promise greater security but less control.

Changes in Living Arrangements, 1978 to 1987

Details concerning the changes in living arrangements that this sample of women actually experienced bring into sharper focus the situations with which they have to contend.

TYPES OF HOUSEHOLDS

The rules for categorizing households in this study take into account both the structural association between living arrangements and social support, and the subjective attitudes of the older women themselves. The categories outlined here reflect a hierarchy of claims to informal support—ranging from strong to less strong—that older women can make on members of their households. The strongest claims can be made on a husband, the weakest on nonkin. The support provided in institutional households is categorized as "formal." Following are the categories of households (Day 1988:3):

1, Lives alone
2, Lives with husband only
3, Lives with husband and others
4, Lives with member(s) of stem family (son or daughter only or with family of son/daughter)
5, Lives with member(s) of extended family (kin other than husband/son/daughter)
6, Lives with nonkin (all others not included above—e.g., friends, boarders)
7, Lives in institution[3]

This hierarchy implies an "other things being equal" qualification. Studies show that claims for care are mediated by the older person's needs, the availability (demographic and social) of potential providers, and preferences for particular relatives to minister to particular needs. The health status of the older person and the marital or employment status of stem family members, for example, will color the choice of caregiver.

In a study of "caregiving portfolios" of disabled older women, Wolf (1988) found, for example, that at every level of caregiving—whether primary, secondary, or tertiary—levels of disability were significant determinants of the choice of caregiver (if any). Given these qualifications, claims for support are strongest from spouses, less strong from stem relations (e.g., son, daughter, grandson, granddaughter), and less strong still from extended family members (uncle, aunt, sister, brother, niece, nephew) (Litwak 1985). The weakest claims over the long term are those on nonkin (e.g., friends, neighbors, and unpaid helpers, such as church workers or volunteers from charitable organizations).

In the sample described here, in 1978 all the women lived in private households. By 1987, 90 percent still did, the remainder having moved into nonprivate households.[4] Altogether, of the 589 women for whom information could be obtained, a net of 39 percent had a living arrangement in 1987 that was different from their household situation in 1978 (table 4.3). The proportions experiencing such a change over this period were: 23 percent among those living alone in 1978, 55 percent among those living with a husband, and 30 percent among those living with someone else (stem family, extended family, and nonkin). In 1978, 39 percent of these 589 women were living alone, 47 percent were living with a husband (with or without others), and 14 percent were living with someone other than a husband. In 1987, the proportion living alone had increased to 52 percent, the proportion living with a husband had declined to 22 percent, and the proportion living with someone else (including living in a nonprivate household) had increased to 26 percent.

IMPLICATIONS OF CHANGES FOR SOCIAL SUPPORT

Regarding these changes, three observations can be made with implications for social support. First, there has been both continuity and flux in living arrangements. On the one hand, substantial proportions of women had remained in households of the same type: nearly 8 in 10 (77 percent) of those living alone in 1987 were also alone in 1978, and nearly 7 in 10 (67 percent) of those living in 1987 with stem family members were living in 1978 with a stem family member as well (table 4.3). On the other hand, a major change in living arrangements can be seen in the 4 out of 10 (42 percent) of those living alone in 1987 who, in 1978, had been living with a husband.

Second, as noted earlier, changes in living arrangements over this interval reflect a time of potentially disrupting status transitions in the lives of these women. The increase in the proportion of women widowed and living alone at these advanced ages has important repercussions for financial security (Holden 1988:S22), family support (Antonucci and Akiyama 1987), and physical and mental well-being (Seeman and Berkman 1988). Such changes have important implications, as well, for dependency and intergenerational support. In 1978, 10 percent were living with a son or daughter or some other member of the stem family; in 1987 this proportion increased to 15 percent, as women moved from living alone or living with a husband to joining an adult child. In a cultural climate in which "intimacy, but at a distance" is the living arrangement preferred by most older people and their families, an increase of this magnitude (although small relative to the increase in those living alone) portends the

Table 4.3 LIVING ARRANGEMENTS OF WOMEN BORN 1990–1910: 1978 SURVEY SAMPLE FOLLOWED UP IN 1987, RESPONDENTS LIVING IN PRIVATE HOUSEHOLDS

Living Arrangements	Total	1987 Living Arrangements						Total
		Alone	Husband Only	Husband and Others	Stem Family	Extended Family	Nonkin	
Alone								
Number	211	178	3	0	22	2	6	211
Percentage	38	84	1	0	10	1	3	100
Husband only								
Number	234	102	108	6	15	2	1	234
Percentage	42	44	46	3	6	a	a	100
Husband and others								
Number	26	3	6	5	11	1	0	26
Percentage	5	11	23	19	42	4	0	100
Son/daughter and/or stem family member								
Number	57	13	1	0	40	2	1	57
Percentage	10	23	2	0	70	4	2	100
Brother/sister and/or extended family member								
Number	20	5	1	0	2	12	0	20
Percentage	4	25	5	0	10	60	0	100
Nonkin								
Number	3	1	1	0	0	0	1	3
Percentage	a	33	33	0	0	0	33	100
Total								
Number	551	302	120	11	90	19	9	551
Percentage	100	55	22	2	16	3	2	100

a. Less than 1 percent.

increasing dependency of women in the later years of old age on their middle-aged children—a transition that is not always easy for either older or younger generations (Brody 1981; Cantor 1983; Zarit, Todd, and Zarit 1986).

Finally, since economic status is a particularly significant determinant of one's ability in old age to afford to maintain a separate household (Wolf and Soldo 1988:389), the increased proportion living with stem family members signifies a growing interdependence in these later years between frailty, financial insufficiency, and the declining options to retain an independent household. Torrey's study (1988), cited in chapter 3, suggested that the aged hold on to their savings as long as possible, not to provide their children with estates, but to cover themselves in case of emergency or "to insure their financial security or independence." Certainly, the link between income and choice of living arrangements is not lost on women in this sample. Three in the qualitative interviews were explicit about the association, as demonstrated in the following examples.

Mrs. Smart, Mrs. Hoffman, and Mrs. Farmer: Income and Choice of Living Arrangements

Mrs. Smart, 82, a widow living alone, swam lengths every evening in the university pool a few blocks from her. Greeting me in a bright pink track suit, she said she had trouble making ends meet, but loved her home and would not want to move in with her only child, a daughter: "I can't seem to save anything on my income. My will's going to say, 'Being of sound mind, I spent it all before I left.' I would like to hold onto my home. I hope I'll be carried out of here."

Aged 88 when I met her, Mrs. Hoffman, a widow living alone, was among the most physically limited of the 20 I visited. She also was among the minority who had an income in the highest category, and could afford to hire a housekeeper to help with meals, cleaning, and getting around outside (tables 3.6 and 3.7). She had three sons to whom she was very close and who were financially quite well-off. One living in the same city had asked her to move into an apartment adjoining his house. But Mrs. Hoffman told me: "I like my independence and I can afford to do what I want. I'd have no alternative if I wasn't financially secure."

Mrs. Farmer, aged 87, sold her house when her husband died and moved into a retirement home. Our meeting was postponed because she was playing in a bridge tournament. Childless, she has three nieces to whom she is very close and who, she says, want her to come to live with them. But Mrs. Farmer was unequivocal: "I live here for independence. I don't want to bother everybody else. But most people don't have the money to do it."

LOSSES AND GAINS IN CLOSE RELATIONSHIPS

Kin are a major source of support for individuals of any age: for people in their late 70s and 80s, a number of studies have shown that close relatives, particularly members of the nuclear family, are the primary source of support (Antonucci and Akiyama 1987; Litwak 1985; Mugford and Kendig 1986; Stone, Cafferata, and Sangl 1987). In tracing the major events in these women's lives over the decade, therefore, losses and gains to their pool of family members are treated here as critical transitions affecting both their personal resources and the availability of social support.

Nonkin also figure prominently in the lives of older people, especially among those who are widowed and childless (Seeman and Berkman 1988). Thus, losses and gains to one's circle of friends are also documented here as major life events.

Death and Dislocation

The impact of deaths to kin at these late ages is exacerbated by the consequences of losing someone with whom one has been sharing a household. In particular, illness or death of a husband who has been providing support often precipitates the need to make alternative arrangements, such as moving in with an adult child or moving to a long-term care facility. Among caregivers in this study who said they had started helping the elderly respondent at a particular time, nearly 3 in 10 (28 percent) mentioned the husband's death as the reason they were called in to help.

Mrs. Grainger:
Illness of Spouse, Widowhood, and Dislocation

In the 1987 survey, Mrs. Grainger told the interviewer that because her husband, who had been helping to care for her following a quadruple by-pass operation, had, himself, suffered a debilitating stroke, she was obliged to do all the things he had previously done for her: "My husband used to do it before he went to the hospital—now I do it on my own—very slowly. I have a call button if I need help. I wear it around my neck."

Two years prior to the 1987 interview, she and her husband had moved away from their cottage by the lake into a high-rise building for people needing comprehensive care. Following her operation, said Mrs. Grainger, the house they had lived in for 17 years was "too much work for us—large grounds to care for."

Mr. Grainger, who, at that time unknown to Mrs. Grainger, was also very ill, made a downpayment and arranged for them to move into the retirement home—without consulting with his wife.

"The moving man called when I was out. My husband said, 'You'll never guess where you're going. What would you think if you didn't go home tonight? You're going to sleep in HT Plaza.' I started to cry. I thought I'd ease out. I didn't go back for a year. I didn't want to see it. We thought that this [the cottage] was going to be *it* for the rest of our life."

The shock of the move for Mrs. Grainger was still palpable when I met her more than two years later. Her sense of dislocation was heightened by the precipitious, unilateral way in which her husband had made all the arrangements, thus effectively removing the decision from her control (see Rodin 1986, also chapter 2, this volume).

Loss of Adult Children

Although less significant than widowhood as a factor precipitating a change in living arrangements, loss of adult children is nevertheless a shattering and potentially dislocating event. Forty-six women in the 1987 survey claimed to have lost a total of 64 children since 1978, a particularly traumatic loss for women in these ages because they expected "to go first." Mrs. Smart, the lively swimmer, described the suicide of her son 10 years previously as having a more shattering impact on her life than having her husband waste away at home with Alzheimer's disease.

The "ripple effects" of death on living arrangements is illustrated by this description of the loss of a son who had been a live-in caregiver, from a woman in the larger survey, not one of the participants in the qualitative interviews:

"My son died and that has affected my life. Having to break up my housekeeping and scatter my furniture and live with someone. Moving in here with my daughter and her family."

Although it may be a somewhat rare event for the death of a child to trigger such a chain reaction, the loss of a caregiver living in the same household often prompts the need for major readjustments.

Gender and Loss of Family and Friends

The proportion of the sample who, over the decade, had lost close relatives (besides their husband) ranged from nearly a third (31 percent), who said that no close member of their family had died, to 5 percent, who claimed that 5 or more close family members had died. One out of five in the 1987 sample had lost three or more close relatives (table 4.1). Those who came from large families, of course, were at risk of experiencing more deaths among their blood relatives—of siblings, nieces, and nephews. In all, more than two-thirds (68 percent) said that over the past 10 years they had lost a close family member besides their husband.

Deaths were particularly heavy among same-generation members of the extended family (i.e., brothers and sisters), and heavier among male members of the same- and second-generation kin (i.e., brothers-in-law, sons, sons-in-law) than among female members (i.e., sisters-in-law, daughters, daughters-in-law). Among the dozen who lost a grandchild, for all 12 that child was a grandson.

As age advances, close social relationships increasingly become confined to women—female kin and female friends. Since male kin, when they are available, tend to be the ones who assist in business and financial matters, the disproportionate depletion of men in these later years shifts the responsibility for managing business matters back onto either the older woman herself or to other female kin who may (or may not) be prepared to make appropriate decisions.

One woman, for example, who was widowed between the time of the two surveys, also lost two brothers, a brother-in-law, and a sister-in-law during this period. She described the main impact of life events at this time as, "Adjusting to being alone . . . making all your own decisions . . . lack of income." On the support roster, she listed two sons, both of whom lived in another state. The people she had most contact with were two daughters (one of whom she designated as the primary caregiver), three sisters, and two female friends.

Increments to Social Networks

A number of women also said they had increased their support networks over time. Forty-four women who were either widowed or divorced in 1978 were remarried in 1987. Mrs. Farnsworth's story (chapter 1) shows that remarriage in later life can close as well as open options for forming new close ties. However, the opportunity to remarry at these ages does at least create the potential for increasing intimate relationships. Forty-nine women in 1987 were recorded as having at least one more living child than they had in 1978. New friends were also added over the period. Asked about people who had come into their lives over the past two or three years, over one-third (N = 200) said they had met someone whom they felt quite close to, could confide in, and who provided emotional support. Although the numbers who had formed such new relationships are small by comparison with those who said they had lost people close to them, the findings deserve attention as evidence that in the later years of life the pool of potential support may expand as well as contract (Hagestad 1987).

FUNCTIONAL CAPACITY

Next to losses from death and moving away from the family home, the most traumatic transition cited by women in this sample involved changes in their own physical capacities—from being able to take care of themselves to relying on others to do the many things they once took for granted. For women in their late 70s and 80s, fear about diminishing capacities for self-help is a realistic concern. Studies of the elderly (Branch et al. 1984; Tennstedt and McKinlay 1987:5) have invariably shown a decline in physical capacities and an increase in the need for help as people have moved into their 80s. Fulton and Katz (1984:7) estimated, for example, that although only about one-tenth of people aged 65 to 74 living at home are dependent on others, among those 85 and older the proportion who need help at home rises to one-third. The percentage of older people who live in nursing homes also increases markedly in this decade: from 1.4 among those 65 to 74 to 21.6 for those 85 and older. Moreover, owing to their longer life expectancy and higher proportion widowed, very old women comprise a substantially higher proportion of the elderly population residing in institutions (Day 1987a; Longino 1987).

Significant Issues

The great value women in these ages attach to independent activity makes the question of declines in functional capacity a central interest in this research. However, I would argue that it is not enough simply to document, yet again, the fact that physical capacities decline with advancing age. For the study of successful aging, it is equally important to determine the capacities that older people, themselves, believe are most important. This subjective view of functional capacity is significant for two reasons: first, older people's priorities are a necessary component of planning services for the elderly and their families; and second, as described in chapter 2, despite the burgeoning literature on the aged and their social supports, the components of well-being in later life remain elusive, and the search for ways to measure success in aging continues (Rowe and Kahn 1987:143–49). Only by understanding the priorities of the elderly themselves can we move from our current position of suspended judgment to a clearer definition of the "good life" for old people.

Priorities about Activities

One way to find out about older people's priorities is simply to ask them. To find out what women in this study particularly like to do, the 1987 survey asked: "Of all the things you do, either as a pastime or as part of your daily routine or work, what one thing do you like to do the most?" Responses to this question reflect not only what these women enjoy doing, but their current capacities (see table 4.4).

Whether active or passive, the pastimes chosen also reflect the adaptation these women are making to changes they perceive in their capacities, rather than the sorts of activities they would necessarily prefer to undertake if they thought they had sufficient energy and physical stamina.

The wide variety of activities represented underscores yet again the great diversity among the age group. The small cell sizes are retained to illustrate the range of specific pastimes mentioned (table 4.4). "Home maintenance" headed the list and is popular among 25 percent of the sample. Ten percent elected gardening and yardwork as their favorite pastime within the home maintenance category, and 9 percent said they liked housework best of their daily activities.

The next two largest categories selected were "home crafts," with 20 percent of the sample, and "social events," with 19 percent of the sample. Under home crafts, "fancy work" was the largest single pastime mentioned in all categories. When combined with sewing and quilting, one woman in five chose this as the thing she liked best to do. A traditional vocation among women in this age group,

Table 4.4 ONE DAILY ACTIVITY WOMEN IN FOLLOW-UP SAMPLE LIKE TO DO
MOST: WOMEN BORN 1900–1910, 1987 SURVEY

Activity or pastime	Number	Percentage
1. Home Maintenance	**147**	**25**
Gardening/yardwork	59	10
Housework	46	9
Cooking/baking	35	6
Shopping	7	2
2. Home Crafts	**119**	**20**
Fancy work (knit, crochet, crafts)	85	14
Sewing	19	3
Quilting	15	3
3. Social Events	**109**	**19**
Dancing/bowling/playing bingo	39	6
Going out with friends/visiting friends	32	5
Going to church/church work	19	3
Seeing/talking to grandchildren	8	1
Work/Volunteer work	8	1
Senior citizens functions	3	a
4. Mental/Artistic Pursuits	**77**	**13**
Reading	60	10
Play the piano/organ	12	2
Writing	5	1
5. Passive Pursuits	**51**	**9**
Television	42	7
Rest/sleep	9	2
Eating	2	a
6. Physical Pursuits	**26**	**4**
Trips	13	2
Walking	11	2
Swimming	2	a
Other	26	4
"Nothing"	20	3
"Everything"	5	1
Don't know/no answer	9	2
Total	589	100

Note: Respondents were asked the following survey question: "Of all the things you
do, either as a pastime or as part of your daily routine or work, what *one* thing do
you like to do the most?"
a. Less than 1 percent.

"fancy work" has many assets: it is a creative pursuit that can range from simple to highly skilled work, it can generate income, and can be done at home. Importantly, home crafts can also be used to repay others for kindnesses and practical help, such as providing a ride to church or shoveling snow off a front walk. Cooking and baking can also be used to this end. For older women who are hard put to pay for extras, crafts and cooking can play an important part in maintaining reciprocity in the exchange of favors.

In the social events category, selected as a favorite pastime by 19 percent of the women, again, Mrs. Silvestri illustrates the particular significance for the aged living alone of activities that bring people together. She recognizes that the companionship of others is a vital counterpoint to a steady diet of one's own company: "Get with the people and talk with them. And that will make your day. When you come back, your house looks nicer, because you've been away for a couple of hours . . ." (chapter 1).

On the whole, women in this sample seemed to prefer activities of the mind, such as reading, writing, and playing a musical instrument, and relaxing activities such as watching television and resting ("passive pursuits"), to the more active physical exertion involved in, for instance, walking, swimming, and taking trips (see table 4.4).

When one combines the activities in four categories—home maintenance, home crafts, mental/artistic pursuits, and passive pursuits—over two-thirds (67 percent) of the sample said they enjoy a home-based pastime. Eighty-one women (15 percent) mentioned housework and cooking as favorite activities, and, if gardening and yard-work are combined with housework, fully one-quarter said they like taking care of their home the best of all.

What do these favorite pastimes imply about the functional capacities that are important to women in this sample?

HOUSEWORK: METAPHOR FOR SELF-MAINTENANCE

Studies I have conducted of people 75 years and older (Day 1985a) suggest that housework as a favorite pastime is a metaphor for the priority placed on self-management. It reflects a strongly held belief that being able to keep up one's own home without help is a key to retaining control over one's affairs. The attitude is that once one opens the door to outside help, one runs the risk of being taken over and managed. As a nearly blind 83-year-old man in Sydney, Australia, put it: "If I don't do it myself, someone else will. And, if that happens: I might drop my bundle" (Day 1985a).

By the same token, the home-centered and housekeeping activities enjoyed by women in this sample indicate their desire for continuity and self-help. These activities require certain minimum levels of functional capacity. For example, good eyesight is required to read, do "fancy work," leave home to visit family and friends, go to social meetings, and take trips. Second, sufficient physical stamina is needed to maintain a home independently, including doing the cooking, shopping, gardening, and housework. Third, underlying these physical necessities, mental acuity is necessary to orchestrate the changes in one's life and to retain control over one's affairs at a time when one's personal and social resources are dwindling.

The fact that much of what older women do takes place within the home does not justify expecting them to tolerate premature deterioration in functioning. One goal of successful aging, then, is to strengthen the match between interests and the ability to perform independently and without avoidable physical constraints. This approach is analogous to that taken by environmental psychologists in stressing the importance to the quality of life of balancing older people's capacities with the demands the environment makes on them (see Lawton et al. 1982a; also chapter 2, this volume). How well do the functional capacities of women in this study keep up with their priorities?

Description of Measures

To examine the match, between the women's functional capacities and their priorities, the 1987 study used a modified form of the measures, *Instrumental Activities of Daily Living* (IADLs) and *Activities of Daily Living* (ADLs), Lawton and Brody (1969).[5] Questions about functional capacity were introduced by the statement: "The next few questions are about activities some people have difficulty doing by themselves". This was followed by questions about performance of specified tasks, prefaced in each case by, "Can you do . . ." (for example, "Can you do the shopping for groceries?"). Respondents were classified into three levels of capacity to perform specified tasks: (1) "Without help," (2) "With some help," and (3) Unable to do without help. The tasks were grouped into two main categories:

1. *Instrumental Activities of Daily Living (IADLs)*: shopping, meals preparation, housework, laundry, managing finances. Managing finances, usually classified with the IADL tasks just listed, was treated separately for some of the analysis. The findings suggest

that the sample distribution regarding capacity to perform this activity was somewhat different from that on other IADL activities. For example, among those living alone, the proportion able to manage their finances on their own was much higher than the proportion who did not need help in activities requiring mobility outside the home such as shopping and anything involving walking a distance. When a husband dies, most widows, if they don't already manage the finances, can—with some initial counseling— take over this function. However, if a woman is unable to drive a car and has difficulty getting around, loss of a husband can severely restrict her outside social activities. It is activities involving going beyond the limits of the private home that those with an "environmental psychology perspective" (see chapter 2) believe are particularly necessary to underwrite if older people are to have an independent social life and not become isolated.

2. *Activities of Daily Living (ADLs)*: eating, getting around inside, bathing, washing, dressing, toileting. As discussed later, very few women in the 1987 sample, were unable to do these personal tasks. Of the five, getting around inside posed the most difficulties for those women who were somewhat disabled (figure 4.1 and notes).

Distribution of Functional Capacities

Figure 4.1 shows the percentage distribution of women in the 1987 sample according to the level of their capacity to manage eight daily activities: five IADLs and five ADLs. Of the five IADL tasks, the women said that shopping presented the most difficulty, and preparation of meals, the least difficulty. Over one-third (35 percent) said they needed some help or were unable to do without help with the former, and less than 1 in 5 (15 percent) said they needed help with the latter (percentages of those needing at least some help obtained by adding columns 2 and 3, statistics and notes for figure 4.1). This indicates the marked difference in capacity for independence between activities that require mobility outside the home and those that can be done inside at one's own pace and discretion. Ninety percent of the sample could take care of their personal needs: only 10 percent were unable to wash and bathe themselves without some help, and an even smaller proportion were unable to dress and undress, get around inside, or go to the toilet without help.

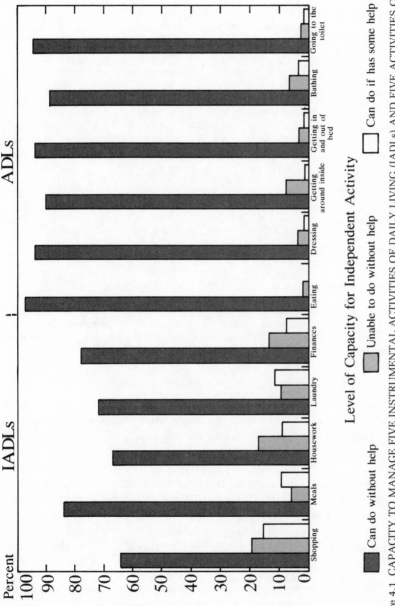

Figure 4.1 CAPACITY TO MANAGE FIVE INSTRUMENTAL ACTIVITIES OF DAILY LIVING (IADLs) AND FIVE ACTIVITIES OF DAILY LIVING (ADLs): WOMEN BORN 1900–1910, 1987 SURVEY

Statistics and Notes for Figure 4.1

	Percentage by Different Levels of Independent Activity				
	Can Do without Help	Can Do with Some Help	Unable to Do without Help	No Answer,	
Task	1	2	3	Not Included	Total
IADLs:					
Shopping	64.2	19.4	15.4	1.0	100
Meals	83.7	5.8	9.5	1.0	100
Housework	66.9	17.0	9.0	7.2[a]	100
Laundry	72.0	9.3	11.7	7.0[a]	100
Finances	77.9	13.4	7.5	1.2	100
ADLs:					
Eating	97.1	1.7	0.2	1.0	100
Dressing	93.7	3.7	1.5	1.0	100
Getting around inside	89.8	7.8	1.4	1.0	100
Getting in and out of bed	93.9	3.4	1.7	1.0	100
Bathing	88.6	6.8	3.6	1.0	100
Going to the toilet	94.6	2.7	1.7	1.0	100

a. On the grounds that the service would be provided for them, the 38 residents of nursing homes were not asked whether they could do their housework and laundry. Excluding these 38 from the denominators would raise the proportion who could do housework without help to 71.5 percent and laundry without help to 76.9 percent.

FUNCTIONAL CAPACITY, AGE, AND LIVING ARRANGEMENTS

The preceding figures, however, are averages for the sample as a whole: there are marked differences in these capacities by age and living arrangements. Even within the relatively narrow age range of 77 to 87 years, a comparison of needs for help in 1987 by age group shows that older age increases the likelihood of dependence on outside assistance. For example, the oldest one-third of women (84 to 87 years) were substantially more likely to be unable to do various tasks without help. Nearly 2 out of 3 (65 percent) of women in their late 70s (77 to 79 years of age) could manage without help, as compared to less than 3 in 10 (29 percent) of those in their mid- to late-80s. Conversely, less than 1 in 5 (16 percent) of those 77 to 79 years of age said they were unable to manage at least one IADL without help, compared with over one-third (35 percent) of those 84 to 87 years of age.

In terms of living arrangements, there were substantial differences in capacities along two lines: between women living in private house-holds and those living in nonprivate households, and between women living alone or with a spouse, and women living with a son, daughter, or other relatives. Those living with people other than their husband needed (or were getting) more help, whether they were living in a home for the aged or the home of a relative.

The association between age and increasing difficulty with man-aging on one's own is borne out in the longitudinal dimension of capacity to manage, as well.[6] Nearly one-third (31 percent) of the women in the 1987 survey were managing less well than in 1978, but 12 percent apparently were managing somewhat better (table 4.1). These net changes in functional capacity over the decade are reinforced by the changes in perceived health status: 31 percent felt that their health had declined compared to others in the age group, whereas 21 percent held a more optimistic view of their health rel-ative to others in their age group.

EXPECTATIONS AND HOPES

The reactions of women in the sample to changes in their lives were recorded in responses to three open-ended questions: two questions asked about the women's expectations and hopes for the future, and one asked them to describe which of the many life events touched upon in the 1987 interview had changed their lives the most.[7] The first two questions, "What do you expect to be doing a couple of years from now?", and "What would you really like to be doing?", are measures of a sense of the future. The third question—"We have talked about many things in your life: death of people close to you, making new friends, changes in your family, illness, changing where you live. In the last ten years, which of these things would you say changed your life the most?"—posed at the end of the interview, is a measure of the perceived salience of life events. Can the expec-tations and hopes of women in these ages be seen to be related in any way to the events that are most salient in their lives?

Salient Events

To explore this relationship, first consider responses to the question about salient events (table 4.5).[8] Sixteen percent of the respondents said that everything was pretty much the same, that is, "there have

Table 4.5 THE ONE EVENT IN THE PAST 10 YEARS, 1978–1987, THAT HAS
CHANGED YOUR LIFE THE MOST: WOMEN BORN 1900–1910

	Number (N = 589)	Percentage
No outstanding events	85	16
Events entailing loss	410	70
Losses to network membership:	236	40
Death of husband	143	24
Death/illness of family and friends	84	14
Lost contact/drifted apart	9	2
Bad health/slowing down: "Can't do as much as I used to."	113	19
Change in residence/relocation: "When I had to give up my home of 50 years. . . ."	36	6
Miscellaneous:	25	4
"Retiring from my job."	16	3
"Family problems."	5	1
"Change in neighborhood—afraid now."	5	1
Events entailing gains	67	11
New kin/new friends/new activity	26	4
Better health/able to do more	16	3
Miscellaneous:	25	4
"Increase in income."	5	1
"Better located/more convenient here."	20	3
Don't know/no answer	27	5
Total	589	100

Source: 1987 survey question J4: "We have talked about many things in your life:
death of people close to you, making new friends, changes in your family, illness,
changing where you live. In the last 10 years, which of these things would you say
changed your life the *most*?"

been no great changes in my life." Of those who did mention changes,
7 out of 10 referred to an event entailing a loss and 11 percent to an
event entailing a gain. Among those citing a loss, the largest category
comprised the 4 in 10 women who mentioned separation events—
losses in close relationships due to death, illness, or drifting apart.
Another nearly 1 in 5 (19 percent) said that deterioration in their
own health and vitality made the most difference. Seven percent
mentioned the effect on their lives of having to relocate—moving to

smaller quarters, moving in with relatives, or moving to a nursing home.

The 11 percent who deviated from the majority and referred to positive changes talked in specific terms about changes in their family situation, health, or activities that had enhanced their social life or improved their life-style—for example: "Made new friends," "A new grandchild in the family," "Better services," "I can do more now." Five women in the miscellaneous positive category specifically mentioned a rise in income, and at least one implied that the improvement in her economic status had enabled her to continue to live independently: "Getting a paid job so I can go on living in this apartment."

Sense of the Future

Turning to the first two questions about expectations and hopes (table 4.6), do the responses provide any insight into the impact of life events on a sense of the future? Over 50 percent said that in a couple of years they expected to be doing much the same thing they were doing now. Often, this desire for continuity was coupled with hope— for example: "hope I am doing the same thing," "hope there won't be any change." Another 3 out of 10 women said that they would be dead or, since they had no control over what happens anyway, they did not want to think about the future (e.g., "Pushing up the daisies," "Looking down on all of you from above," "Not in my hands," "Don't know, no idea"). Only 13 women expressed their future expectations in terms of being involved in a specific activity. Again, this was often couched in terms of hope (e.g., "Still going to music club and playing cards with friends, I hope").

INTERPRETATION OF RESPONSES

The tenor of these remarks reveals four broad orientations toward the future: (1) Control over events in old age is limited; (2) Change is the enemy, and time is the elderly's friend; (3) Consolidation and optimization are the relevant goals rather than growth and personal development; and (4) Death and physical finitude are a reality and are unavoidable. These women appear to be saying that when you are overtaken by events you cannot control or alter, such as death of a husband, child, or sibling; slowing down in physical energy; illness of family and friends; and the threat of having to move from your home—the best you can do is hope that things will stay the same. You hope that you will be able to consolidate your gains,

Table 4.6 EXPECTATIONS FOR THE FUTURE—WOMEN BORN 1900–1910: 1987
SURVEY ("WHAT DO YOU EXPECT TO BE DOING A COUPLE OF
YEARS FROM NOW?")

	Number (N = 551[a])	Percentage
Same as doing now "Just what I'm doing now, I recken." "Doing the same thing, I hope."	295	54
Fatalistic view: **"Nothing I can do about it"**	173	31
"Don't know." "No idea."	77	14
"Probably be dead. A person 85 can't expect to live too long."	68	12
"Not in my hands." "Take one day at a time." "I live day by day with the Lord."	28	5
Doing a specific activity	69	13
a. *Domestic pursuits* "Taking care of my home." "Reading, watching TV, sewing."	26	5
b. *Active, outdoor pursuits* "Walking, swimming." "Going on trips."	16	5
c. *Social pursuits* "Involved with my children." "Working with church group." "Going to Senior Citizens."	15	3
d. *Employment* "Still working/still doing my job."	6	1
Miscellaneous	4	[b]
No answer	4	[b]
Total	551	100

a. Women living in private households only.
b. Less than 1 percent.

optimize your resources, and keep what you are and what you have right now from being diminished by further losses.

Juxtaposing the three questions regarding hopes and expectations (see table 4.7) illustrates the ambiguity expressed by these women about expectations and their uncertainty about what will happen next. Three of the four women, Mrs. Danburger, Mrs. Fleishmann, and Mrs. Wright, mentioned deaths in the family as being the event that has affected their lives the most. In their close familiarity with death, women in their 80s are distinguished from all other groups in modern urban societies.

Table 4.7 EXPECTATIONS, HOPES, AND SALIENT EVENTS: WOMEN BORN 1900–1910

Mrs. Danburger

Expectations: "Pushing up the daisies."
Hopes: "Sitting on the porch swing as good as I am today."
Salient events: "Deaths in the family."

[Married, husband disabled. Very poor health. Needs help with shopping, laundry, transportation. Deaths to five family members in the last 10 years. Divorced son lives with them. Other son dying of cancer.]

Mrs. Worth

Expectations: "Breathing, I hope. Feel like I won't be living here."
Hopes: "Living right here."
Salient events: "Nothing has changed in the past 10 years."

[Married. Husband having trouble with stairs. Says her health has worsened in the last three years. Thinks they may soon have to give up their apartment and move to a retirement home to be nearer their one child, a son.]

Mrs. Fleishman

Expectations: "Not much more than I'm doing now. I'll be 80 years old. What does a person 80 years old do? I'll be happy if I can keep my eyesight and my health."
Hopes: "Just what I'm doing now."
Salient events: "My husband dying."

[Widowed three years. Living alone in large, suburban house. Having difficulty keeping up maintenance, housekeeping, and social activities.]

Mrs. Wright

Expectations: "I hope I'll be doing just like I am now. I don't want anything to change. I don't expect anything much to change."
Hopes: "Nothing great, I imagine just about the same old thing, staying right in the building here because I don't intend to move."
Salient events: "I had family members die and get divorced, but that didn't change my life. It changed most when I had to give up my house of 50 years. I had rooms of furniture and I gave it all away."

[Widowed over 10 years. Living in a high-rise, state-run home for the aged. Developed new health problems over the past year. Eight children.]

Source: Examples in this table are taken from the 1987 interview schedules of the 20 women followed up in the 1988 qualitative study.

MOVING RESIDENCE

Wanting to Stay Put

The findings on moving residence reinforce the observation that this is a group of women who want above all to stay put, to stay as they are and where they are. This is reflected both in the length of time they have stayed in the same place and in their attitudes toward relocation. Six out of 10 (66 percent) said they had not moved in the past 10 years. When interviewed in 1987, nearly half (46 percent) had lived where they were for 20 years or more (table 4.1). Over 8 in 10 (83 percent) said they "definitely" did not intend to move, and another 9 percent that they "probably" would not move. As though to stress determination to stay on, 7 out of 10 (73 percent) said they had "just the right amount of room." Mrs. King's situation provides a case in point.

Mrs. King:
Desire to Stay Put

Mrs. King was living alone in the house she and her husband purchased 48 years ago. "I don't like change," she said, "I want to stay in my home as long as possible." This is her wish—yet realizing it is becoming increasingly hard. Her only child, a daughter, lives on the West Coast and wants her mother to move out there to be with her. Mrs. King's answers to the questions on expectations, hopes, and major events reflected the growing tension she feels between the desire to stay put and the desire to see more of her daughter and two grandchildren. Her options are fading as angina and deteriorating eyesight reduce her capacity to get around by herself:

Expectations: "Probably doing the same as I am now. Hopefully, living in fairly good health."

Hopes: "I'd like to be able to travel more—go see my children."

Salient events: "Illness. Nothing severe, but it makes a difference."

MAJOR DILEMMAS

The dilemmas associated with major transitions over the decade are well illustrated by the experiences of women in the qualitative interviews.

1. Changes in social relationships. Over the 10 years, substantial changes had occurred in the social relationships of these 20 women. Five had lost their husband, 4 of the 6 who were still married were concerned that their husband's health was deteriorating to the point that he would soon be unable to manage in their present home. Eighteen had lost close family members besides their husband (for half of these women, the number of deaths was three or more).

2. Disasters to children loomed large in their concerns. One woman was mourning the rape of an adopted grandaughter, and two others were anxious about the diagnosis of cancer in a son. Six out of the 16 who had living children were distressed by divorce and family breakup among them. (Two, Mrs. Fleischmann and Mrs. Hammerstein, had taken major responsibility for rearing the child of a son or daughter's broken marriage.)

For the majority who saw their own marriage as stable and essentially happy, divorces among their children were particularly devastating. Mrs. Eisenstein, for example, described her son's and daughter's divorces as "a hurdle that I had to pass through. "When my son was divorced he lived with us. It was the hardest thing I ever did. He wasn't accustomed to the food we eat. There was added laundry, packing lunches—but I never complained." These marriage breakdowns made Mrs. Eisenstein feel, she says, that divorce "is worse than death, especially since I am happy with my husband . . . a few arguments but no serious quarrels."

3. Slowdown in functional capacities. Capacity to function adequately was an increasing source of anxiety. In the 1987 survey, 12 women said that health problems stood a little in the way of what they wanted to do, and when I talked to them over a year later, 15 reported that their capacity to help themselves had been further compromised by the onset of disabling conditions. Three had moved into homes for the elderly because of faltering strength and altered family circumstances. For those living alone, failing vision was a particular nightmare because it affected their ability to drive themselves to do the shopping and to keep up with social activities that they had been attending for years.

Maintaining past standards of housekeeping was a main area of activity affected by slowing down. For the 11 living in a house (rather than an apartment or retirement home), upkeep was becoming an increasing burden and physical strain. Mrs. Fleischmann told me it was hard to get help to paint her house and repair her roof. When maintenance men do come, she said, "They won't listen to how an old woman wants things done. My husband would have kept them in line."

4. To stay or to go. Worries about capacity to do housework and keep up their homes, in turn, were at the core of the dilemma about whether to stay or go. The 16 women who had children were wondering how long they should struggle on in their homes before "letting go" and relinquishing their privacy and autonomy for the greater security of living with or near a son or daughter.

Humanitarian Issues of Aging

The United Nations World Assembly on Aging, which convened in Paris in July 1982, released a document on the "humanitarian issues of aging" that captures the dynamic processes underlying the deepening dilemmas women face with advancing age.[9] The central thesis was that, as age advances, issues that involve basic human needs and human welfare become increasingly interdependent:

> The relation between income, food and nutrition, housing and living relationships, family status, health and health-care needs is such that a change in one area may affect any or all of the others. A reduction of income may lead to a decision to reduce food and nutritional levels in order to meet housing needs. Such reductions, however, may in turn affect the older person's ability to function or remain in a familiar household or may require greater care by family members or providers of services. This may in the long run, result in increasing separation and isolation from family and community. Because of this interdependence of needs, older people are socially more vulnerable than other adult groups. (United Nations 1982:6)

An illustration of this thesis from this book's study is the rising proportion of intergenerational households between 1978 and 1987, suggesting that as age advances there is an increasing interdependence between frailty, financial insecurity, and declining options for maintaining a separate household.

Limits to Self-Help: Social and Demographic Constraints

The circumstances of women in the qualitative interviews illuminate the nature of these interdependent relationships and the processes that increasingly circumscribe older women's choices about their living situation. Except for the three women who had already moved into homes for the elderly, all were concerned about what they would do if they could no longer manage without substantial help. They were uncertain about the alternatives available to them or about how to time their withdrawal from the life they had been leading since the early years of retirement. All 20, however, had resources of one sort or another to help them get by—at least, "for the moment": a person to care, a house they owned, financial resources to buy services, or sufficiently good health "to do for myself." Outside of the 20, however, Mrs. Peres's situation illustrates a starker pool of social supports. I did not visit her personally, but the 1987 interview conveyed her plight, as follows.

Mrs. Peres:
The Limits to Self-Help

Mrs. Peres's predicament reveals, finally, the rock-bottom limits to self-help and efficacy in old age that are set by conditions over which one has no control. The manager of the retirement home where Mrs. Peres lives was designated by her as her primary caregiver. She described Mrs. Peres as an independent person who struggles to maintain her dignity and to overcome the hardships of her circumstances. "She's a real inspiration. Maria is so independent and she could allow herself to be dependent, and that's why she's such an inspiration. There are people in better shape than she that allow themselves to behave more disabled."

Strong motivation for independence, however, does not compensate for the ineluctable constraints against self-help that Mrs. Peres's circumstances impose upon her. Her functional capacities, family composition, level of income, support network, and living arrangements all interact negatively to deny her the autonomy she so desires. Widowed 30 years and losing her eyesight, she is childless and has no living relatives except for an adopted brother who lives out of state and telephones once a year. Her support roster contains only two persons, the apartment manager and the distant brother.

Mrs. Peres says there is no one in whom she can confide and no one with whom she shares social activities: "I'm so limited in what I can do." To these already potentially isolating conditions is the added constraint imposed by meager income ($5,000 to $6,999). "My main problem," says Mrs. Peres, "is financial. I can't afford to go out."

Fading eyesight, little money, and no one to care make Mrs. Peres profoundly vulnerable and place her in a category that Kotlikoff and Morris (1987), researchers at the National Bureau of Economic Research, claim describes a substantial minority of elderly in the United States today—those "who are very poor and either have no children or have no children who provide significant time or care."

Here is a classic case of the interdependence of humanitarian issues. Widowed and childless, Mrs. Peres has no sources of informal support, and low income makes it difficult for her to pay for formal services. Yet, capacity for independent maintenance is a major criterion of eligibility for residents of her retirement home. Over the last decade, these interdependent forces have increasingly isolated her. She is reduced to relying on her own resilience. That she is near the end of her personal resources is reflected in what she says about her expectations, hopes, and the things that have mattered most over the past 10 years:

> Expectations: "I expect to be still taking care of myself, if it's possible. But I doubt it. I pray for it."

> Hopes: "I'd really like to see better, but this is a degenerative thing and it's not going to be."

> Salient events: "I wouldn't want to do anything different about my living. The things that I can't change are the things that bother me most . . . my money and not being able to see. Sometimes it gets tough."

The picture that emerges leaves no doubt that, with all the will in the world, the circumstances of some older women undermine their desire not to ask for, or be the recipient of, outside help. Women in these ages define public welfare as charity. Community services for the elderly, such as Meals on Wheels, home help, assisted transportation, or visiting nurses were not available to their aged parents, and they prefer not to use them. They tend to feel that they have no special claim on public assistance. A typical attitude is, "There's always someone worse off than me."

TRANSITIONS AND STATUS CHANGE

This review of the major transitions experienced by women in this study suggests that the challenges associated with aging are most readily discernible, and have the greatest potential for causing distress, at times of acute change in status, that is, married woman to widow; strong and hardy to frail and easily fatigued; independent home manager to dependent on help with housekeeping tasks; owner-occupier of the family home to sojourner in another's household or a group residence. These status changes all involve having to make decisions about living arrangements, life-styles, and environmental settings—decisions that profoundly affect autonomy, financial resources, preservation of close ties, opportunities for independent social activity, and continuity of self. The increase in life expectation has heightened the likelihood that American women, white and black alike, will have to confront one or more of these wrenching transitions in their lifetimes.

The Many Faces of Aging

In the effort to establish that chronological aging is a process distinct from biological deterioration (Rowe and Kahn 1987) and social disengagement (Cumming and Henry 1961), scholars of the aging process may unwittingly have fostered a new set of stereotypes—that old age is a time of fruition, release from responsibilities, and involvement in postponed creative activity. This is certainly the ideal. It may also describe the life-styles of an increasing number of rich "young olds." But as a description of the collective experience of the survivors among women born 1900 to 1910, such a picture is clearly one-sided. Contrary to current stereotypes, for women in their late 70s and 80s, the transitions associated with these years can be seen to rock the very foundations of self and security.

To suppress "the bads" of aging is as incorrect and dehumanizing as to fail to acknowledge "the goods." This is a group of women facing an uncertain and finite future—for the most part, realistically, and without flinching. What they expect is that things will get no better, what they hope is that things will get no worse, and what they fear is that things over which they have no control will rob them of their husbands, health, home, and power to remain in charge of their own affairs.

That a clear majority express their hopes for the future in terms of "staying as I am," might be seen as an eclipse of horizons and an end to the faith that things can get better (see Bearon 1989 and chapter 8, this volume). But it can also be seen as a sign of integrity, not despair—an acceptance, as Erikson says (1951:232), of "their one and only life cycle as something that had to be and that by necessity permitted of no substitution." The wish to "just be doing the same thing—keeping my health and independence," may reflect not so much a giving up as an appreciation of what one has and the deter-

mination not to give way to despair before the erosion of one's resources.

Notes

1. A more comprehensive version of the material in this section on living arrangements and social support is presented in (Day 1988).

2. For material on trends in living arrangements among older American women, I
have drawn heavily on the Census Monograph Series, *American Women in Transition*
(Bianchi and Spain 1986: 95–99), which includes extensive references to studies of
the effects of income on the propensity to live alone.

3. Different types of institutional settings were represented: 23 of those interviewed
were living in retirement/life care communities, and 6 were residents of comprehensive care nursing homes. To obtain an estimate of the incidence of institutionalization
prior to death, persons acquainted with the deceased were asked whether she had
ever been a patient in a nursing home, convalescent home, or rest home, the dates of
admission of the first and last times, and the duration of stays. According to the
informants, one-third (33 percent) of the deceased had been in an institution at least
once prior to death.

4. This calculation of the living arrangements in 1987 is based on a population from
which two groups of women from the initial sample were excluded: the 307 women (29
percent) known to have died, and the 112 for whom there was no information in 1987
(table 3.1—not located (30 women), refused to be interviewed, or were incapable of being
interviewed; no interview, 82 women). Given the likelihood that a disproportionate
number of those excluded were frail or seriously ill (Maddox 1987; Streib 1983), the
shift from private households to institutions over the decade is likely to be understated.
For the same reasons, the transition from living alone or with husband only to living
with someone else may also be underreprsented by the experiences of this sample.

5. These measures have been developed and refined over the years for use by cli-
nicians and researchers in assessing the physical capacities of older people (see, for
example, Lawton and Brody 1969; Lawton et al. 1982a; Lowenthal 1964).

6. Data on functional capacity in the two surveys are not strictly comparable: only
four tasks were included in 1978 (i.e., shopping, going up and down stairs, getting
around outside, and managing finances). Furthermore, the wording in the two surveys
is slightly different. The decision to forego strict comparability between the 1978 and
1987 surveys was made on the grounds that it was preferable in 1987 to use measures
of functional capacity that correspond to current practices.
    Instead of asking "Can you do" the shopping, and so forth, "with help," "with
some help," "unable to do without help," the 1978 survey asked: "Do you have
difficulty with." ["Now we have a few questions about certain activities some people
have difficulty doing by themselves. The first activity is going up and down stairs.
Do you have no difficulty with this, some difficulty, or are you completely unable to
do this by yourself?"]
    Given the strong value women place on managing independently, there may be a
difference between asking "Can you do?" and "Do you have difficulty with?" An
older person may see herself as having difficulty with a particular activity (e.g., it
causes her discomfort, she can only do it slowly, she feels that doing it may place

her at risk of injury). And yet she can still consistently define herself as able to manage the task without help. Other things being equal then, it is likely that the 1987 data on functional capacities underestimate changes over the decade in the proportion who need at least some help if they are to continue to live in their own homes.

7. It is important in interpreting the findings to know that women residing in institutions were not asked: "What do you expect to be doing a couple of years from now?" At the time I was developing the questionnaire, I was urged to exempt women in institutions from this question, on the grounds that it was insensitive and inappropriate to ask what they thought they would be doing in the future. The rationale was that people who are institutionalized could not be considered as people living "in the community." They are in a twilight zone, considered socially already half dead.

Joy Spalding, former research director of the National Citizens Coalition for Nursing Home Reform, whom I consulted about the questionnaire for nursing home residents, had quite a different perspective. She recommended that except in cases where the questions were clearly inapplicable, women in institutions should be asked the same questions as women living in private households. Dr. Spalding felt that older women in institutions have the same right to a future as have older women living in private homes. In hindsight, I agree, and another time would not exclude them, both for reasons of justice and science.

On the side of justice, women in institutions have the right to be considered on equal terms with women living in private households. Older women residents of institutions have as much right to a claim on the future as do women living in other types of arrangements, and, moreover, if the level of morale and independent activity is to be raised, residents in institutions should be actively encouraged to look upon themselves as having a stake in the future.

Second, from the viewpoint of social research, people living in institutions are an important part of the older population. After talking to women living in institutions, myself, I believe that there is much variety among them in their sense of well-being, physical capacities, and expectations about the future. Some are able to manage quite well, others are very ill. Some are able to retain "a resilient self-hood," while others succumb to the dehumanization of institutional living. Some have a sense of the future, others are simply waiting to die. There is even great diversity among institutional residents in their reserves of private support. Like those not living in institutions, some are affluent, others are poor. Some can pay their own way and afford quite luxurious accommodations, while others must rely on Medicaid and live under very stark conditions. Some have family members or friends who visit regularly, others are isolated and alone. The distributions of these characteristics among institutional residents are different from those among older women living in private households, but the views and life conditions of women in residential facilities need to be aired if we are to have an informed understanding of the human consequences of national policies and social arrangements regarding the elderly.

In this book's study, entering a nursing home is not defined as a sign of unsuccessful aging. Therefore, the fact that the 38 women residing in institutions were not asked the question about future expectations does not substantially alter the significance of orientations toward the future among the 551 women living in private households.

8. As in table 4.4's answers to "What one activity do you like to do the most?" the responses in table 4.5 include some very small cells. This is to indicate the diversity in the content of replies. I wanted to avoid burying in a "miscellaneous" category the rich detail reflecting the impact of events on women in this sample. This is not to suggest, however, that the proportions in these categories are generalizable to the larger population of women born at the turn of the century.

9. The United Nations statement defines "humanitarian issues" as those arising out of the nexus between basic human needs and the conditions of a society. Implicit in the definition is the fact that addressing issues of this kind requires a society to make decisions about the allocation of collective resources—financial, human, and natural.

Chapter Five

PEOPLE WHO MATTER

*We have each other when we're sick
because you have to go through so much.
That's what friends are.
To have a friend, you've got to be a friend.*

—Mrs. Carlton, age 78

Throughout this book, the contribution of social relationships to health and well-being has been a central interest. This chapter brings into sharper focus the core relationships of women in the sample— members of their families, as well as other people they confide in, share activities with, perform small services for, and turn to when in need of help. Of particular note is evidence of the significance of interdependence to successful aging. Interdependence, which is vital at all ages, assumes added weight in very old age because, as people move into the late years, practical help and emotional support become more necessary to sustain the management of day-to-day activities (chapter 4).

KEY QUESTIONS

A key question about the social relationships in this study is what they show about the support available to women in their late 70s and 80s—the strengths and limits of families to sustain mutual support over the entire life cycle, as well as the reserves of nonkin that

This chapter is a revised version of a paper presented with Lincoln H. Day, titled "Continuity and Change in Household Composition," at the European Population Association Conference on "Ageing Populations: Determinants and Consequences," Prague, July, 3–10, 1989.

are available to older women whose family members are in short supply. To what extent do the findings reflect Riley's (1983) observation that the unprecedented increases in longevity over the past two decades have changed the "configurations" of kinship structure? Has kinship structure become more extensive and complex and have the temporal and spatial boundaries of the family been altered? Have "the opportunities for close family relationships proliferated?" Do we find confirmation of Riley's claim that "these relationships are no longer prescribed as strict obligations. They must rather be earned—created and recreated by family members over their long lives"?

The phenomenon of longer life has existed, historically, for too short a time to determine the long-range effects on kin of changing patterns of family building and dissolution. The topic of intergenerational relations has attracted lively research interest in recent years (National Institute on Aging-National Institute on Child Health and Development [NIA-NICHD] Workshop 1987). Yet, as is the case with many topics in this comparatively new field of aging, there are differences in viewpoints on many issues—the unmet needs of the elderly, the role of families as an ultimate source of support, and the influence of social change on "a loss of community" among the aged.

The contribution of kin to care of the elderly also has important policy implications (Day 1989). In all industrialized countries, the projected costs of health care of older people and, in particular, of providing long-term residential care for rising numbers of people 85 years and older (Manton and Liu 1984) raise the stake individuals and society have in the efficacy of families as the helpers of last resort—the bulwark against institutionalization of the frail and impaired aged.

The data in this study raise three crucial questions regarding current issues about support in later life: First, do women in this sample have needs that are not being met by members of their family circle? Second, to whom do these women turn for particular kinds of help? And, third, in the longer term, what is the possible impact of social change on the integration of older Americans into their communities?

UNMET NEEDS

Concern about who will care for the elderly in the future (Day 1985b) has prompted extensive research to identify the special needs of the elderly in specific social categories: the very old, women living alone, people with disabilities, and members of minority groups (Soldo and Manton 1985). These categories of older people are particularly vulnerable to a downward cycle of isolation, poverty, and breakdown in health (Kasper 1988). In part, this research on special needs has also been stimulated by a growing conviction among gerontologists that the practice of allocating entitlements on the basis of chronological age is ill-advised (Binstock 1985; Neugarten 1979). Appreciation of the great diversity within the older population, so the argument goes, calls, instead, for restructuring age-based policies and allocating collective assistance on the basis of need.

Unfortunately, so far as policy intervention goes, replacing age-based with needs-based entitlement may not provide a simple solution. The data in this study are full of anomalies about needs—their existence and their definition. Two main findings, however, are relevant to ongoing policy considerations: first, a substantial minority of the sample in this book do have needs that elude the ministrations of family members, and second, there are areas of need that may remain invisible to current research methods, but that are important to consider in policy development.

Perceptions on Need

Women in this study have two kinds of needs. One type is the sort measured in standard survey instruments described in chapter 4, and is related to the capacity to manage independently, that is, to perform household tasks and look after one's personal upkeep. The other kind emerged when women talked about their hopes and fears in open-ended questions on the 1987 survey and in the qualitative interviews. These needs are difficult to measure in a structured interview format, but are just as real and are closely related to psychological well-being and functional performance. They consist of basic human requirements for interdependence (see, Erikson 1982, and chapter 2, this volume).

SURVEY PERSPECTIVES

Type of Task and Need for Help

Chapter 4 examined functional capacities in terms of major transitions between 1978 and 1987 and the implications of changes for women's chances to implement their goals. Here I look at the same measures from another perspective—that is, in terms of the type and adequacy of the support women in this sample are receiving.

First, in terms of measures of need from the survey data in 1987 over half (53 percent) of the women said they could manage all five activities of daily living without help. The flip side of this, however, is that, in all, over 4 in 10 said they needed some help with at least one of these routine housekeeping tasks.

Levels of capacity, however, differed markedly according to the particular task. A third of the sample (34 percent) said they could do the shopping only if they had some help, one in five (21 percent) said they needed at least some help to handle their finances, and 16 percent said they needed help preparing meals (table 5.1). Only 83 women (13 percent) in the sample as a whole said they needed help in their personal upkeep, the largest proportion (10 percent) being those who required assistance with bathing.

What is the relationship between the nature of the need and the availability and sources of help? To address this question, I first looked at supportive arrangements in 1978 when women in the survey were 66 to 77 years old, and then at how the situation appeared 10 years later in 1987. Whom did women in 1978 rely upon for assistance when they had difficulty managing their housework and personal care?

Table 5.1 PERCENTAGE DISTRIBUTION OF 1987 SAMPLE: LEVEL OF HELP
NEEDED TO PERFORM FIVE IADL TASKS AND ONE ADL TASK—589
WOMEN BORN 1900–1910, 1987 SURVEY

	Percentage Can Do Without Help	Percentage Need at Least Some Help
IADL^a Tasks		
Shopping	64	34
Housework	72	28
Laundry	77	23
Financial matters	78	21
Meal preparation	84	16
ADL^b Tasks		
Washing and bathing	87	10

a. IADL, Instrumental Activities of Daily Living.
b. ADL, Activities of Daily Living. On the 1987 survey, washing and bathing were combined into one question.

Sources of Support: 1978 Survey Findings

The 1978 survey data in table 5.2 yielded four overall findings. First, there is a wide range in the proportion of the total sample who experienced some difficulty with three IADLs (going up and down stairs, shopping for groceries, and managing finances) and one ADL (washing and bathing): from 34 percent who they said had difficulty managing stairs to only 6 percent who said they had trouble with washing and bathing.

Second, there are marked differences between activities in regard to the availability of helpers—from less than half (47 percent) who said they had someone to help with stairs to 9 out of 10 (90 percent) who had help with shopping and, again, nearly 9 out of 10 (86 percent) who had help managing their finances. Turning around these proportions shows that 51 percent had no help with stairs,

Table 5.2 DISTRIBUTION OF RESPONDENTS WITH SOME DIFFICULTY, BY SOURCES OF HELP WITH DAILY ACTIVITIES, 1978

	Instrumental Activities of Daily Living						Activities of Daily Living	
	Going Up and Down Stairs		Shopping for Groceries		Managing Finances		Washing/ Bathing	
	No.	%	No.	%	No.	%	No.	%
Total in sample with some difficulty	351	100	191	100	74	100	67	100
Sources of Help Total with some difficulty who have help	165	47	172	90	64	86	40	60
Husband	74	45	44	26	20	31	13	33
Son/daughter	47	29	59	34	32	50	15	38
Other relatives	29	18	31	18	10	16	2	5
Friends/neighbors	13	8	31	18	2	3	5	13
Formal (paid)	2	1	7	4	2	3	2	5
Total with some difficulty who have no help	179	51	16	8	8	11	24	36
DK/NA[a]	7	2	3	2	2	4	3	4
Total in 1978 sample with some difficulty (N = 1049)	351	34	191	18	74	7	67	6

a. DK/NA, Don't know./No answer.

compared to only 8 percent who had no help with shopping and 11 percent who had no help managing their finances.

Third, there are marked differences between activities in the sources of assistance: husbands are the most important sources with stairs (45 percent), but are less prominent in assisting with shopping than are sons and daughters (26 percent as compared with 34 percent, respectively). In 1978, one-third of the sources of help with finances were husbands (31 percent), compared with one-half (50 percent) who were sons and daughters. Since husbands, of women in these ages if they are able, usually take responsibility for managing finances, the high proportion of adult children helping out in this way reflects the fact that over half (51 percent) of the sample in 1978 were already widowed. Although friends and neighbors played much less of a role than kin in helping with these four activities, nevertheless, they constituted nearly one in five (18 percent) of the total helpers with shopping.

Finally, summing the proportions who were receiving help from someone other than a husband or adult child (that is, in table 5.2, "Other relatives, Friends/neighbors, or Formal [paid]"), a total of 4 in 10 (40 percent) women were relying on sources outside the nuclear family. In a confirmation of the results of previous studies (see Kendig 1986:183), only about 5 percent of these women in their late 60s and 70s used formal help of any kind with these four activities.

Sources of Support: 1987 Survey Findings

How do these findings compare with patterns of support a decade hence? Chapter 4 reported that, between 1978 and 1987, there were fairly substantial declines in the proportions of women saying they could manage without difficulty. Taking the two activities that were comparable between the two surveys in terms of need for assistance—shopping and financial management—in the former, the proportion who could manage independently declined from 81 percent in 1978 to 64 percent in 1987, and in the latter from 92 percent to 78 percent. In all, the proportion of the sample saying they needed at least some help to manage the shopping more than doubled between 1978 and 1987 (from 16 percent to 35 percent).

Between 1978 and 1987, there were substantial shifts, as well, in the balance of help provided—on the one hand, by husbands and sources outside of close family relations (i.e., "Other relatives, Friends/ Neighbors, and Formal" support) and on the other hand, adult children. In general, sources comprised mainly of same-generation helpers (such as husbands, siblings, and friends) lost ground, to be replaced by adult children (table 5.3).

Table 5.3 PERCENTAGE DISTRIBUTION OF WOMEN BORN 1900–1910 WHO SAY THEY NEED SOME HELP WITH SHOPPING, BY SOURCES OF HELP WITH SHOPPING: 1978 AND 1987 SURVEYS

Source of Help	1978 (N = 1,049)	1987 (N = 589)
Husband	26	19
Daughter or son	34	53
Other (other relatives and nonkin)	40	22
Number who need help	172	208
Percentage of total sample	16.4	35.3

The proportion with husbands as helpers with shopping declined from 26 percent in 1978 to 19 percent in 1987, and sons and daughters as helpers with groceries increased as a proportion of the total from 34 percent to 53 percent. Likewise with regard to managing finances, the importance of husbands as helpers declined from 31 percent in 1978 to 20 percent in 1987, and help from an adult child had increased from 50 to 55 percent. Sources other than nuclear family members represented a much smaller proportion of all those helping with shopping in 1987 than in 1978, declining from 40 percent to 16 percent.

Another change was in the proportion of women in the 1987 survey who said they needed help with shopping, but, nevertheless, were doing most of the work themselves. Taking into account that the wording of questions on the two surveys was not exactly the same (see chapter 4), in 1987 one-third (33 percent), compared with 8 percent in 1978, claimed that they were doing without the help they need. This apparent increase in unmet need may reflect the larger proportion in 1987 who were widowed and living alone, as well as the aging of friends and relatives who 10 years earlier had more reserves to contribute to exchanging favors.

Finally, in 1987, it appeared that a somewhat larger proportion of the follow-up sample than 10 years previously were using paid help, particularly with housework and laundry. But the proportion was still under 10 percent.

FAMILIES—THE ULTIMATE RESOURCE?

Are families capable of taking the main responsibility for care of frail and dependent aged members? Can they meet the needs of an elderly population increasing in age and possibly also in frailty? This is still an unsettled question in the gerontological literature. On the one hand, many have looked to the family "as a financial or in-kind service solution" to the problem of increasing costs for care of the dependent aged (Binstock 1985:444). On the other hand, it has also been pointed out that many older people have no children, while others have children who are unable or unwilling to provide personal care or financial assistance (Kotlikoff and Morris 1987; Rosenwaike 1985). Moreover, the notion that family care can be stretched further has been challenged by a number of studies conducted over the past two decades (Doty 1986; Horowitz 1985; Horowitz and Dobrov 1982). Brody (1985) concludes, for example, that families, not formal service systems, provide 80 percent to 90 percent of medically related and personal care, household tasks, transportation, and shopping to disabled persons who are not in nursing homes. The stories of Mrs. Smith, Mrs. Peters, and Mrs. Sergio in chapter 7 of this book illustrate the limits of kin care under different conditions, for example, where the older person is frail and needs round the clock attention, where families are geographically separated, and where children and parents do not get along.

Kinship Structure, Living Arrangements, and Caregiving

To explore the issue of family care in this study, I examined three factors affecting the nature of social support: household composition, living arrangements, and availability of kin. First, I made a detailed tally of household composition and looked at the people selected as primary caregiver by women living in various kinds of household structures. Did women living with their husband invariably select him as the person most responsible for their care? What about those living with a daughter or son? Was the person(s) with whom an older person lives, invariably the one she selected to rely upon for help? Then, I compared available kin in 1987 with the person selected by the women in the sample as primary caregiver. How many close family members did women participating in this study have in their kin networks, and how many of these close kin were actually serving as a major source of care? The answers to these questions throw light on the extent of assistance provided by family members, as well as the possible constraints on families as an ultimate source of support.

Household Composition, 1987

A detailed breakdown of the household composition of women living outside institutions in 1987 is presented in table 5.4. The findings

Table 5.4 HOUSEHOLD COMPOSITION OF 551 EVER-MARRIED WHITE WOMEN BORN 1900–1910 LIVING IN PRIVATE HOUSEHOLDS, 1987

	Number of Persons in Household												Total Households	Total Persons
	1	2	3	4	5	6	7	8	9	10	11	12		
Living Alone	305												305	305
Not Living Alone														
Living with husband														
Husband only		117											117	234
Husband and other														
Kin only														
Daughter			4	1									5	16
Daughter and son-in-law				1									1	4
Son			1										1	3
Granddaughter			1										1	3
Kin and nonkin														
Grandson and friend				1									1	4
Nonkin only—friend			1										1	3
Not living with husband														
Living with kin only														
Living with sibling														
Sister														
Sister only		7											7	14
Sister and brother-in-law			1										1	3
Sister and son-in-law and grandchild						1							1	6
Sister and niece and greatniece				1									1	4
Brother only		5											5	10
Sister-in-law														
Sister-in-law only		1											1	2

continued

Table 5.4 HOUSEHOLD COMPOSITION OF 551 EVER-MARRIED WHITE WOMEN BORN 1900–1910 LIVING IN PRIVATE HOUSEHOLDS, 1987 (continued)

	Number of Persons in Household												Total Households	Total Persons
	1	2	3	4	5	6	7	8	9	10	11	12		
Sister-in-law and nephew and greatniece and greatnephew						1							1	6
Brother-in-law only		1											1	2
Living with child														
Daughter and son			1										1	3
Daughter														
Daughter only		20	1										21	43
Daughter and son-in-law														
Without grandchild			12										12	36
With grandchild				4	4	1	1						10	49
Daughter and other kin														
With grandchild			3										3	9
With brother			1										1	3
With nephew			1										1	3
Son														
Son only		19	1										20	41
Son and daughter-in-law														
Without grandchild			5										5	15
With grandchild					2							1	3	22
Son-in-law and grandchild							1						1	7
Living with grandchild														
Granddaughter		1											1	2
Grandson		5											5	10
Living with kin and nonkin														
Living with sibling and other														

Sister and grandson and friend				2				2		8
Sister and friend				1				1		3
Living with daughter and friend				1				1		3
Living with son and friend			2	1				3		11
Living only with nonkin										
Partner				1				1		2
Friend		7		1				9		21
Total	305	184	37	13	6	3	2	1	551	910

Notes: Household composition is presented here in full detail because of the unique opportunity these data afford to see the distribution of living arrangements among women aged 77 to 87 in these cohorts. This distribution, including the proportion of the sample living in different generational combinations, is summarized in the data following:

1. The predominant living arrangements are living alone (55.3 percent) or living with husband (21.2 percent).

2. A very small proportion (2.7 percent) live with nonkin; only 2.0 percent live exclusively with nonkin.

3. Among those living with an adult child, there was essentially no difference between the proportions living only with a son (3.6 percent) or daughter (3.8 percent); but there was much less tendency to live with a son if he had a family (wife, child, partner) than with a daughter if she had a family (husband, child, partner): 2.0 percent and 4.7 percent, respectively.

4. Few (11.3 percent of total of 551) lived with more than one other person:
   —Of the 246 not living alone, 25.2 percent lived with two or more persons;
   —Of the 129 not living either alone or with a husband, 48.1 percent lived with two or more persons.

5. There are 35 different combinations of households represented in the table:
   —Thirty-three of these relate to persons not living either alone or with a husband;
   —Only 14 of these 33 combinations occur more than once;
   —The most frequent combinations involve living with an adult son or daughter (87 women were in 15 household combinations that included a child; 9 of these combinations occurred more than once).

from table 5.4 on the generational composition of households are then summarized in table 5.5.

The most striking features of these household patterns are:

1. The prevalence of one-person households—over 55 percent of the respondents were living alone.
2. The fact that nearly all those living with a husband were living with no other person (thus, over three-fourths [77 percent] were living either alone or only with a husband).
3. The infrequency of living in two- and three-generation households (17 percent and 5 percent of the total, respectively).
4. The great variety of household types among the 23 percent who were living neither alone or with a husband: 33 types altogether (although only 14 of these 33 occurred more than once).

Another factor deserving mention is the preponderance of small household size. Nearly 9 out of 10 of these women lived with no more than one other person, and in two out of three cases, that other

Table 5.5 DISTRIBUTION OF 551 WOMEN LIVING IN PRIVATE HOUSEHOLDS BY GENERATIONAL COMPOSITION OF HOUSEHOLD, COHORTS BORN 1900–1910

Type of Household Arrangement, 1987	Percentage of Total Households (N = 551)		Percentage of Total Not Living Alone (N = 246)
	No.	%	
1. Living with:			
Someone of own generation	158	29	64
Someone of children's generation	92	17	37
Someone of grandchildren's generation	30	5	12
2. Living exclusively with:			
Someone of own and children's generation	8	1	3
Someone of own and grandchildren's generation	4	1	2
Someone of own and children's and grandchildren's generation	3	1	1
Someone of children's and grandchildren's generation	18	3	7

Notes: Household categories are not mutually exclusive. See also notes to table 5.4. Data in table 5.5 summarizes the data in table 5.4 in terms of broad categories of generational composition. All the notes in 5.4 pertain equally to 5.5, but the patterns described are not observable in the aggregated categories in table 5.5.

person was the husband. Intergenerational shared households were infrequent. If a husband was still living, the outstanding tendency was to live with him alone, not with members of the first- or second-descendant generations. In only nine (7 percent) of the 127 households that included a husband was there also a child or grandchild (table 5.4).

These data also show that grandchildren have little experience living with a grandparent in these very old ages. (At this late stage of the life cycle, grandchildren are often in their 20s and 30s, completing vocational training, entering jobs, and beginning their own families.) The great majority of grandmothers in this study were living apart from their grandchildren, communicating with them mainly by telephone and occasional visits centered around holidays.

Finally, these patterns show the abiding importance of kinship in household formation: only 3.1 percent of the total lived with any nonkin, and only 1.8 percent solely with nonkin.

Household Composition and "Primary" Caregiver

The impact of living arrangements on patterns of caregiving is reflected in the distribution of primary caregivers by household type (table 5.6).

DESIGNATION OF PRIMARY CAREGIVERS

The primary caregiver was designated at the end of a series of questions about help needed and help received as "the one person" most responsible for giving "practical help and support" (Appendix 5-A). Only a small minority of women (3 percent of those living in private households) failed to mention someone who fulfilled this role.

However, choosing a primary cargiver was difficult for women in a number of situations, such as those who were not receiving practical help, but had people around them who were providing emotional support; those who felt that they, themselves, were actually the ones providing the practical help and emotional support to others, but were not receiving any kind of support in return; those who were receiving practical help from more than one person and had to choose between them.

Furthermore, among those not receiving practical help, but who designated a primary caregiver, anyway, that designated person, when interviewed, sometimes denied the role, saying that he or she actually did little, that really Mrs. "X" took care of herself. A few of the older women, when they discovered that we intended to interview the

Table 5.6 PRIMARY CAREGIVER BY LIVING ARRANGEMENTS

Living Arrangement of Respondent	Caregiver Living in Same Household as Respondent						Caregiver Living in Different Household from Respondent										
	Hus-band	Dau-ghter	Son	Other Kin F[a]	Other Kin M[b]	Friend	Dau-ghter	Son	Other Kin F	Other Kin M	Friend	Neigh-bor	No One	Other	Don't Know	No Data	Total
Living alone							89	66	68	14	32	11	12	9	1	3	395
Living with husband																	
With husband only	81						16	7	7	2	1	1			2		117
With husband plus others																	
Kin only	4	3		1			2		1								11
Other	2																2
Living with other than husband																	
With kin only																	
With daughter		39						1	1	1				1			43
With son			15				2	3	3	3			2	2			26
Other		2		9	3		3		3	1	1	1		1			25
Other			1			6	1		3		1			1			14
Total	87	44	16	12	2	6	113	77	84	20	35	13	14	13	3	3	543[c]
Percentage of Total	16	8	3	2		1	21	14	15	4	6	2	3	2	1	1	100

a. F, female.
b. M, male.
c. Excludes 8 cases for which there was no matching information for respondent and caregiver.

primary caregiver, withdrew the name, changed their minds, or refused to give permission. To determine the meaning of these various situations for estimating the availability of support would require a content analysis of the reasons given in each instance. As in the case of defining living arrangements (chapter 4), the designation of primary caregiver is at heart a subjective judgment. Therefore, the following findings, summarized in table 5.6, incorporate the women's choice of caregiver at face value.

Results. Women living alone have greater diversity in their primary sources of informal support than do those who live with others. They rely more on friends and distant relatives (such as cousins and in-laws), and to a greater extent on male relatives. A higher proportion also said that "no one" was responsible for providing support (but this was only 2.2 percent versus the 0.4 percent for everyone else).

These differences between the primary caregivers of those living alone and those living with others are what one would expect, given the strong preference of older women for maintaining independent households, and the fact that sharing a household usually reflects both the need for more comprehensive help and the existence of fewer financial resources to pay for services within the home. Moreover, perhaps because they were at least somewhat dependent on others for personal care, those who were living in another person's household were considerably more likely (about two and a half times more likely) to designate as the primary caregiver a daughter or other female relative rather than a son or other male relative.

Distinction between Living Arrangements and Care Arrangements

Recent research (Soldo, Wolf, and Agree 1986) has called attention to the importance of distinguishing between living arrangements (household structure) and care arrangements (the organization of helpers). Living with a family member (e.g., a husband or daughter) from whom one can, in theory, claim strong support does not necessarily guarantee the receipt of support to match the need. Almost one-third of those who were not living alone chose a primary caregiver from outside the household. The proportion was the same even among those women living solely with their husbands. In Wolf's study (1988:28) of the care arrangements of frail older women, although 71 percent of the sample had some problems with Activities of Daily Living (ADLs), only 44 percent of the children serving as primary caregivers were providing this type of assistance.

Thus, availability of support is not ensured by any particular type of household structure. For example, an elderly woman living alone may have strong support from family members living outside the household, while an elderly woman living with a husband who himself needs care may have no one in the immediate family to help out and have to turn for substantial help with day-to-day needs to others (e.g., friends or neighbors) on whom she has a weaker claim. A woman in the latter situation may be more vulnerable to deteriorating health and institutionalization than is her counterpart living alone, yet living alone is commonly seen as the most vulnerable situation for women of very advanced years.

Available Kin and Social Support

Both living and care arrangements are affected by a third structural variable: the availability of kin—in particular, the number and characteristics of siblings and adult children in the older person's family network. Kin are a major source of support for individuals of any age, but among those in their late 70s and 80s, a number of studies have found the primary source of support to be blood relatives, particularly members of the nuclear family (see, for example, Litwak 1985). The number of brothers and sisters, for example, influences both the types of shared households potentially available in later life and the potential availability of nieces and nephews as a source of support, particularly if one is childless oneself.

It is particularly interesting, therefore, that 3 out of 10 ($N = 150$) of the nearly 9 out of 10 ($N = 523$) women in this study who had a husband, son, or daughter did not designate one of these nuclear family members as their major provider of support. Instead, 12 women nominated no one, while the 138 others mentioned a wide variety of people, including kin by marriage, such as a daughter-in-law and a nephews's wife, and nonkin, such as friends and an unpaid companion. The proportions in the major categories were almost equally spread between members of the stem family, the extended family, and nonkin.

Content analysis of 92 questionnaires of women who did not nominate a close family member suggests that these women represent a substantial minority who experienced grave difficulty in sustaining the type of family relations that would permit someone to take major responsibility for supporting an older person at home. Some in this category had sons but no daughters, and were reluctant to turn to a son and daughter-in-law for help where they might have felt freer to approach a daughter and son-in-law. Others lived a half hour to two hours away from the nearest adult child. Fourteen had husbands who were ill or whom for some other reason the women considered unable to take responsibility for support. In some cases, the son or daughter who might have provided support was ill. In a few cases, the older woman said she did not get along with either the adult child or the son-in-law or daughter-in-law. Whatever the reason, the husband or adult child was not viewed by these people as an appropriate source of support.

QUALITATIVE PERSPECTIVES ON NEED AND SOCIAL SUPPORT

What light do perspectives from the qualitative approach shed on the questions about need and sources of support among these cohorts? Do these women believe they are able to manage independently? From their own perspective, the answer of the great majority is, "Yes . . . at the moment." Nearly 9 out of 10 (89 percent) in 1987 said they did not need (more) help. Data on functional capacities from the survey, however, raise questions about these subjective assessments. As noted earlier, a third of those who said they needed some help to do the shopping also said that they were getting the groceries mostly on their own; half (54 percent) said they have help going places beyond walking distance.

Repeatedly, when I asked women in the fieldwork interviews what they would do if they could no longer manage on their own, they replied in effect, "I'll cross that bridge when the time comes." "What would you do if you could no longer drive?" I asked Mrs. Smart, who drives herself to the pool every evening to swim laps. "I'll think about that tomorrow," she said. And others replied in a similar vein. They also felt that when one needs services, there are places one can turn no farther away than the yellow pages, or the senior citizens club, or one's church. Always, though, the attitude was that these services are fine for someone else, but not for them: "I'm not ready for that yet. . . . Besides, I have friends."

Although the role of friends and neighbors appears small with respect to the particular activities measured by standard IADLs and ADLs, when it comes to helping out for a short time in case of illness, nearly 7 in 10 (68 percent) of women in this sample said they have friends or neighbors whom they can turn to in such an emergency. Time and again in talking to the 20 women in the qualitative study, when I inquired, "Do you need any help or services you don't have?" they answered, "No, I have friends." It was neighbors and friends, not children, that they mentioned in terms of, "We help each other." The relationship rests on reciprocity—"You do something for them, and they do something for you." By means of a variety of carefully nurtured arrangements, a woman like Mrs. Silvestri, who lives alone on a small budget and does not drive, has constructed a system of support relationships with neighbors and friends on which she can rely for everything from help with shopping and getting to church, to installing light bulbs and shoveling snow off her walk in winter time. Friends and neighbors help each other with shopping, with driving to church or to play bridge, with providing a haven in which to recuperate after surgery, with getting library books, with checking to see whether everything is all right on a regular basis and in the event of illness or distress about family problems.

Mrs. Carlton:
Friends and Reciprocity

Mrs. Carlton, for example, had a friend staying over when I visited her. When I asked about this, she explained that the friend was recovering from breast surgery. The doctor said that she needed someone with her. However, the friend lives on her own and her son and daughter-in-law live 25 miles away, so Mrs. Carlton invited her friend come to stay with her.

"You can't hardly get someone to come. And when they do—it's 10, 12, and 14 dollars an hour. You can't compete with that—so we try and help each other. She came when I had my operations. (I can do better in my own home than in someone else's.) We have each other when we're sick because you have to go through so much. That's what friends are. To have a friend, you've got to be a friend."

On the 1987 survey, Mrs. Carlton designated the oldest of her two daughters as the person most responsible for providing practical help and support. But this daughter lives in another state and is aged 55 herself. Also, she has rheumatoid arthritis. A mathematics teacher, she has recently retired because she can no longer write on the blackboard or get out of bed in the morning without help. Mrs. Carlton says her family is "very close knit," but cataracts and six heart attacks have slowed her down. She isn't able to visit out-of-town relatives as much as she used to. Rather than go to live with one of her daughters, she says she would choose to go to a nursing home. But she wants to stay in her own home as long as possible:

"I would hate to be a burden. I don't want to go to a nursing home, but I can if I have to. If I get to the point where I can't do for myself, I'll go, but I want to be here as long as I can. I'd like to be taken out feet first.

Meanwhile, I stay busy, that's the main thing. Comin' and goin'. People take me places. The main thing you've got to remember is to keep in touch, and to keep in touch with the time—because it can outrun you in a hurry."

Going Places Beyond Walking Distance—Elderly's Achilles' Heel?

These findings raise several points about the use of standard measures of functional capacity as indicators of potential need. The Instrumental Activities of Daily Living (IADLs) and Activities of Daily Living (ADLs) instruments are used mainly to measure the minimum support necessary to maintain an older person, that is, just to meet daily requirements of survival—eating, grooming, shopping, housekeeping, and managing finances. The convention has been to make no distinction between these activites in terms of what they suggest older people can or cannot do to realize their goals, or in terms of what they suggest about their access to activities that enhance the quality of life (chapter 4). The activity that was most difficult for the highest proportion of the 1978 sample was going up and down stairs. This was also the activity with which the highest proportion had no help. From the point of view of basic maintenance, for most old people it is not essential to use stairs. But, although stairs can be avoided or circumscribed, to the extent that they are present in most public places and in most public transportation, they must be negotiated to have access to outside activities, personal development, recreation, and contact with the mainstream of community life.

An older woman can often remain in her home if she cannot maneuver stairs, but she must eat and also pay the bills. In fact, in both 1978 and 1987, shopping and managing finances were the activities with which the highest proportion of women who need help have help. But as for getting out and about, and retaining one's interdependence in the community, the 1987 cohorts were having difficulty. Describing her obstacles to getting to bridge club and historical society meetings, Mrs. Carter remarked, "My car and I are getting old."

IS THERE A "LOSS OF COMMUNITY?"

Is there evidence that in the future older people will be less protected by community ties? As in so many aspects of the rapidly developing field of gerontology, there are differences in findings and in their interpretation. James House and his colleagues (1988:544) forecast that changes in marital and childbearing patterns and in the age structure of American society may lead to a steady decrease in the number of older people who have spouses or children. In the declining ratio of family caregivers to older people, they see a potential increase in the number of older people who are alone and isolated. On the other hand, Wellman and Hall (1986:191) presented findings from their extensive study of social networks among East Yorkers in Canada purporting to show that social ties among the aged are complex, strong, and persistent. How does the current study's research on older women speak to these diverse conclusions?

Elasticity in Care Provision

On the one hand, the great variety of distant kin and nonkin whom a third of the women in 1987 designated as primary caregivers suggests that there may be more elasticity in caregiving relationships than has been previously appreciated. There are grounds for optimism in the fact that if a member of the primary stem family kin (e.g., a daughter or son) is not available, an extended family member (e.g., a sister, daughter-in-law, or niece) may be available to serve as an acceptable substitute.

On the other hand, the reasons why women who, despite having a husband, son, or daughter, turned to another less closely related person cast the issue of kin efficacy in a more pessimistic light. The findings suggest that for a substantial minority of the women, the nuclear family was lacking as the ultimate resource in late life.

Variety of Households and Care Arrangements

The detailed analysis of household composition in 1987 (tables 5.4, 5.5, and 5.6) provides some perspective on the relation between the people older American women are living with and the type of care potentially available to them. First, the great variety of household types found among those not living alone or with a husband suggests that standards about who should live with whom in American society, far from being rigidly determined, are defined by family circumstances and personal and social resources as these evolve over the life course. Given shrinking family size and the increasing complexity of family types as a consequence of divorce and remarriage, more research is needed to ascertain what combinations of households under what conditions work best for all generations concerned.

Constraints on Family Care Provision

A second key finding about family support is the substantial proportion of women who designated caregivers outside the household in which they were living. This highlights again the pitfalls (Day 1985b, 1989) associated with equating "availability" of support with the actual receipt of support. Failure to distinguish between living arrangements and an older person's system of support obscures factors that place constraints on the capacity and willingness of family members to be responsible for long-term care—factors such as geographic separation, poor health, competing demands of employment and family responsibilities, and preferences dictating who should perform services of various kinds, such as the well-documented fact that daughters are preferred for personal care, and sons for financial advice and practical help.

Third, a major finding confirming the results of other studies is the reluctance among women in this survey to share a household with an adult son or daughter. Three-fourths of the sample were either living alone or only with a husband. Nevertheless, three trends point to an increase in the need for shared households in the future: 1) the aging of the older population, 2) the association between advancing age and declining capacity for independent activity, and 3) the fact that rising costs may make institutional care an option only for the disabled poor and the very rich. Under the circumstances, there is a need to develop specific strategies to deal with the deep uncertainty many older women now experience when they confront the need to move from unassisted living in their own homes to comprehensive help in a more protected environment.

Friends, Neighbors, and Community Ties

Finally, the qualitative findings support Wellman and Hall's (1986:211) claim that "gerontologists may have focused too narrowly on studying supportive ties with kin." In 1987, nearly 4 in 10 (36 percent) of women in the sample had one child or none. Others had children too far away to help with day-to-day activities, children who were in their 50s and ill themselves, or children with busy lives whom they did not want to bother. Given the prevalence of widowhood and diminishing mobility (which reduces access to kin who do not live close by), the role of friends and neighbors as anchors allowing older women to remain in their homes is very important in these later ages. However, the significance to older women of interdependence with nonkin and with people in one's local community highlights the crucial nature of place as a context of aging, and raises concerns about changes in American society that may jeopardize community ties (see chapter 9).

Social Supports—A Dimension of Successful Aging

The findings presented here anticipate the key role to be played by social relations in the model of successful aging (see chapter 6). The data show that although an increasing proportion of old women are living alone, no woman is an island, even in old age. All but a small minority of women in this study had someone outside the four walls of her home with whom she shared a relationship (see chapter 8 for discussion of that minority). An important element in women's adaptation to growing old, therefore, is their relationships with family members, friends, neighbors, and social groups. Thus, in terms of public policy implications for older women in the diverse circumstances represented, we need to look beyond personal feelings of well-being and to ask: What demographic and social conditions foster or deter the opportunities of older women to interact with others? And What are the implications of these conditions for the role of families, friends, and service providers in contributing to the well-being of the elderly?

INVENTORY OF KIN AND
INFORMAL SUPPORT

An inventory of the respondents' informal support was compiled by adding people to a "support roster" as their names arose in connection with various kinds of practical help and emotional support. [A survey of people 60 years and older living in Sydney, Australia, conducted in 1981 by the Ageing and the Family Project, Australian National University, Canberra, used a similar design to collect information about informal support among the elderly living in private households (Kendig et al. 1983).] The study described here collected information on kin in various amounts of detail according to degree of closeness to the respondent. Three criteria of closeness were used: intimacy of kinship tie, physical location, and type of support provided. In terms of amount of information sought, priority was given to primary stem family members (husband, sons, daughters) and primary extended family members (brothers, sisters). All these kin were included on the roster, regardless of where they lived or whether they were mentioned as support providers. Next in order of priority were persons living in the same household with the respondent and persons the respondent mentioned as providing her with support of various kinds. All persons meeting any one of the three above criteria were listed on the roster and, for each person, respondents were asked (where applicable) to furnish the following basic information: relationship, location, distance in travel time, sex, age, marital status, employment status, number of living children, frequency of time spent with, frequency of correspondence with, and frequency of telephone contact.

Given these rules of data collection, primary stem and primary extended family members are the only kin for whom information was obtained with which to determine the association between "availability" in terms of actual presence in these older women's kinship networks and the provision of informal support. The amount of information collected on secondary stem and extended family members (e.g., daughters-in-law, sons-in-law, grandchildren, sisters-and brothers-in-law, nieces and nephews) was determined not by kinship ties but by living arrangements and supportive relationships (that is, whether they lived in the same household with the respondent and whether they were specifically mentioned as support providers). Thus, for example, information is not available on the characteristics of *all* the respondents' grandchildren—only for those living in the same household or for those whom respondents particularly singled out as persons they turned to for help or emotional support.

Chapter Six

THE MODEL OF SUCCESSFUL AGING

Whether in the long run the concept of successful aging will remain a scientifically viable topic, is perhaps less significant than its power in identifying and organizing questions and research directions which reflect the current dynamics of the field.

—Paul and Margret Baltes, "Psychological Perspectives on Successful Aging"

The previous chapters have laid the groundwork for developing a model of successful aging. Key issues and research approaches have been reviewed. Major life transitions and the specific dilemmas facing individual women have been documented, and the quandaries such dilemmas pose for American women in their late 80s have been brought to light. The people who matter to women in these cohorts have been described, and the strengths and limits of families to support each other throughout the aging process have been examined.

In this chapter I look at the meaning of successful aging in the context of the major changes in these women's lives in the decade following their late 60s and 70s.[1] Some of the questions I address include: What is the impact of changes in marital status and living arrangements on satisfaction with life and the continued capacity to look after oneself? How do we distinguish women who are aging effectively from those who are aging less well? What is the ratio of those who are fit and in control of their own lives to those who are frail and highly dependent on others? What background factors differentiate those who are happy and leading rewarding lives from those who are depressed and have time on their hands? A framework is presented here for answering these questions under three main headings: the meaning of success, the measurement of success, and the modeling of success.

MEANING OF SUCCESS

Before discussing measurement, it is important to define *success* on the bases of both theoretical perspectives and the qualitative insights derived from the fieldwork interviews.

Theoretical Perspectives

As applied to the women in this study, success has four major features. It is: normative, relative to time and place, defined by the variables measured in the 1978 and 1987 surveys, and directed toward strengthening our knowledge about older women in order to identify a hierarchy of needs.

NORMATIVE

"Successful aging" is, by definition, a normative concept. On one level, it involves images about old age and the social roles appropriate to women and men in their later years. On another, it involves values about what constitutes "the good life" for people of different gender and different age groups.

CULTURALLY RELATIVE

Because it is a normative concept, successful aging, as described in this study, relates to conditions that pertain to a particular time in American history (the late 1980s), and to a particular milieu of economic and political priorities. The relativity of success to time and place means that particulars of the model may be outdated by the time women now in their 60s move into the current ages of these cohorts. We cannot know for sure, for example, what American women who became wives and mothers in the affluent 1950s will expect of their children and the larger society when they are in their 80s. The requisites of contentment in old age for a generation that has known material affluence, advanced technology, and Social Security entitlements may be quite different than those for women who still vividly recall the Great Depression as a dark shadow casting hardship and uncertainty over the nation. Asked if she recalled those times, Mrs. Silvestri sighed: "The depression? Who can forget it?"

CRITERIA TIED TO SURVEY DATA

A third point about success in relation to the model is that the criteria are tied to the specific measures included in the 1978 and 1987 surveys. A successful ager is a woman who does better in terms of available measures than do other women in the sample. This means that not being categorized as "successful" is not necessarily tantamount to being an "unsuccessful" person, in a conventional sense. Some qualities we greatly admire in older people, such as fortitude in the light of grave personal loss or taking a philosophical approach to profound disability, were not measured directly in this research. Mrs. Grainger, for example, ranked low on some criteria because she is going blind and has trouble managing a number of aspects of her life without at least some help. But she is facing her situation resolutely, cheerfully making friends in the home for the frail and disabled where she has had to move, and learning new skills to compensate for failing vision (see chapter 8).

POLICY APPLICATIONS

Finally, in line with George Maddox's (1987) strong stand in favor of social reform (see chapter 2), the model developed here is regarded as a tool for improving the opportunities of older women to age effectively. It implies that increasing our understanding of different individual experiences of aging can contribute to changing social institutions in ways that increase the chances for older people to lead rewarding lives.

Qualitative Perspectives

In addition to these theoretical perspectives, success was illuminated in this study by a qualitative look at the lives of women. Women who appear to be aging most effectively ranked high on each of three life domains: a sense of well-being, the capacity to manage on their own, and the availability of private means of support—that is, resources to call upon if necessary.

In any individual situation, the character of the aging experience will be determined by the nature of the interrelationship between all three domains. But, although the three interact and reinforce one another, they are not necessarily related in a strictly linear sense. For example, as defined in this study, a sense of well-being is a psychological orientation identified by a number of different measures: positive attitudes, a sense of control, a liking for the company of others, and so forth. Numerous studies (see Rodin 1986, and chapter 2, this volume) show that psychological well-being among older people tends to be associated with managing one's own affairs and controlling one's environment. Persons capable of independent activity are likely to have a sense that the environment is responsive to actions they take to achieve their ends. Nevertheless, "a sense of well-being or control" can coexist with what an outsider might see as a very minimal capacity for independent behavior. The following situations illustrate the complex relationship between contentment, self-management, and private supports.

Mrs. Crawford:
High Subjective Well-being, Strong Private Safety Net, Weak Capacity for Independent Activity

Mrs. Crawford, an 87-year-old retired teacher, has a high score on psychological well-being. Yet, of all the women in the qualitative interviews, she was among the most dependent on help from others with daily tasks. One of the 20 percent minority in this sample who requires assistance with Activities of Daily Living (ADLs), as well as with Instrumental Activities of Daily Living (IADLs) (chapter 4), she depends on her husband for bathing, dressing, and getting around the house, as well as for shopping, preparing meals, and housekeeping. The issue is: Can Mrs. Crawford be considered to be aging successfully? From her point of view, yes, unequivocally. Her responses on the 1987 survey indicate that, although confined to a wheelchair most of the time, she is happy with every aspect of her life. My visit to her 16 months later confirmed this high level of contentment. From the point of view of her husband, the answer is also yes. He is the designated primary caregiver, and, when interviewed, he indicated his total willingness to provide the support his wife requires. He showed me with pride how he had rearranged the house, setting up the bedroom downstairs in the living room to make it easier for him to help Mrs. Crawford dress, bathe, and move about. I have no information about how the couple's only son, who lives within eight miles of his parents, feels about the quality of his mother's aging, since the 1987 survey conducted interviews only with the primary caregiver. However, since her son was the first person Mrs. Crawford called for help, when three months prior to my visit she fell downstairs and broke her arm, it is quite likely that he and his wife are anxious about the older couple's continued capacity for independent activity.

From the perspective of the wider society, would Mrs. Crawford also be seen to be aging successfully? The answer is probably yes, but with a significant qualifier—"for the moment." She would be considered successful, not only because she defines herself as a happy woman, but because she has a reserve of private resources that she can call upon for support. She has a husband to care for her daily needs, a son and daughter-in-law who live close by, and she and her husband own their home. Family members and a comfortable financial position keep Mrs. Crawford from having to call upon public assistance.

———————————

Mrs. Peres:
Fair Subjective Well-being, Weak Private Supports, Weak Capacity for Independent Activity

In contrast, Mrs. Peres, described in chapter 4, is coming close to losing her capacity to maintain herself by private means. Failing eyesight is eroding her capacity to get around and to do housework, and she lacks even one person she can rely upon if her own efforts prove inadequate. She neither owns her house nor has the income to hire paid help. In spite of her hardships, her sense of well-being is fairly strong. However, that, too, must be seen as unstable. In 1983, she began to experience hemorrhaging in the retina. The threat of blindness puts her courage to a hard test. On the 1987 survey, Mrs. Peres listed "walk and read" as activities she most likes to do, but she adds "I like to read better, but can't do it much . . . can see just a little bit."

Mrs. Peres can be seen to be aging "unsuccessfully," not so much because she will probably have to go to a nursing home and be supported on Medicaid, but because she will be obliged to do so *involuntarily*. She lacks the resources to choose any other alternative. The home where she is now living does not cater to "aging in place." It has no services to provide for people with profound disabilities who lack the means to hire help. However, if her eyesight deteriorates further and she experiences a further decline in the capacity to help herself, Mrs. Peres might actually be relieved and adjust very well to moving to a more sheltered environment. Many people can make a good adjustment to living in an institution, especially if (as discussed in chapter 2), they participate actively themselves in making the necessary arrangements (Krantz and Schulz 1980; Rodin and Langer 1977).

———————————

DYNAMICS OF "SUCCESS"

Mrs. Crawford's and Mrs. Peres's stories highlight three aspects of the aging experience that affect the interpretation of success. First, the definition of *capacity for self-management* involves a subjective as well as a functional component. Mrs. Crawford and Mrs. Peres both had severe functional disabilities, but they defined themselves as still being in control of their activities. Second, among people in their late 70s and 80s, successful aging is an unstable condition, identified at a moment in time and subject to unpredictable and precipitous change. Mrs. Crawford's fall on the stairs deepened her dependence on her husband's help. If Mr. Crawford suddenly became ill and unable to provide for his wife, their son and daughter-in-law might have to be called upon for substantial assistance. The lives of the whole Crawford family could change overnight.

A third point illuminated by these two stories is that successful aging is not wholly a matter of individual experience or aptitudes. It is interdependent with an individual's social relations over the life course, and can be perceived differently by people who occupy different positions in relation to the older person. Mr. and Mrs. Crawford were content that they were managing well; their son and daughter-in-law may have been less sanguine. The manager of the retirement home admired Mrs. Peres for her courage and independence (see chapter 4). However, she might have exaggerated the success with which Mrs. Peres was dealing with aging. Since her relationship with Mrs. Peres was formal, not that of a confidant, the manager probably was unaware of Mrs. Peres's deepening sense of isolation and despair about the prospects of going completely blind.

In Mrs. Crawford's and Mrs. Peres's stories, we see how the three domains of contentment, independent activity, and private supports interact to produce a particular constellation of subjective feelings and objective circumstances. These and other qualitative insights suggest that weakness in any one of the three domains substantially destabilizes a woman's prospects for long-term continuity in her current living arrangements and life-style. Mrs. Silvestri's and Mrs. Farnworth's narratives (chapter 1) reinforce this observation. Of all the women I visited, Mrs. Farnworth seemed to be doing the least well and to have the least stable future prospects. Extreme dissatisfaction with home and community, painful hips, and alienation from her husband were making her life intolerable, even though she had strong support from her four children—one of whom, a widowed daughter, was prepared to take her mother into her home.

Strength in all three domains, on the other hand, conveys an aura of balance and stability. After 11 years of widowhood, Mrs. Silvestri still missed her husband, but she was happy with her life and able to manage for herself all the activities that she especially wanted to do. Moreover, she had abundant social supports: family, friends, and comfort in the knowledge that she owned her own home. Her long-term future seemed to hold continuity and security.

MEASUREMENT OF SUCCESS

Overview of Steps in Model Development

To measure success involved developing a model in four steps. To provide an overview of the approach, these steps are summarized next, with a more detailed description following.

DEPENDENT VARIABLES

Step 1. Defining dependent variables. The dimensions of successful aging were defined and justified on the basis of theory and findings from research on aging.

Step 2. Selecting empirical measures to form indexes of three dimensions. For each of three major life domains—psychological well-being, capacity for self-management, and private means of social support—a set of empirical measures was selected from the 1987 questionnaire. Appendixes 6-A through 6-C present the list of measures used to construct each of the three dimensions.

Step 3. Performing factor analysis on the three sets of measures, and, for each dimension, computing a numerical index from the first factor. The empirical measures were entered into a program to determine the contribution of each one—net of the others—to defining each of the three dimensions. Using principal components and factor analysis, linear combinations of the variables were calculated to establish the relative contribution of each measure to explaining the variation between positions or scores on the composite scales.

For each of the three dimensions, an index was constructed from coefficients on the first factor. Table 6.1 shows the coefficients or weights on the set of measures that contribute most to defining the three dimensions. The set that best defines each of the three dimensions comprises the "markers" of successful aging.

INDEPENDENT VARIABLES

Step 4. Using the indexes as dependent variables in regression equations to reveal the background characteristics correlated with successful aging. Background characteristics— hypothesized as associated

Table 6.1 MARKERS OF SUCCESSFUL AGING

A. Dimension 1: Perceived Well-being	
Marker Name	Weights[a]
1. R[b] feels health not good compared to others.	−0.24
2. R feels health worse compared to 3 years ago.	−0.19
3. R feels health problems stand in the way.	−0.24
4. R feels things keep getting worse as she gets older.	−0.90
5. R feels less useful as she gets older.	−0.40
Bradburn Affect-Balance Scale: Markers 6–15:	
6. R feels excited or interested in something.	0.13
7. R feels too restless to sit for long.	−0.19
8. R feels proud because complimented for something.	0.12
9. R feels very lonely and remote from other people.	−0.21
10. R feels pleased about having accomplished something.	0.07
11. R feels bored.	−0.24
12. R feels on top of the world.	0.21
13. R feels depressed or very unhappy.	−0.09
14. R feels things are going her way.	0.21
15. R feels upset because someone criticized her.	−0.13
16. R overall is unhappy with life these days.	−0.34
17. R never or almost never has time on hands.	0.19
18. R is not satisfied with neighborhood.	−0.15

Notes: On all three dimensions in the table, the first factor is the set of markers that explains the highest proportion of the variation among five factors in the general linear model procedure (see Appendix 6-C). Also, on all three dimensions, a minus sign denotes a negative influence, and no sign denotes a positive influence on the scales of successful aging.

a. The weights are the unrotated coefficients of the first factor, which explains 60 percent of the variation in the 18 markers. For a discussion of the statistical procedures used in assigning the weights, see Appendix 6-C.

b. R, respondent.

continued

with variations between the women in levels of successful aging—were selected from the 1978 and 1987 surveys. Table 6.2 lists those characteristics selected. Regression was used to calculate the relative significance of sociodemographic characteristics as correlates of successful aging. Regressions were run separately for each index.

Step 1. Defining Dependent Variables—The Dimensions of Successful Aging

The first step in building the model was to operationalize the meaning of success. On the basis of theory derived from research on aging

Table 6.1 MARKERS OF SUCCESSFUL AGING (*continued*)

B. Dimension 2: Capacity for Independent Activity

Marker Name	Weights[c]
1. R walked at least once a week in past year.	0.21
2. R made trips away from neighborhood in past year.	0.28
3. R helped a family member with housework/laundry.	0.08
4. R's eyesight is fair or poor.	−0.27
5. R needs help to go outside walking distance.	−0.38

Instrumental Activities of Daily Living (IADLs): Markers, 6–10

6a. R can do shopping for groceries without help.	0.79
b. R needs some help with shopping for groceries.	−0.32
c. R cannot do the shopping without help.	−0.66
7a. R can prepare own meals.	0.79
b. R needs some help to prepare meals.	−0.42
c. R cannot prepare meals without help.	−0.63
8a. R can do the housework without help.	0.73
b. R can do the housework with some help.	−0.29
c. R needs help to do the housework.	−0.70
9a. R can do the laundry without help.	0.79
b. R needs some help to do the laundry.	−0.27
c. R cannot do the laundry without help.	−0.73
10a. R can manage own money.	0.71
b. R needs some help to manage own money.	−0.44
c. R cannot manage money without help.	−0.52
11. R needs (more) help with any IADL tasks.	−0.09

c. The weights of the first factor explain 53 percent of the variation in the 11 markers. Markers 6 through 10 have been made into three separate, dichotomous variables corresponding with the three levels of capacity to perform IADLs: 1, With help; 2, With some help; and 3, Cannot do without help.

C. Dimension 3: Private Safety Net

Marker Name	Weights[d]
1. R does not have relatives to help with major medical expenses.	−0.11
2. R does not have a primary caregiver.	−0.12
3. R does not have a secondary caregiver.	−0.26
4. Number of living children, 1987.	−0.24
5. Income, 1987.	0.18
6. Number of persons on support roster.	−0.21
7. Number of rooms in R's 1987 residence.	−0.14
8. R does not own her home.	−0.62
9. Name in which R's home is owned/rented:	
a. Self/spouse	0.95
b. Relative	−0.37
c. Other (e.g., lives in nursing home, lives with relative)	−0.35

d. The weights of the first factor explain 49 percent of the variation in the 9 markers.

Table 6.2 INDEPENDENT VARIABLES: SURVEY MEASURES, 1987 AND 1978,
USED AS CORRELATES IN REGRESSION ANALYSIS

1987 Survey, N = 589:
1 Living arrangements, 1987
2 How many times married?
3 Marital status, 1987
4 Year of husband's death
5 Living brothers and sisters
6 Close members of family (besides husband) died last 10 years
7 Lost contact with friends and neighbors last 10 years
8 New person in last 2 or 3 years who gives emotional support
9 Worked for pay in past 10 years
10 Voted in elections for president last 10 years
11 How often attend church or synagogue in past year?
12 Someone you confide in
13 Someone who makes you feel needed and appreciated
14 Someone with whom you share interests and activities
15 Friends/neighbors who would help if sick for a short time
16 Number of times changed residence in the last 10 years
17 What do you expect to be doing a couple of years from now?
18 Interviewer evaluation: respondent's overall attitude toward interview

1978 Survey, N = 1049:
19 Respondent's year of birth
20 Respondent's birth cohort
21 Respondent's age at first marriage
22 Respondent's farm residence before marriage
23 Urban/Rural residence respondent ages 6 to 16
24 Respondent's religion when aged 6 to 16
25 Respondent's highest grade completed
26 Respondent's other educational training
27 First husband's education
28 Inside toilet first 10 years after marriage
29 Ever use diaphragm?
30 Number of live births respondent had
31 Couple use any nonsurgical method of contraception?
32 Number years respondent worked for pay since first marriage
33 Is respondent currently employed?
34 Respondent's degree of worry about family future during depression
35 How would respondent rate own health?
36 Does respondent have difficulty going up/down stairs?
37 Does respondent have difficulty going shopping?
38 How many including respondent live in household?
39 Size of community respondent lived in, 1978
40 Interviewer evaluation: respondent's level of cooperation, 1978
41 Interviewer evaluation: was respondent at ease with contraception/pregnancy
    questions, 1978?

(chapter 2), as well as findings from the two surveys and the qualitative interviews, I determined that three major domains were fundamental to the quality of life of older women: psychological well-being, capacity for self-management, and a private safety net of social supports.

WHY THREE SEPARATE DIMENSIONS?

Although the three dimensions have been defined as separate properties of successful aging, they and their markers are joint elements of the larger phenomenon, successful aging. The question arises, Why were the three dimensions considered separately in the first place? Why not enter all the variables in the data matrix into a program and let the analysis determine the configuration of the factors?

The answer is that the model is only one of a number of approaches I used to analyze data in this study. Before designing the model, I had already explored the nature of successful aging using several other approaches. I had searched the literature on aging from a number of perspectives (chapter 2), made extensive bivariate analysis of data from the 1978 and 1987 surveys (chapters 4 and 5), and closely monitored what the women in this study said themselves—both in the open-ended questions in the 1987 survey and in the qualitative fieldwork interviews (chapters 1 through 5). The evidence from these various sources strongly suggested that successful aging could be conceptualized in terms of the three distinct dimensions described here. The purpose of the model was to determine whether empirical measures available from the two surveys would substantiate the view that these three domains together can account for differences in individual experiences of aging. Further statistical exploration of the data to define the dimensions did not seem necessary or expedient.

In addition to the strong research support and theoretical basis for retaining the three dimensions as distinct entities, I saw two other major advantages of this approach: first, as shown in the preceding comparison of the four women's circumstances, it enables one to differentiate between women who might be strong in one domain but weak in another. And, second, it permitted a look at the background characteristics associated with success in particular life domains.

Dimensions and markers. The model makes a distinction between "dimensions" and "markers" of successful aging. The former are major life domains that are used to approximate areas fundamental to the quality of life in old age. The term, dimension, is used here in its broad sense as a major component or characteristic of the phenomenon of successful aging, not in its more technical sense as an element in a system with certain mathematical properties. The "markers" are the empirical measures from the 1987 survey that compose the best set of variables for defining each dimension.

PUBLIC DIMENSION OF SUCCESSFUL AGING

Missing from this framework is a fourth dimension, the public dimension of support. This can be defined as a safety net of community services and public entitlements. Examining the relationship between private and public supports is, in fact, a key research interest in the field of aging today. One prominent goal is to ascertain the impact of formal services on informal care (Edelman and Hughes 1990), and the stresses on families of providing long-term assistance to frail and homebound elderly members (Braithwaite 1990; Crisp and George 1990).

In chapters 8 and 9, I stress that public supports are essential to the well-being of all older people, and, particularly, to those who are frail, poor, and deficient in private supports—such as those having no husband, children, or responsible nonkin. In view of the current research interest in the topic, and its importance to older people and to American society, generally, why omit consideration of the public safety net in this model as a substitute (however imperfect) for private means of support?

The reasons are at once conceptual and heuristic. The concept of successful aging proposed here reflects the situation represented by the great majority of women in this sample—that is, they are getting along, for the most part, on their own with a little informal assistance from family and friends (for exceptions, see chapter 7). Very few are being supported by public services. True, the overwhelming majority (95 percent) are receiving Social Security. However, only 12 women (2 percent) have ever received health care paid for by Medicaid (or a comparable state program). In addition, the proportion using community services was quite small, the highest proportion in this regard being the 10 percent who use senior citizens centers and take communal meals. No more than half that many used community services of any other kind, such as special transport (5 percent), adult day care (0.3 percent), or a checkup telephone service (2 percent).

The 1987 survey aimed to study the informal care provided by family, friends, and neighbors: it did not seek to examine variations in the types of community services used or the possible reasons for the low proportion using them: was it lack of accessibility, reluctance to accept charity, or poor information about the services available? The data offer few empirical measures to answer these questions. However, the life stories (chapters 1 and 2) suggest that sorting out the factors underlying the use of public resources can be complex. For example, Mrs. Farnsworth had a need for formal services and she knew they existed in the community, but because she desperately wanted the excuse to leave her husband, she was unwilling to try to ease her hardships by seeking public assistance. Mrs. Silvestri's liberal use of the senior center, communal meals, and special bus service illustrates, on the other hand, how intelligent use of community services can implement and extend one's capacity for independent activity. A major theme throughout this book is that knowing how and when to use community resources may both reflect and contribute to successful aging.

Summary: The Public Safety Net. That women in this sample survived into their 80s sets them apart from the 307 women in the initial sample who died over the decade, and makes them less likely to have resorted to a public safety net. As a group, the nonsurvivors may have needed more outside assistance and, prior to death, relied upon public supports.

To assess the relationship between successful aging and use of public resources, one would have to distinguish between the types of services used. I would suppose, for example, that communal meals and subsidized transportation would have very different implications as measures of successful aging than, say, adult day care and Medicaid payments. In any case, the number of women in this sample saying they used these resources was too small to make such an analysis.

As a final note, in excluding the public dimension from the model, I do not mean to suggest either that it is inconsequential to successful aging or that use of public resources is an indicator of aging less well.

RELATIONSHIP BETWEEN MODEL PARAMETERS

Figure 6.1 is a simple flow chart of the relationships between the model parameters. The three main boxes are arranged in temporal sequence and in the order in which the main components are presumed to influence each other. At the top of the chart (box 1) are the "correlates," the sociodemographic characteristics of women in the sample that are hypothesized as playing a role in shaping the three dimensions of successful aging (box 2). In the column below each dimension are listed examples of the measures selected as markers of that particular domain. These are not arranged in any hierarchical order of influence. Box 3, at the foot of the chart, represents the likely consequences or outcomes

Figure 6.1 MODEL FOR THE STUDY OF SUCCESSFUL AGING

1.

CORRELATES
Demographic and Social Background Factors (e.g., size of community when growing up, schooling, marriage and childbearing patterns, use of birth control, employment history, attendance at religious services, living arrangements, major gains and losses since 1978)

2.

DIMENSIONS

PERCEIVED WELL-BEING	↔	CAPACITY FOR INDEPENDENT ACTIVITY	↔	PRIVATE SAFETY NET

Some Markers for Successful Aging

Attitudes towards Self	Capacity to manage daily tasks: meals,	Children, number of Caregivers
Health	shopping,	Primary
Family relations	housework, laundry,	Secondary
Activities	finances, etc.	Supports, affective:
Living arrangements	Mobility, level of	persons to confide
Neighborhood	Physical activity,	in, share interests
Perceived adequacy of	involvement in:	with, make one feel
income	walking, swimming,	needed and
Reaction to interview	etc.	appreciated
Satisfaction with	Social activity,	Supports,
housing	involvement in:	instrumental:
Perception of time:	clubs, visiting,	persons to give help
R is occupied	playing games, etc.	when sick, to help
R has time on hands	Eyesight, adequacy of	with medical costs
		Homeownership
		In whose name?
		Rental?
		Income, level of

3.

CONSEQUENCES OF SUCCESS

PERCEIVED WELL-BEING	↔	CAPACITY FOR INDEPENDENT ACTIVITY	↔	PRIVATE SAFETY NET

Life satisfaction	Extended independent	Sense of security
Greater autonomy	action	Improved quality of
Sense of self-worth	Longer life	life
	Greater social	Sense of control over
	integration, less	life events
	social isolation	

associated with success in the different dimensions. The longitudinal design of the study permitted an examination of the association between the correlates (box 1) and the dimensions of successful aging (box 2). However, analyzing the consequences (box 3) was outside the scope of this study. Research into the consequences of occupying different positions on the successful aging indexes would require conducting an additional survey—to see how women who scored "very effective" or "not so effective" in 1987 would rank on the three dimensions at some future time. This would entail the kind of longitudinal prospective approach that Rodin (1986) conducted in examining the effects of a sense of control on the health and morale of older residents of nursing homes (see chapter 2).

INTERDEPENDENCE OF MARKERS AND DIMENSIONS

The direction of the arrows in figure 6.1 indicates that, for the most part, the variables in the chart are interdependent and mutually influence one another. For example, there is a close connection between feeling bored and having time on one's hands, or between needing help to go shopping and needing help to go beyond walking distance.

The dimensions, too, are interrelated. For instance, a sense of contentment is linked to the capacity to manage one's own affairs; the capacity for self-management is linked to ability to purchase services such as transportation within the community; and having access to community events is, in turn, linked with a sense of satisfaction that one is still part of the ongoing stream of social life. These interdependencies were discussed in chapter 2 in relation to "the person-environment-services system" and, in chapter 4, in relation to the value that women in the sample attach to having an adequate income—namely, that it contributes to their capacity to choose how they want to live and, in particular, may enable them to maintain a household separate from their children or other relatives. The United Nations World Assembly on Aging (1982), in its statement on humanitarian issues, described conditions very like these as being interdependent (see chapter 4).

Step 2. Selecting Empirical Measures to Form Indexes of the Three Dimensions

The second step in building the model was to examine all the potential empirical measures from the 1987 survey and to assign each to one dimension only, on a conceptual basis.[2]

In selecting the measures, my aim was to include as many as possible from the 1987 survey, so that each domain would represent a composite of many different indicators.[3] In most cases, there was no doubt about where to assign a particular item. For example, "Do you feel less useful as you get older?" or "Taking all things together, how happy would you say you feel these days: Very happy, Pretty happy, Not so happy?" are both clearly measures of perceived well-being. Likewise, "Can you do the shopping for groceries (meal preparation, laundry, housework, finances): Without help, With some help, or Are you completely unable to do?" are measures of the capacity for self-management. And income and home ownership can certainly be seen as indicators of private means of support.

However, a few measures were borderline, and I was obliged to make a decision about assigning them on theoretical and subjective grounds. For example, it was difficult to say whether the item, "Compared to others in your age group, would you say that your health is: excellent, good, fair, or poor?" defined more a sense of well-being or the capacity for self-management. I assigned it to "Perceived Well-being," on the grounds that it indicates how satisfied a woman feels about her physical condition.

This type of decision making is by no means unusual in social science research. The task of setting up indicators of social phenomena always involves some degree of subjectivity (Diamond and Garner, forthcoming). In this study, in most cases, the assignment of measures to one or another of the three dimensions involved very little ambiguity. The approach used to select and assign the measures to each of the three dimensions is described more fully next.

MEASURES OF DIMENSION 1: PERCEIVED WELL-BEING

Taking first the dimension "Perceived Well-being," I wanted to measure differences among women in the sample in terms of a sense of satisfaction with their lot—their general feelings of being happy or sad, and of being in good or poor physical shape, as well as their attitudes with respect to a number of specific aspects of their current physical and social environments. The 1987 survey included questions measuring a variety of such attitudes—for example: satisfaction with the amount of space in one's home and with facilities in the neighborhood, attitudes toward the adequacy of one's income, and feelings about the use of one's time.

To form the dimension, Perceived Well-being, an index was developed based on scores on measures of how a woman feels about herself, her home, and her activities. For example, on the survey item, "Do you feel less useful as you get older?" (table 6.1, item 5), if a woman answered yes—that is, "I do feel less useful"—she would receive a relatively lower score on the scale of Perceived Well-being than if her answer was no—that is, "I do not feel less useful as I get older."

Another example relates to attitudes toward health, as just described. Those in the sample who described their health as "excellent" (21 percent) would contribute a high mark to their composite score on Perceived Well-being; the 39 percent who described their health as "good" would contribute a next lower mark to their composite score on this dimension, and so on. In this fashion, the women's responses to selected survey items were combined to develop the three indexes. Each dimension is thus a composite of multiple survey items.

MEASURES OF DIMENSION 2: CAPACITY FOR INDEPENDENT ACTIVITY

The second dimension, "Capacity for Independent Activity," was measured by both subjective and objective survey items. "Independent" activity implies a combination of physical and mental conditions, some of which are more or less objectively determined (e.g., "Can you do the shopping? Can you do the housework?"), and some of which reflect the woman's subjective perception of her physical capacities. In this dimension, as in the other two, subjective perceptions such as "How good is your eyesight: excellent, good, fair or poor?" were included on the same basis as more objective assessments of functional capacity, such as "I can do the shopping without help." The reader may wonder, in terms of the latter example, how can a woman's capacity to do various kinds of activities be accurately assessed? In fact, studies (see, for example, Maddox 1987) have shown that older people's subjective views about how they feel and what they can do are often the best measures of their general health and physical capacities.

MEASURES OF DIMENSION 3: PRIVATE SAFETY NET

Measures selected to construct the third dimension, "Private Safety Net," consist of supports an older person can claim in case she is unable to meet the demands placed upon her. These supports are of two main types: (1) persons available to provide informal help of various kinds, and (2) economic assets and housing characteristics. The items selected include measures of informal support, such as "Do you have help with medical bills?" and income and other material assets such as ownership of a home and number of rooms in one's dwelling.

Table 6.1 lists the set of empirical measures used to construct the index for each dimension. As determined by factor analysis, these are the measures from the 1987 survey that contributed the most to defining the three dimensions. Step 3 describes the procedures used for the factor analysis and the explanation of "the weights" in Table 6.1.

Step 3. Performing Factor Analysis on the Three Sets of Measures and, for Each Dimension, Computing a Numerical Index from the First Factor

One approach to developing the indexes would simply have been to total the raw scores for each woman on the relevant empirical measures. In effect, this was the method used in figure 6.1 to illustrate the marked differences between Mrs. Silvestri and Mrs. Farnsworth in terms of their general sense of well-being. However, the contributions of different measures to defining the three dimensions are unlikely to be all the same. Some can be expected to have more influence than others in explaining the variation in the women's positions on the indexes.[4] Therefore, principal component and factor analysis were used to differentiate between the indicators in terms of their relative contribution to the underlying structure of the three main dimensions. Based on "the weights" or coefficients assigned to the measures, an index was constructed for each of the dimensions separately. The statistical procedures are outlined next.

PRINCIPAL COMPONENT AND FACTOR ANALYSIS

The "unrotated coefficients" in table 6.1 represent the weights generated by using algebra to calculate the linear combination of the items that explains the greatest variation in each of the three domains. The program used principal component and factor analysis to identify the five factors or sets that explain most of the variation. The process involves calculating the average of the scores, a weighted sum, for each set of items. The proportion of the variation explained by each of these linear combinations of markers sums to 100 percent.

For the purposes of this analysis, I used the first factor only, the one set of items in the data matrix that is the most robust in explaining the variation in each of the domains. Table 6.1 lists the "weights" for this first factor. For the purposes of this study, this set of variables and their "weights" are called "markers."

Proportion of variance explained by first factor. Table 6.1 shows that on dimension 1, Perceived Well-being, 18 markers explain 60 percent of the variation; on dimension 2, Capacity for Independent Activity, 11 markers explain 53 percent of the variation, and on dimension 3, Private Safety Net, 9 markers explain 49 percent of the variation.

Assignment of scores. To assign women in the sample to various positions on the three indexes, the coefficients were amalgamated to produce a score for each dimension. The mean of this score is zero. The scores constitute interval scales ranging from negative to positive, an unbroken continuum representing degrees of successful aging. These scores, as such, admit of no simple classification, and by themselves are meaningless. They make sense only in relational terms; that is, as defined by this model, "this woman is relatively more or less successful as compared to that woman."

Continuums of successful aging. The product of the factor analysis is three continuums representing the three domains of successful aging. A fourth continuum, not shown in the tables, can also be computed representing the overall average of the three.[5] The continuum for "Perceived Well-being," for example, is shown in figure 6.2. Going from high on the negative pole to high on the positive pole, the scores on the indexes represent a continuum ranging from less-successful aging to more-successful aging. As defined in this model, the higher your position on the index, the more successful you are. Simply from an operational viewpoint, women who are defined as effective agers are distinguished from those who are less effective by having higher positive scores on the three continuums.

Best set of markers. The results of identifying the best set of markers are shown in table 6.1. What do these data reveal about the contri-

Figure 6.2 CONTINUUM OF SUCCESSFUL AGING—DIMENSION 1: PERCEIVED WELL-BEING

Less Successful —	More Successful +
High Negative Score	High Positive Score
For example, respondent feels that she is less useful as she gets older.	For example, respondent does *not* feel that she is less useful as she gets older.

bution of the different empirical measures to defining the three dimensions? Essential to interpreting the best set of markers is the assumption that the measures included do, indeed, give some approximation of the three major dimensions.[6] Thus, the coefficients in table 6.1 can be interpreted as weights that sort the measures selected to define each dimension into a hierarchy indicating their importance relative to the others in the set.[7]

For example, a negative weight of -0.34 on feeling unhappy, marker 16 ("R overall is unhappy with life these days") (table 6.1) indicates that in this model to say one is unhappy is a relatively robust marker in terms of its power to discriminate variations in feelings of well-being. The important point is that, net of *all the other* measures from the 1987 survey included in the factor analysis, feelings about general happiness do well in enabling us to distinguish between women who are feeling quite well satisfied and those who are feeling discontented with their lot.

STRUCTURE OF THE THREE DIMENSIONS

The three sections following describe the contribution of "the best set of markers" to understanding the underlying structure of each of the three dimensions.

Perceived Well-being. Table 6.1, part A, shows 18 markers in the best set for defining Perceived Well-being, accounting altogether for 60 percent of the variation. In general, these markers reflect a constellation of feelings that include believing that things get worse as you get older, that aging makes one less useful, and that time hangs heavy on one's hands. Markers 6 through 15 are items from the Bradburn Affect-Balance Scale (Bradburn 1969). This instrument has been used for many years in surveys of older people to measure global feelings of depression or contentment with life. The odd numbers 7, 9, and 11 show the negative impact on a sense of well-being of feeling restless, remote from other people, and bored, respectively. In contrast, the even numbers 6, 8, and 10 show the positive contribution of feeling, respectively, excited, proud because someone complimented you for something, or pleased about having accomplished something. Images of one's health (markers 1, 2, and 3) are also important to defining perceived well-being. A poor image of one's health contributes to a lower sense of well-being.

With a weight of (-0.90), marker 4 ("R feels things keep getting worse as she gets older") is by far the strongest in the set. Feeling that things are getting worse as you get older is, in a sense, a watershed. A positive attitude toward aging is part of a larger group of optimistic orientations, such as a sense of control over one's life, that one is still useful to others, and that one's time is full and well occupied rather than empty and meaningless (see chapter 2).

In summary, these 18 markers show that, among this sample, a high level of perceived well-being is defined by the following markers: (1) positive attitudes toward one's health and the belief that health problems do not limit one's activities, (2) feeling interested, stimulated, and connected with others, rather than bored, lonely, and remote, and (3) above all, having an optimistic view about aging itself.

Capacity for Independent Activity. The best set of markers describing Capacity for Independent Activity consists of 11 variables, accounting for a total of 53 percent of the variation (table 6.1, part B). The most powerful markers are numbers 6 through 10, indicating the woman's ability to manage without help the routine activities of daily living—that is, shopping, preparing meals, doing housework, doing laundry, and handling financial affairs.[8] By the same token, not being able to carry out these tasks without help makes a strong negative contribution to defining the dimension. Other markers of functional performance, such as taking walks at least once a week and making trips outside the neighborhood, contribute less than do the more traditional IADL and ADL measures (see chapter 4). The great importance of eyesight as a constraint on independent activity is seen in the negative impact of defining one's eyesight as only fair or poor.

The presence of marker 5 ("R needs help going places out of walking distance") as a negative characteristic in this set underlines the importance to the independence of older women of being able to get out and about on their own. It also highlights the significance of the person-environment service system described by Lawton and Hoover (1981), namely, that older people's independence is often linked to the support provided by family, friends, neighbors, and community workers. Mrs. Silvestri, for example, is thoroughly capable of looking after herself, but she does not drive, and requires the assistance of her neighbors and the community bus to go beyond walking distance. This means that her score on Capacity for Independent Activity will be lower than that of a woman who can drive her own car and get places out of walking distance without help from others.

This is an instance where the appropriateness of the tools used to measure levels of functional capacity can be legitimately challenged.

We need measuring instruments that take into account the important distinction between availing oneself of assistance in order to attain independence and relying upon the help of others as a sign that one cannot manage for oneself.[9]

Two other features of this index deserve brief comment: the distribution of the sample on functional capacities, and findings concerning older women's perception of need.

Distribution of sample on functional capacities. The distribution reinforces the fact that a majority of women in this sample can manage quite well and do not need substantial outside help (Appendix 6-C). A small number of very badly off women (28 in all) scored highly dependent, whereas the majority were fairly adept at managing for themselves. Only 15 percent were unable to shop for groceries without help, 9 percent needed assistance to prepare their meals, and 7 percent needed help to manage their money (Appendix 6-A).

Perception of need. Also of interest is marker 11, the respondents' perceived need for help (table 6.1, part B). Relative to others in the set, marker 11 ("R needs (more) help with any IADL tasks") makes only a small negative contribution. In other words, to say that one needs more help, apparently, is a relatively ineffectual means of discriminating between high and low levels in the capacity to manage independently. The reason may lie in the fact that this is a measure of the woman's subjective assessment—both of the adequacy of help she actually receives and of help she thinks she needs. As such, it is a misleading indicator of how well one can actually manage on one's own. From evidence in this survey, it seems likely that many women say they need no help when in reality they may be having quite a hard time. Mrs. Peres, with failing eyesight and no family or friends to give her a hand, still claims she needs no more help. She is proud and has a fighting spirit. Moreover, she has no private support to draw upon, and dislikes the idea of asking for public assistance.

The high concentration of the sample in the "Can do" and "Need no help" categories suggests that a useful direction for future research would be to develop measures of functional capacities that differentiate more closely between levels of ease and difficulty in performing everyday activities. An example is that of distinguishing between light and heavy housework—often used now in studies of the elderly. A similar disaggregation of daily tasks could be tried with respect to shopping, laundry, financial management, and getting around outside the house. Some older people with poor vision, for example, hesitate to ride an elevator alone because they cannot read the floor numbers and are afraid of getting stuck or losing their way. Better ways to distinguish between levels of competence could contribute to more effective ways to identify those who need support of particular kinds.

Private Safety Net. The set of nine markers describing private safety net is in some ways the most interesting. Clearly, with a weight of (-0.62), marker 8 ("R does not own her home") is the most powerful in discriminating levels of resilience in private resources (table 6.1, part C). The significance of this marker was, in fact, foreshadowed in chapter 1 by Mrs. Silvestri's strong statement about the fundamental importance of her home to maintaining her independence and allowing her to continue with her favorite activities. This theme, as we have seen, is echoed by many other women in the survey, as well. By comparison, as will be discussed later, income (marker 5) is a much less robust measure with which to account for variations in private safety nets.

Because children are usually seen as a major source of support in old age, the negative impact of marker 4 ("Number of living children") is rather unexpected. Among women in this sample, having borne a large number of children is associated with a relatively weak—rather than strong—private safety net. Apparently, in the course of these women's adult lives, and in the times they lived through, having a large family came to be associated with conditions not conducive to strengthening one's reserves in old age.

The negative impact of large family size in this model may also be indicative of the relationship of family planning during the Depression to other social characteristics, such as social class, level of schooling, religion, and motivation to control the events in one's life. Women who were college-educated, urban-dwelling, white-collar, and non-Catholic were the most likely to have used contraception to limit their family size (Dawson, et al. 1980:76). The association of these characteristics with income, home ownership, and modes of informal support in old age deserves further investigation in future research.

Markers 1, 2, and 3 show the negative contribution to the private safety net of not having informal supports of particular kinds, such as someone to help with medical bills, or a caregiver to take responsibility for practical help and emotional support. That having no *secondary* caregiver is a more powerful marker of a safety net than having no primary caregiver can probably be accounted for largely by the fact that very few women in the sample (3 percent) had no primary caregiver, while nearly a fourth (24 percent) had no secondary caregiver.[10]

Finally, how to account for two other findings: the small negative contributions of marker 6 ("Number of persons on support roster"), and marker 7 ("Number of rooms in R's 1987 residence")? One might expect that both these markers would make a positive, rather than a negative, contribution to defining private supports. However, since all living children were listed on the support roster, there is a correlation between the number on the roster and the number of children. As was seen in the Mrs. Farnsworth case, children may or may not play a supportive role, and, besides, as noted above, among these women who raised their children during the Depression, large family size may be associated with life chances (such as the risk of experiencing the death of a child or of not being able to afford to live in a separate household) that entail greater hardship in coming to terms with aging.

The negative impact of marker 7, number of rooms, has two possible explanations: first, the larger the house, the more potentially difficult it is for an old person to keep it up without help, and the greater the chance that she may be persuaded to sell and relocate. Second, a large number of rooms may be associated with living with persons other than one's husband, a situation that again places an old person in a precarious position in terms of continuity of residence and control over what happens in the future. The great importance of having one's home in one's own name is highlighted by the power (0.95) of marker 9a, which designates "Self/Spouse" as the "Name in which R's home is owned/rented." The contribution of this marker to defining a strong private safety net may reflect the association between owning one's home and the retention of control over one's decisions in later life.

SCORE POSITIONS OF WOMEN IN 1987 SAMPLE ON THREE DIMENSIONS

The percentage distribution of the sample by scores on the three indexes is presented in table 6.3, and the distribution is shown graphically in figures 6.3, 6.4, and 6.5. The pattern of scores on all three indexes looks a little like a normal distribution, with a majority clustered in the middle three of the five-category range and less than 20 percent scoring in the top and bottom of the range. Nearly 50 percent of the women scored in the middle of the range on Capacity

Table 6.3 PERCENTAGE DISTRIBUTION OF SCORES ON THREE SCALES OF
SUCCESSFUL AGING, 1987 SAMPLE

Score Range	Percentage Sample in Score Range
Dimension 1: Perceived Well-being	
0.7 to 1.0	3.8
0.3 to 0.6	20.6
−0.1 to 0.2	43.7
−0.5 to −0.2	23.1
Less than −0.5	8.8
Dimension 2: Capacity for Independent Activity	
More than 0.9	4.0
0.2 to 0.9	12.5
0.01 to 0.19	49.1
−0.7 to 0.0	28.3
Less than −0.7	6.1
Dimension 3: Private Safety Net	
0.7 to 1.2	7.7
0.1 to 0.6	42.5
−0.5 to 0.0	38.9
−1.1 to −0.6	9.4
Less than −1.1	

Note: This table was prepared with the assistance of Lincoln H. Day and Ian Diamond, both of the Department of Demography, Research School of Social Sciences, Australian National University, Canberra, ACT.

for Independent Activity, whereas scores on Safety Net were skewed toward the higher range. The pattern on Perceived Well-being fell somewhere in between these two, with higher scores than on Independent Activity, but not as many scores in the upper ranges as on Safety Net. The high scores on Safety Net may reflect the large proportion of women who still lived in homes that they owned and had occupied for well over 10 years.

POSITIONS OF WOMEN IN QUALITATIVE STUDY

The distributions of sample scores (table 6.3) show mainly that on each of the three dimensions, a majority of the women were clustered around the mean. However, the locations of the women relative to each other on the qualitative interviews (see table 6.4) highlight two other important features of the model: first, that a discrepancy may occur between one's personal impressions and a woman's position

Figure 6.3 DISTRIBUTION OF 1987 SAMPLE SCORES ON THE PERCEIVED
WELL-BEING DIMENSION

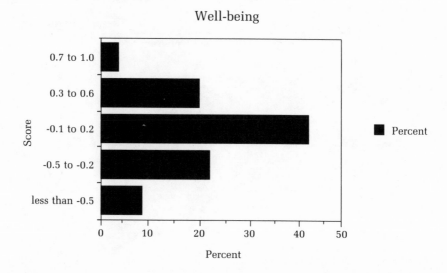

on the continuum of successful aging; and, second, that the women's scores reflect a configuration of many different factors.

Personal impressions and score positions. The personal impressions I obtained from the qualitative interviews about aging effectively did not always fully mesh with the women's scores on the three dimensions. This was partly due to the fact that changes in the women's circumstances had taken place in the 16-month interval between the 1987 survey and my visit to their homes. As noted in chapter 3, some of these changes were profound. Mrs. Crawford, for example, who, though using a wheelchair, was managing meals and some housework when interviewed in 1987, was more dependent when I saw her in 1988, because she had broken her arm in a fall downstairs and needed help with personal care as well as with cooking and getting around.

To be sure, my strongest impressions are well reflected in the model scores. Mrs. Silvestri, for example, who so impressed me with her calm, good sense, and control over her affairs, ranked in the top 95th percentile in the sample as a whole, and, among women in the qualitative interviews, scored at the top of the combined data index.

Figure 6.4 DISTRIBUTION OF 1987 SAMPLE SCORES ON THE CAPACITY FOR
INDEPENDENT ACTIVITY DIMENSION

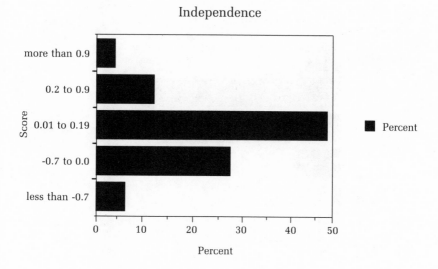

Mrs. Farnsworth, whom I found in pain and despair, ranked in the bottom 30th percentile in the sample as a whole and was among the bottom third of the women in the qualitative interviews in all three domains. However, there were other women, who were less obviously aging well or poorly, who had moderate to low scores in the model, and seemed when I met them to be handling the challenges of aging very well, and vice versa—some, who appeared unexceptional, had higher scores than I would have expected.

The discrepancy between personal impressions and the quantitative scores may be due not only to changes between the interviews but also to differences between my personal values and the norms about aging underlying the empirical measures.[11] An example is the measurement of functional dependence and independence. As noted earlier (see note 9), driving a private automobile, because it implies not having to depend on others to get around outside the house, is interpreted as an indicator of a higher capacity for independent activity than using public transportation or getting lifts from friends and neighbors.

Multiple paths to success. A second feature of successful aging suggested by table 6.4 is "the supreme individuality in adaptation to

Figure 6.5 DISTRIBUTION OF 1987 SAMPLE SCORES ON THE PRIVATE SAFETY
NET DIMENSION

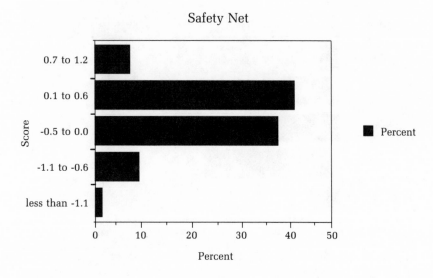

Safety Net

aging (see Baltes and Baltes 1988, chapter 8 in this volume)." Relationships between these women's rankings on the three dimensions
reveal no uniform pattern or simple interpretation. One can, like
Mrs. Carlton, have a high position relative to others in terms of
Perceived Well-being and a lower rank on Private Safety Net. This
suggests that no *single* condition, such as marital status, functional
capacity, or type of living arrangement is invariably associated with
level of perceived well-being or strength of private safety net. High
levels of satisfaction are found among widows living alone as well
as women still living with their husbands, among childless women
and those with three or four children, and among those with one
friend and those with many. The women's scores reflect a mix of
diverse elements.

This result could have been anticipated, given what we know
about aging from previous research. West German psychologists
Margret and Paul Baltes (1988:32), for example, stress that there
are many different ways of achieving a successful adjustment to
old age. They see successful aging as a "creative" blending of
individual traits with a unique combination of social circumstances (see chapter 8).

Table 6.4 SCORE POSITIONS OF 20 WOMEN IN QUALITATIVE STUDY: THREE
DIMENSIONS OF SUCCESSFUL AGING AND COMBINED DATA SCORE

1. Perceived Well-being	2. Capacity for Independent Activity	3. Private Safety Net	4. Combined Data Score
1 Esherman	1 Crawford	1 Farmer	1 Silvestri
2 Silvestri	2 Worth	2 Dewitt	2 Dewitt
3 Smart	3 Eisenstein	3 Porter	3 Crawford
4 Carlton	4 Carter	4 Farnsworth	4 Carlton
5 Dewitt	5 Wright	5 Silvestri	5 Smart
6 Hammerstein	6 Carlton	6 Crawford	6 Porter
7 Crawford	7 King	7 Smart	7 Farmer
8 Porter	8 Farmer	8 Carlton	8 Carter
9 Worth	9 Dewitt	9 Carter	9 Esherman
10 Farmer	10 Silvestri	10 Danburger	10 Hammerstein
11 Eisenstein	11 Porter	11 Fleischmann	11 Farnsworth
12 Grainger	12 Esherman	12 Esherman	12 Fleischmann
13 Carter	12 Smart	13 Grainger	13 Worth
14 Danburger	12 Tyler	14 Worth	14 King
15 King	13 Hammerstein	15 Wright	15 Danburger
16 Fleischmann	14 Farnsworth	16 Hoffman	16 Wright
17 Farnsworth	15 Danburger		17 Grainger
18 Wright	16 Grainger		
Missing:	17 Hoffman	*Missing:*	*Missing:*
Tyler		Tyler	Tyler
Hoffman		Eisenstein	Eisenstein
		King	Hoffman
		Hammerstein	

Notes:
1. The 20 women in the qualitative interviews are listed here from the highest to the lowest in the order of their scores on the three scales of successful aging, and the Combined Data score which is an average of the other three.
2. In many cases, the difference between these scores is quite minimal. Particularly in Dimension 2: Capacity for Independent Activity, the scores were highly concentrated around the mode, with Mrs. Danberger, Mrs. Grainger, and Mrs. Hoffman falling considerably behind the rest. In addition, Mrs. Dewitt, Mrs. Silvestri, and Mrs. Porter were virtually tied, and Mrs. Esherman, Mrs. Smart, and Mrs. Tyler drew identical scores.
3. A comparison of the distribution of scores for 20 women in the qualitative study with the scores for the sample as a whole showed that the former generally are overrepresented in the proportion, with high scores on Perceived Well-being and on the Combined Data score. They are about on a par with their cohorts on Independent Activity and Safety Net. It is possible that the positive orientation toward life reflected in psychological well-being was a factor selecting these women over others when I telephoned a selection of women from the 1987 survey to request a third interview.
4. Among women selected for the qualitative study, none were in the lowest 20 percent of the scores on the four scales. (This comparison is not shown in the table.)

Step 4. Using the Indexes as Dependent Variables in Regression Equations to Reveal the Background Characteristics Correlated with Successful Aging

The final stage in the research strategy called for analysis of the background characteristics associated with aging well or aging poorly. For example, are the women who rank relatively higher on the indexes likely to have endured fewer recent deaths of close family members? Do they have more years of completed schooling? Have they been employed longer? Do their attitudes during the Great Depression or their family planning practices appear to have any bearing on their position relative to others in the three domains of successful aging?

To examine these questions, regressions were run using the three numerical indexes as the dependent variables and a long list of background attributes as categorical, independent variables. The purpose was to determine which sociodemographic characteristics were most strongly associated—net of each other—with each of the three indexes. All the items selected from the 1978 and 1987 surveys are listed in table 6.2.

SELECTION OF INDEPENDENT VARIABLES

In selecting items to be used as independent variables, the goal was to estimate the impact of the older women's backgrounds (e.g., demographic characteristics, functional capacities in 1978, life events between the two surveys, and living arrangements) on the dependent variables (e.g., current attitudes, functional capacities in 1987, and private means of support).

Relationship between dependent and independent variables. Underlying all the independent variables is the theory that, in one way or another, the background characteristics selected affect opportunities for, or constraints against, successful aging. For example, a woman's age, education, work history, living arrangements, and capacities for managing daily tasks in 1978 are regarded as influences that may foster or deter her chances of having good morale, the capacity to manage independently, and various kinds of private supports available to her in later life.

Most of the background data come from the 1978 survey. However, to update the survivors' family structure and living arrangements, a few measures from the 1987 survey were included as well, such as marital status, number of living brothers and sisters, and number of persons living in the household. Moreover, since a major theme in this research is the impact on aging of life transitions between the two surveys, I counted as independent variables losses and increments to one's social network, year of husband's death, and number of times the respondent changed residence in the past 10 years (see Appendix 6-B).

Several other measures from the 1987 survey were selected as rough indicators of a woman's political and religious commitment (e.g., "Have you usually voted in the elections for the president of the United States?" and "In the past year, how often did you attend a church or synagogue service?").

Affective support: Reasons underlying selection as independent variable. The selection of the four indicators of affective support (Appendix 6.B, item 7), that is, does the woman have someone to confide in, someone who makes her feel needed and appreciated, someone to share interests with, and someone who would help out if she were ill for a short time, illustrates the reasoning underlying the relationship between dependent and independent variables. Why were these measures of affective support defined as background characteristics rather than as dimensions of successful aging? What differentiates them from measures such as someone to pay for medical bills or the availability of a secondary caregiver, both of which were included as dependent variables in Private Safety Net?

The distinction is based on differences between the characteristics of affective support and the characteristics of the type of support I see as underlying the concept of private safety net in this model. The private safety net is defined as a reserve of social and financial resources available to an older woman in case her capacity to manage on her own becomes attenuated. Support of this type has the following characteristics: it is available over the relatively long term, it covers comprehensive needs, it may involve a substantial commitment of time and money, and the elderly woman has a strong claim upon it. The kind of assistance entailed in help with payment of medical bills is usually provided by a close family member.

In contrast, as described in the literature (Litwak 1985), affective support generally tends to be emotional, short term and fleeting, and involves a less binding commitment on the provider. Support such as sharing interests and activities is usually exchanged with someone in an older woman's peer group, that is, with friends, neighbors, or siblings, usually sisters.

On the basis of the characteristics of these different types of support, and of the different relationships to the older woman of the people who provide them, I designated affective support as a background characteristic hypothesized as influencing the three dimensions of successful aging. Instrumental support, such as payment of medical bills, was designated a dependent variable—a component of private safety net. Is the availability of affective support, I asked, significantly associated with a woman's sense of well-being, capacity for handling daily activities, and access to instrumental means of support? In brief, is affective support correlated with successful aging?

Future expectations: an independent variable? Finally, worthy of note is the inclusion as an independent variable of item 17 in table 6.2 ("What do you expect to be doing a couple of years from now?"). On what grounds were future expectations selected as a background characteristic influencing successful aging?

"A sense of the future" has been hypothesized as a determinant of behavior in a number of studies—involving, for example, the commitment of young people to social causes (Mead 1967), the motivation for a couple's bearing children (Day and Day 1984), and an older person's desire to continue to grow and develop (Erikson 1982; Maslow 1971). The literature on child and adult development suggests that a feeling of optimism about the future and the sense that one has a personal stake in it are associated with a sense of well-being and an active orientation toward determining the events in one's life. Conversely, pessimism about the future goes hand in hand with lassitude about one's potential and inertia about social activity (Mead 1967). As studies of depression among children and young adults make abundantly clear, if one has no "sense of the future," one feels old and defeated—whatever one's age. These sorts of considerations contributed to the definition of future expectations as an independent variable in this model.

CORRELATES OF SUCCESSFUL AGING

Table 6.5 lists the sets of sociodemographic characteristics that constitute the most significant correlates for each of the three numerical indexes.

Procedures Underlying Regressions

The following procedures were used to generate these relationships. To construct an economical model, two stages of model selection

Table 6.5 CORRELATES OF SUCCESSFUL AGING

Background Factor	Coefficient	Standard Error (coeff.)	t-Score
A. Dimension 1—PERCEIVED WELL-BEING			
1 R's[a] worry about family future in depression, 1978			
At least some worry	−0.19	0.07	−2.71
Not at all worried	0.00	—	—
2 Perception of health compared to others, 1978			
Excellent, good, or fair	0.45	0.15	3.00
Poor	0.00	—	—
3 Difficulty going shopping, 1978			
No difficulty	0.66	0.29	2.28
Some difficulty	0.27	0.31	−0.87
Unable to do	0.00	—	—
4 Living arrangements, 1987			
Living alone, with husband or with kin	0.63	0.25	2.52
Living with husband and others	0.00	—	—
5 Year R's husband died			
Still living or more than 5 years ago	0.38	0.10	3.80
1 to 5 years	0.00	—	—
6 R worked for pay in last 10 years			
Yes	−0.23	0.11	−2.09
No	0.00	—	—
7 R has friends/neighbors who would help if sick			
Yes	0.31	0.08	3.88
No	0.00	—	—
Constant	1.62	0.39	4.15

Notes: R^2 = 0.14. See Appendix 6-C for notes on regression analysis.
a. R, respondent.

continued

were used for the categorical variables. The first involved testing whether a given categorical variable was a useful correlate of the dependent variable, and the second considered whether the individual categories of the variable were different from each other. If there was no statistical evidence that two categories were different, then they were collapsed. This saved on degrees of freedom and, more importantly, aided in interpreting the effects of a variable. There may be cases when sociological sense requires that a variable be left "uncollapsed," but this possibility was carefully monitored

Table 6.5 CORRELATES OF SUCCESSFUL AGING (continued)

B. Dimension 2—CAPACITY FOR INDEPENDENT ACTIVITY

Background Factor	Coefficient	Standard Error (coeff.)	t-Score
1 R has worked for pay since marriage			
Never	−1.49	0.32	−4.66
Sometime	0.00	—	—
2 Perception of health compared to others, 1978			
Excellent, good	0.19	0.09	2.11
Fair, poor	0.00	—	—
3 Size of community in which R lived, 1978			
Central city, 1970 population of 1 million or more	−1.84	0.27	−6.81
All other sized places	0.00	—	
4 Living arrangements, 1987			
Living alone, with husband or with relatives other than adult children	0.65	0.11	5.91
Living with husband and others or with adult child(ren)	0.00	—	—
5 R's attendance at church or synagogue in past year, 1987			
Never attended	−0.58	0.09	−6.44
Attended at least some	0.00	—	—
Constant	0.42	0.13	3.23

Notes: R^2 = 0.23. See Appendix 6-C for notes on regression analysis.

continued

and was not indicated by the data in this model. A description of the specific assumptions underlying the R^2 values is presented in Appendix 6.C.

NOTES ON INTERPRETATION

Two general points should be made here in interpreting the findings. The first is that the search for an explanation goes beyond accounting for the significance of a particular variable in isolation from other possible influences. To understand why a particular sociodemographic characteristic is significant, one needs to consider a web of other factors that may be associated with it. For example, looking at the correlates of Perceived Well-being (dimension 1, table 6.5, part A), one sees that a household arrangement consisting of living with a husband and others (correlate 4, "R lives with husband and others," 1987) is significantly correlated with a low score on Perceived Well-

Table 6.5 CORRELATES OF SUCCESSFUL AGING (continued)

C. Dimension 3—PRIVATE SAFETY NET

Background Factor	Coefficient	Standard Error (coeff.)	t-Score
1 R's year of birth			
1900 to 1901	−0.35	0.16	−2.19
1902 to 1910	0.00	—	—
2 Number of years R worked for pay since first marriage			
Less than 1 year	−0.90	0.31	−2.90
1 to 39 years	−0.46	0.16	−2.88
40 years or more	0.00	—	—
3 Current employment status, 1978			
Never worked for pay	−0.59	0.18	−3.28
Currently employed or currently not employed	0.00	0.00	—
4 Number, including R, living in household, 1978			
1 to 4	1.19	0.22	5.41
5 to 8	0.00	—	—
5 Living arrangements, 1987			
Living alone, with husband or in institution	0.29	0.19	1.53
Living with stem family[b]	−0.51	0.20	−2.55
Living with more distant relatives or with nonkin[c]	0.00	—	—
6 R's attendance at church or synagogue in past year, 1987			
Never, a few times, or 2 to 3 times per month	−0.26	0.07	−3.71
Once a week and more than once a week	0.00	—	—
7 R has someone with whom to share interests and activities			
Yes	0.19	0.08	2.38
No	0.00	—	—
8 Number of times R changed residence in last 10 years, 1987			
Never	0.92	0.08	11.50
Once or more	0.00	—	—
Constant	1.48	0.34	4.35

Notes: R^2 = 0.39. See Appendix 6-C for notes on regression analysis.
b. Stem family in this study consists of the first-, second-, and third-generation nuclear family members: adult children and grandchildren (for discussion, see chapter 4).
c. Extended family relatives consist of aunts and uncles, brothers and sisters, nieces and nephews (for discussion, see chapter 4).

being (significant at the 0.05–0.10 level, Appendix 6-D). Recalling the discussion in chapter 4, a plausible explanation is that for a couple to live together in someone else's home is often a consequence of low income, frailty, and the wife needing more comprehensive care than an elderly husband can manage on his own. So strong is the convention in the United States for married couples to live alone that only under conditions of extreme adversity and absence of other options does one find such a couple—even one in their upper 80s—living with others. Not unexpectedly, these conditions are associated with a negative impact on life satisfaction.

Following from this example, the second point about interpretation is that the model is not the last word, but the first. The findings reveal relationships between the background characteristics and the three life domains, about which we need to gain deeper understanding to penetrate the real meaning of the conditions facilitating or deterring aging well.

Given these points, what do the regression results indicate about the conditions that have an important impact on life chances and the quality of the aging experience?

Regression Results

CORRELATES OF PERCEIVED WELL-BEING

The set of seven factors that constitute the "best" correlates for Perceived Well-being can be grouped into three general categories: (1) perceived health and capacity to manage in 1978, (2) the nature of social relationships and modes of social support, and (3) optimistic or pessimistic orientations. The coefficients and standard errors of the seven independent variables that comprise the regression line for Perceived Well-being are shown in table 6.5, part A.

Correlates 2 ("Perception of health compared to others," 1978) and 3 ("Difficulty going shopping," 1978) show the importance of health conditions at ages 66 to 77 to how women in the sample feel in their 80s. This finding confirms the conclusions of earlier studies that perceptions of health and functional capacities in old age are traceable to earlier stages in a person's life history. Those who felt their health was poor or reported having difficulty doing the shopping in 1978 also had less of a sense of well-being in 1987.

A second category of influences on sense of well-being is reflected in correlates 4 through 7 (table 6.5). All relate to the nature and quality of the women's social relationships—people she lives with, is married to, works with, or depends upon to help if she becomes ill. The devastating effect on perceived well-being of losing one's husband at these late ages is shown by the strong negative impact of correlate 5 ("Year R's husband died"). The duration of loss is particularly telling. After five years, an older woman has had time to adjust to the major changes incurred in being without her partner, and the traumatic impact of the loss on her sense of well-being is less significant.

On the brighter side, correlate 7 ("R has friends/neighbors who would help if sick") makes a strong positive contribution to one's psychological well-being at these ages. As shown in chapter 5, the supportive role of friends and neighbors is well illustrated in the stories of women in the qualitative study. The significance of correlate 7 highlights the importance to perceived well-being of having people around who can provide practical help when one's own resources prove less than adequate (see Syme 1988, and chapter 2 in this volume).

Although not as significant as others in the set, of particular interest is the negative influence of correlate 1 ("R's worry about family future in depression," 1978). There are two possible interpretations: (1) that women who worried about their family's future during the depression were particularly hard hit and that this setback has had a lasting effect on their lives and attitudes, or (2) that pessimism is a stable orientation with lasting effects over the whole life course. Whatever the reason, in this sample there is a significant association between worry over the future of one's family during the depression, as expressed by women in 1978, and their level of well-being in 1987. Those who said they did not worry at all about the future in those years generally do better than those who say they worried at least some.

Finally, the model shows that a woman's work history has an influence on psychological well-being, but not perhaps in the direction expected by today's committed young career women. The negative sign of correlate 6 ("R worked for pay in the past 10 years") indicates that, for a woman in her late 70s or 80s, having worked at some time in the last 10 years is a factor detracting from a sense of well-being. This is probably because working for pay in these ages is likely to be associated with economic hardship and with having to earn an income to supplement, or substitute for, Social Security. Pressure to work of this sort does not sit well with a sense of overall happiness or a feeling that things are going your way. Material in the interviews suggests that working for pay at these ages is often driven by the desire to maintain one's independence, by, for example, struggling to keep up payments on one's home or to hire services to help with the increasingly unwieldy tasks of heavy housework and keeping up a yard. The observation that work for pay at these late ages is often associated with a struggle to maintain autonomy coincides with Torrey's (1988) research (cited in chapter 4), showing that older people tend to husband their assets to ensure control over their own affairs, rather than putting aside a nest egg for their children.

CORRELATES OF CAPACITY FOR INDEPENDENT ACTIVITY

The five background factors in this set all reflect the influence of a complex interaction between older people's demographic characteristics and life-styles, on the one hand, and level of physical functioning, on the other. The processes underlying these relationships are somewhat obscure. Rather than clearly indicating the pathways to capacity for independent activity, they suggest the need for deeper exploration of the mechanisms linking past and present experience.

Accounting, first, for the more straightforward of the five factors in table 6.5, part B, correlate 4 ("R living arrangements," 1987) demonstrates again the strong association between living arrangements and capacity for independent activity. The relationship between the ability of older people to manage on their own and the structure of the households in which they live has been the subject of much research on the elderly (see chapters 4 and 5). In this model, two types of arrangements, living with a member of the stem family or living with nonkin, are associated negatively with capacity for independent activity. This highlights the often-cited preference of participants in this study to maintain separate households. Only if one cannot look after oneself, it appears, do women in this sample tend to live with people other than their husbands. Older women can find sharing a kitchen with another woman stressful, for example—especially if that other woman is a daughter-in-law (Day 1985a). "You get in each other's way," they say, and, "It makes for bad feelings."

According to women in this sample, having one's family move in with you is also stressful, although not as bad as having to move in with kin (see chapter 3). A woman who had very low scores on the four scales of successful aging, and refused my request to visit her at home, had this to say in 1987 about her chaotic household: "These folks stay with me. . . . they have no place else to go. My preference would be to live alone if I could, with outside help, because I don't want to bother anyone and I don't want to be bothered either."

The importance of correlate 2 ("Perception of health compared to others in 1978") to capacity to manage in 1987 is, again, not hard to explain. Rating one's health as poor or only fair in 1978 is associated with a lower level of independent functioning 10 years later. However, the forces connecting the other three correlates in this set to independent activity are less easy to discern. Why, for example, does having lived in a central city predict low independent activity among the few women in the 1987 sample who did so in 1978? It is possible that these were women who, in 1978, were already frail, poor, and had no alternative but to move into rental accommodation or the homes of relatives.

Likewise, the negative impact on independent activity in 1987 of correlate 5 ("R's attendance at church or synagogue in past year," 1987) is open to diverse interpretations. Low attendance at religious services could be related both to a declining ability to get out and about on one's own and to the negative effects on health of lack of access to social contacts. The latter explanation ties in with theories about the beneficial effects of social relationships for health and longevity, and the harmful potential for older people of social isolation (House et al. 1988, and chapter 2 in this volume). Or it could be that women who attend religious services are sustained by spiritual values that mitigate the emotional distress of the losses of later life?

Finally, there is the presence to explain of correlate 1 ("R has never worked for pay since first marriage"). The number of women in 1987 who had never worked for pay since first marriage was very small (N = 13), but the negative relationship of this to capacity for independent activity suggests the need for further investigation of the work histories of the women in this study. Questions to raise would include: How many women in the original sample had never worked after marriage? How many in this never-worked category died in the 10-year interval between 1978 and 1987, and what were their demographic backgrounds and health characteristics in 1978? Such questions might provide clues to the relationship between women's work experience, health, and social ties. To understand the role of women's paid work in the management of aging, we need to distinguish between the relative influence of health, contact with others, and personal skills and attitudes acquired as a consequence of having occupied roles outside the family in paid employment.

CORRELATES OF PRIVATE SAFETY NET

Three out of the eight most significant correlates of Private Safety Net (table 6.5, part C) overlap with those in the best set for Capacity for Independent Activity. They are correlate 2 ("R has never worked for pay since first marriage"), correlate 5 ("R living arrangements," 1987), correlate 6 ("R's attendance at church or synagogue in past year," 1987). The association of these factors with both independent activity and a private safety net makes sense in view of the connections of both these dimensions with living arrangements, on the one hand, and ability to take care of one's home, on the other hand. Since homeownership and having one's place of residence in one's own name are both important markers of private supports, any background conditions militating against such control over one's accommodation will have a negative impact on one's safety net.

The link between functional capacity and safety net is also seen in the significance of age in this set. The negative impact of correlate 1 ("R's year of birth") shows that the oldest women in the sample, those aged 86 or 87 in 1987, on the whole do less well in terms of availability of private supports than do younger women, those born 1902 to 1910. The oldest women in this sample experience greater difficulty in managing daily activities, and have less resilient sources of backup support.

Two correlates in this set point to the role of social relationships as influences on a private safety net. These are correlates 7 ("R has someone with whom to share interests and activities") and 8 ("Number of times R changed residence in the past 10 years," 1987). The companionship of a person with like interests, and having stayed put for the last decade, are significant correlates of stronger reserves of private social resources. Staying in the same place, of course, increases the likelihood that an older woman will know people in the community with whom she has close personal bonds. As noted in chapter 5, those mentioned by women in this sample as people with whom they share interests were more likely to be friends, neighbors, and relatives of like age, than children or younger kin.

Significance of future expectations. Expectations about the future did not turn out to be significantly correlated with any of the three indexes taken individually. However, when an overall index averaging the three separately was computed (see note 5), the measure, "What do you expect to be doing a couple of years from now?" (item 17, table 6.2) was found to be significant at the <.01 level. This suggests that an older woman's own orientations toward her future prospects is a condition affecting the quality of the aging experience.

As discussed in chapter 4, responses to "What do you expect to be doing a couple of years from now?" ranged along a continuum of orientations from a passive-fatalistic view of life to an active, self-determining one. Responses typical of the former were, "I'll be dead," "I hope I won't be here," or "I don't know. There's nothing I can do about it, anyway." Responses to the latter went something like, "Being as busy as I am now," or "I'll be doing what I'm doing now—taking care of my house, visiting my family, reading books, going to the senior citizens club."

The expectation that one would be alive and active in a couple of years was significantly correlated with a high overall score on successful aging. Women who took this active approach tended also to be satisfied with their home, their social relations, and neighborhood facilities. They tended to disagree with the statement, "Things are getting worse as you get older."

SIZE OF CORRELATIONS

In assessing these results, two crucial considerations must be borne in mind. The first is that all the variables listed in table 6.5, parts A–C, are significantly associated with the three dimensions of successful aging (Appendix 6-D). The second point is that the overall regression correlations are not spectacular. Particularly in the case of Perceived Well-being ($R2 = 0.14$) (table 6.5, part A), the seven background characteristics in the "best" regression line explain only a small proportion of the variation in sense of well-being. Why might this be so?

Reasons for Low Association between Background Factors and Well-being

There are a number of reasons why the sociodemographic characteristics used as categorical variables might account for relatively little of the difference in these women's levels of contentment. Generally, the explanations have to do with the nature of the dependent variable and the measurement of key independent variables such as income and social status.

a. *Large random component.* The phenomenon of perceived well-being may, itself, be characterized by a large random component. In other words, there may be so much variation in the elements that contribute to satisfaction in later life that it is difficult to pinpoint the salient characteristics. Thus, among women born at the turn of the century, the dependent variable, a sense of well-being, may vary so unsystematically across the sample that this model (despite the large number and variety of measures used in the program) was unable to detect any strong pattern of association of categorical variables with variations in psychological satisfaction.

b. *Measurement of independent variables.* The source of low association may lie in the measurement of the background factors. Although the independent variables used in the regressions covered a diversity of indicators of social background (see table 6.5), they may not have been sufficiently robust to establish a strong association with psychological well-being. Take income, for example. This study found that net of other variables, income in 1978 did not correlate significantly with any of the three dimensions of successful aging in this model. How might one account for this lack of a discernible pattern of relationship between well-being, subjectively defined, and income, one of the prime quantitative indicators of social position and advantage?

Studies of income reveal two commonplace types of errors: first, many people (especially, perhaps, women in these ages) tend to be quite unsure about what the size of their income really is; and, second, there is a tendency for people on surveys to fabricate their income level to suit various purposes—either to inflate a low income to make it look better or to deflate a high income to conceal their actual financial worth. Reluctance to report income is demonstrated in this study by the fact that fully 12 percent of women in the sample in 1978 refused outright to answer the question on income. If to these missing data we add the other types of errors, it is quite possible that the gradations between income levels were blurred, thus reducing the chances of documenting distinctions in financial status that might predict levels of perceived well-being.

c. *Age, gender, and the salience of income.* Finally, in looking for reasons for the apparent low order of relationship between income and a sense of well-being, I returned to the special characteristics of these women themselves. Studies comparing the levels of satisfaction among different age groups suggest that older people alter their expectations to accommodate to changes in their life circumstances (see chapter 8). The convention is to see this process as a lowering of aspirations, a "downward" shift in expectations. However, data presented in this study suggest that women in their 80s may have a different set of priorities from those in younger ages—one linked more closely to the requirements of raw survival and the challenge of keeping up when one is slowing down.

Recall that I am talking here about how the older woman sees well-being from her own particular perspective, not about how an outsider might characterize her circumstances. Assuming, then, a hierarchy of priorities, when one sees at stake one's very survival as a person in control of one's own affairs, one's main aspiration may become to safeguard the capacity for self-respect and self-management. For women in their 80s, success in doing this is often associated more with owning one's home than with gross income level. And, indeed, in this study (table 6.1, part C), net of other variables, not owning one's home is one of the most significant variables negatively associated with a private safety net.

In their model, "selective optimization with compensation" (chapter 8), the Balteses (1988) described the process of adjustment to aging in terms of a paring down of nonessentials, choosing to live simply, and concentrating on one's particular strengths. One implication of this process of simplification and optimization may be to loosen the tie between perceived well-being and socioeconomic background factors such as income, education, and occupation. "Waste not, want not" and "Don't live beyond your means" (table 8.1), aphorisms for successful living described by the older women themselves, would seem to be independent of size of income.

Thus, it would seem that material acquisition, conspicuous consumption, and enhancing one's social prestige are to women in this sample relatively less important than conserving one's capacity to function independently and retaining control over the remaining vestiges of one's kingdom—ownership of one's home. If this observation has validity, it raises a number of intriguing questions about the association in later life between subjective well-being and financial circumstances (see Espenshade and Braun 1983). Is the apparent lack of a strong relationship between income and well-being a function of old age, as such, or is it peculiar to these particular women who lived through the Great Depression (an era in American history very different from the postwar and affluent 1950s)? Does the association of income and a sense of well-being vary according to gender, and is it related to differences in men's and women's roles throughout the life course? Is a sense of well-being among older men, for example, less random and more closely tied to factors such as social class, income, and occupational prestige? These latter questions about gender differences in the experience of aging are, unfortunately, not answerable in a sample composed exclusively of older women. To answer the former requires a study of succeeding cohorts of women in their late 70s and 80s—women not immediately affected by the economic hardships experienced by their mothers and grandmothers.

d. *Interdependence of reasons for low association.* In the end, it seems likely that these various explanations are interrelated. That is, the low correlation of background factors with a sense of well-being may be due in part to imperfect techniques of measurement, which, in turn, are based on the failure of the survey instruments to take account of the very qualities of women in their 80s that affect the nature and intensity of their satisfaction with life. There is still a tendency, for example, to focus on paid work as an indicator of productivity (see chapter 3), when the important work older women do in providing support to husbands, adult children, grandchildren, friends, and neighbors is unpaid. To women in this sample, helping others is a major source of satisfaction. And by the same token, seeing oneself as less useful than in former years is one of the most important markers negatively associated with a sense of well-being (table 6.1, part A). Thus, it may be that the explanatory power of the background variables is low because we have yet to measure adequately what really matters to women in their ninth decade.

HIGHLIGHTS OF MODEL

I have used the concept of "dimensions" here in a nonstatistical sense to indicate three major attributes of a larger phenomenon, successful aging. Each dimension is constructed of multiple markers. The markers of Personal Well-being include: a global sense of happiness, a feeling that one is useful and well occupied, and a sense that life does not get worse as one gets older. Capacity for Independent Activity is marked by being able to do one's shopping, meal preparation, and housework, without help, and maintaining one's eyesight. Private Safety Net is marked by social supports, such as living with one's spouse, having someone to help with one's medical bills, knowing friends and neighbors who would help for a short time if one were ill, and the ownership of one's own home.

Early in this chapter I noted that the markers of success in this model are tied to the specific information older women in this study provided on the 1978 and 1987 surveys. Does basing the concept of success on such information limit the practicality of the model as a tool for understanding the needs of older women, generally? The answer is yes and no. In chapter 3, I discussed the bias introduced by excluding three categories of older women from the 1978 sample: black women, never-married women, and those too ill or too infirm to tolerate a personal interview. These limitations still hold true with respect to the model presented here. Including women in these other categories, undoubtedly, would have produced a somewhat different picture of success. Given this qualification, however, I believe this model has wide applicability to women in the ages represented in the sample.

The model has three special assets. First, it employs both quantitative and qualitative measures to estimate the quality of life among a little-known segment of the elderly population. Second, it provides a tool to differentiate systematically between those aging well and those experiencing hardship. Like all such tools in social science, this one can be developed and refined using measures of the three dimensions in different contexts and with different populations of old people. Third, although pioneering in relatively unexplored territory, the model incorporates many standard indicators of the aging experience. Measures such as self-perceived health, use of time, the capacity to manage daily activities, and primary modes of social support have been used in many other surveys, and are fundamental to defining the condition of older people in American society today.

Finally, although I do not claim that all areas of importance to women have been covered, or that all the significant issues have even been raised, I am confident that the model offers a useful approach to identifying and organizing concepts of aging that reflect the current dynamics of the field (Baltes and Baltes 1988:7).

NOTES

1. As noted in the acknowledgments, I am indebted to Ian Diamond in the Department of Demography/Research School of Social Sciences, Australian National University, Canberra, for his collaboration on the statistical procedures, and to Douglas A. Wolf for his comprehensive comments on the content and organization of this chapter.

2. The full list of responses to each item in the 1987 survey that was included in the

model is presented in Appendix 6-A, enabling the reader to review the distribution of sample responses for all the variables from which the three composite dimensions were constructed.

3. Use of multiple indicators of broad life domains is the technique recommended by Lawton and colleagues (1982) in their discussion of the Multi-Level Assessment Instrument (MAI) for estimating the quality of life among the elderly.

4. An example of the different results obtained by using weighted items rather than raw scores is shown in table 6.1, Dimension 1: Perceived Well-being, where marker 18 ("R is not satisfied with the neighborhood") is shown to make considerably less of a contribution to defining well-being ($-.15$) than marker 1 ("R feels health not good compared to others") ($-.24$).

5. A fourth index was computed, representing the overall average of the three indexes, thus producing a single score for each respondent. Tables showing the results were not included here, on the grounds that since the three dimensions are interdependent, combining them is additive and contributes little additional information to understanding the conditions of successful aging.

6. The usefulness of the model as an instrument for discriminating between women in the sample with respect to successful aging depends on the belief there are indeed phenomena underlying the markers that we can conceptualize as "well-being," "capacity for independent activity," and "a private safety net."

7. The principal components program identifies the five sets (or factors) that together add up to 100 percent of the variation. To simplify the model, only the coefficients for the first factor, the one that explains the highest proportion of the variation, are shown in table 6.1.

8. For the purposes of this model, these capacities were treated as three separate dichotomous variables, corresponding to the three levels of independent activity— 1, Can do without help; 2, Need some help; and 3, Cannot do without help.

9. In terms of preventive planning, Mrs. Silvestri should be considered more, rather than less, functionally independent than a car driver because she makes use of public transportation, a community service specifically earmarked for the elderly to facilitate their access to community events. In the longer run, if Mrs. Silvestri's eyesight worsens, she will be more independent than car drivers in the sample because she has learned to use alternative methods of transportation. However, her position on the scale of Capacity for Independent Activity (table 6.4) is lower than that of other less-independent women because she does not drive a car and relies on a "person-environment service system" for getting beyond walking distance.

10. Those who did not designate a primary caregiver were not asked if there was anyone else, if the need arose, who could take responsibility for their practical support.

11. The different perspectives gained from quantitative scores versus personal impressions demonstrates the need to refine indicators such as capacity for independent activity, and to use multiple methods in research on the aged. The same lack of a complete fit, for example, is frequently found between scores on objective tests and the personal interviews conducted with job applicants and candidates for admission to colleges and universities. Increasingly, both objective tests and personal observation are considered desirable in determining how well a given applicant fits a particular set of criteria.

DEPENDENT VARIABLES:
SURVEY MEASURES USED TO CONSTRUCT
THREE INDEXES OF SUCCESSFUL AGING

A. Dimension 1: Perceived Well-being

	No.	%
1 Health compared to other people your age		
1—Excellent	123	20.9
2—Good	227	38.5
3—Fair	160	27.2
4—Poor	75	13.7
DK/NA[a]	4	1.0
2 Health now compared to three years ago		
1—Better	64	10.9
2—Same	240	40.7
3—Not as good	282	47.9
9—NA	3	*[b]
3 Do health problems stand in way of doing things you want to do?		
1—Not at all	184	31.2
2—A little	188	31.9
3—A great deal	215	36.5
9—NA	2	*
4 Attitude toward space in house/apartment/nursing home		
1—More than I need	97	16.5
2—Just the right amount	429	72.8
3—It is too small	54	9.2
9—DK/NA	9	1.5
5 Do things keep getting worse as respondent gets older?		
1—Yes	300	50.9
2—No	272	46.2
9—Ref.[c]/DK/NA	17	2.9
6 Does respondent feel less useful as she gets older?		
1—Yes	334	57.0
2—No	236	40.0
9—Ref./DK/NA	19	3.2

continued

Appendix 6-A DEPENDENT VARIABLES (continued)

A. Dimension 1: Perceived Well-being

	No.	%

Bradburn Affect-Balance Scale: Markers 7–16

During the past few weeks, did you feel:

7 Excited or interested in something?

	No.	%
1—Yes	257	43.6
2—No	320	54.3
3—Ref./DK/NA	12	2.0

8 Too restless to sit long?

1—Yes	123	20.9
2—No	457	77.6
3—Ref./DK/NA		

9 Proud because complimented for something done?

1—Yes	369	62.6
2—No	210	35.7
3—Ref./DK/NA	10	1.7

10 Very lonely or remote from other people?

1—Yes	153	26.0
2—No	426	72.3
3—Ref./DK/NA	10	1.7

11 Pleased about having accomplished something?

1—Yes	405	68.8
2—No	168	28.5
3—Ref./DK/NA	16	2.7

12 Bored?

1—Yes	144	24.4
2—No	434	73.7
3—Ref./DK/NA	11	1.9

13 On top of the world?

1—Yes	193	32.8
2—No	382	64.9
3—Ref./DK/NA	14	2.4

14 Depressed or very unhappy?

1—Yes	154	26.1
2—No	422	71.6
3—Ref./DK/NA	13	2.2

15 Things going your way?

1—Yes	394	66.9
2—No	174	29.5
3—Ref./DK/NA	21	3.6

16 Upset because someone criticized you?

1—Yes	55	9.3
2—No	522	88.6
3—Ref./DK/NA	12	2.0

continued

Appendix 6-A DEPENDENT VARIABLES (continued)

A. Dimension 1: Perceived Well-being

	No.	%
17 How happy overall these days?		
1—Very happy	171	29.0
2—Pretty happy	343	58.2
3—Not too happy	64	10.9
4—Ref./DK/NA	11	2.0
18 How often time on hands don't know what to do with?		
1—All the time	34	5.8
2—Quite often	58	9.8
3—Just now and then	160	27.2
4—Almost never	327	55.5
5—Ref./DK/NA	10	1.7
20 Satisfaction with neighborhood		
1—Very much	453	76.9
2—Somewhat	88	14.9
3—Not much	30	5.1
4—Not at all	10	2.0
5—DK/NA	8	1.4
21 Attitude toward getting along on income		
1—Can't make ends meet	9	1.5
2—Just manage to get by	152	25.8
3—Have enough to get along and a little extra	197	33.4
4—Money is not a problem	214	36.3
5—Ref./DK/NA	17	2.9

a. DK/NA, Don't know/no answer.
b. Asterisk (*), less than 1 percent; applies throughout table.
c. Ref., Refused.

B. Dimension 2: Capacity for Independent Activity

	No.	%
1 How often did respondent take walks in past year?		
1—Never	218	37.0
2—A few times	92	15.6
3—2 to 3 times a month	31	5.3
4—Once a week	34	5.8
5—More than once a week	212	36.0
6—DK/NA	2	*
2 How often did respondent do unpaid community or volunteer work?		
1—Never	431	73.2
2—A few times	53	9.0
3—2 or 3 times a month	38	6.5
4—Once a week	28	4.8

continued

Appendix 6-A DEPENDENT VARIABLES (continued)

B. Dimension 2: Capacity for Independent Activity

	No.	%
5—More than once a week	37	6.3
6—NA	2	*

3 How often did respondent go away from neighborhood for day or night trips?

	No.	%
1—Never	179	30.4
2—A few times a year	317	53.8
3—2–3 times a month	51	8.7
4—Once a week	25	4.2
5—More than once a week	14	2.4
6—NA	3	*

4 In past 6 months, did respondent help a family member with housework/laundry?

1—Yes	79	13.4
2—No	468	79.5
3—Inapplicable/nursing home	38	6.5
4—NA	4	1.0

5 How good is eyesight (with glasses, if used)?

1—Good or adequate	441	74.9
2—Poor (partially blind)	145	24.6
3—Unable to see at all	1	*
4—NA	2	*

6 Does someone help go outside walking distance?

1—Yes	318	54.0
2—No	265	45.0
3—DK/NA	6	1.0

7 Can respondent do the shopping for groceries?

1—Without help	378	64.2
2—With some help	114	19.4
3—Completely unable to do	91	15.4
4—NA	6	1.0

8 Can respondent prepare own meals?

1—Without help	493	83.7
2—With some help	34	5.8
3—Completely unable to do	56	9.5
4—NA	6	1.0

9 Can respondent do own housework?

1—Without help	394	66.9
2—With some help	100	17.0
3—Completely unable to do	53	9.0
7—Nursing home resident	38	6.5
9—NA	4	1.0

continued

Appendix 6-A DEPENDENT VARIABLES (continued)

B. Dimension 2: Capacity for Independent Activity

	No.	%
10 Can respondent do own laundry?		
1—Without help	424	72.0
2—With some help	55	9.3
3—Completely unable to do	69	11.7
7—Nursing home resident	38	6.5
9—NA	3	*
11 Can respondent manage own money?		
1—Without help	459	77.9
2—With some help	79	13.4
3—Completely unable to do	44	7.5
9—NA	7	1.2
12 Does respondent need (more) help?		
1—Yes	68	11.5
2—No	515	87.4
3—NA	6	

C. Dimension 3: Private Safety Net

	No.	%
1 Does respondent have a relative to help with major medical expenses?		
1—Yes	322	54.7
2—No	267	45.3
3—DK/NA	10	2.0
2 Does respondent have a primary caregiver?		
1—Yes	566	96.1
2—No	16	2.7
3—NA	4	*
3 Does respondent have a secondary caregiver?		
1—Yes	431	73.2
2—No	141	23.9
3—DK/NA	17	3.0
4 Number of living children respondent had in 1987		
0—None	70	11.9
1—One	142	24.1
2—Two	170	28.9
3—Three	91	15.4
4—Four	52	8.8
5—Five or more	63	10.7
6—NA	1	*
5 Total income that respondent and husband received last year		
01–Under $4,000	47	8.0
02 $4,000 – <$5,000	81	13.8
03 $5,000 – <$7,000	94	16.0
04 $7,000 – <$10,000	95	16.1

continued

Appendix 6-A DEPENDENT VARIABLES (continued)

C. Dimension 3: Private Safety Net

	No.	%
05 $10,000–<$15,000	65	11.0
06 $15,000–<$25,000	69	11.7
07 $25,000–<$35,000	29	4.9
08 $35,000 or more	22	3.7
97 Refused	37	6.3
98 Don't know	41	7.0
99 No answer	9	1.5
6 Number of persons listed on respondent's support roster		
1—None to two	31	5.3
2—Three to five	184	31.2
3—Six to eight		
4—Nine to eleven		
Twelve +		
7 Number of rooms in respondent's residence: kitchen but not bathroom		
1—One to two	22	3.7
2—Three	83	14.1
3—Four	108	18.3
4—Five	147	25.0
5—Six	105	17.8
6—Seven and more	83	14.1
7—Nursing home resident	38	6.5
9—NA	3	*
8 Does respondent own or rent, or is she living with others?		
1—Own	343	62.3
2—Rent	145	24.6
3—Living with relative/other	60	10.2
4—Nursing home resident	38	6.5
5—NA	3	*
9 Name in which respondent's house/apartment is owned/rented		
1—Self/spouse	443	75.2
2—Relative	34	5.8
3—Other/inapplicable	61	10.4
4—Nursing home resident	38	6.5
5—NA	1	*

CATEGORIES OF SURVEY MEASURES
SELECTED AS INDEPENDENT VARIABLES

Measures Selected from 1978 Survey:

1 Sociodemographic characteristics:
(e.g., age, number of years of completed schooling, work history, size of community between ages 6 and 16)
2 Family structure and living arrangements, 1978:
(e.g., number of persons in respondent's household, number of children in 1978)
3 Attitudes and orientations:
(e.g., as reflected in data on family planning, degree of worry about family during the depression, perceived health compared to others, reactions to the 1978 interview)
4 Capacity to manage daily activities:
(e.g., degree of difficulty going up and down stairs, shopping, washing and bathing, and managing finances in 1978)

Measures Selected from 1987 Survey:

5 Family structure and living arrangements, 1987:
(e.g., number of brothers and sisters when growing up, marital status, number of living children, number of persons in household)
6 Life transitions between 1978 and 1987:
(e.g., years since husband died, number of deaths among family and friends 1978 to 1987, new close contacts since 1978, number of times moved since 1978)
7 Characteristics of affective support:
(e.g., someone to confide in, make respondent feel needed and appreciated, share interests with, help for a short time)

8 Orientations toward the future:
(e.g., "What do you expect to be doing a couple of years from now?")

NOTES ON REGRESSION ANALYSIS: EXPLANATION OF R^2

1. The R^2 values measure how much variation in the dependent variable can be accounted for by the model. R^2 is the sum of squares for the model divided by the total sum of squares for the dependent variable, and can range from 0 to 1. The 00 values in table 6.1 can be considered as reference categories.

2. To estimate models such as these, it is necessary to place some constraints on the values of the coefficients. This is because there can be too many coefficients to estimate for the data available. All statistical packages make some assumptions, and the one SAS (a statistical analysis program) uses is to set the upper level of any categorical variable equal to zero.

3. Two main points should be made about the data in table 6.5, part B: Capacity for Independent Activity. First, the scores on Capacity for Independent Activity are clustered toward the positive pole of the index (discussed in the text); and, second, two women had negative scores that were substantially higher than all the rest. Regarding the first point, 28 women had scores greater than two standard deviations from the mean. A small minority of women were severely functionally dependent, but the majority were quite well off, and variation in their functional capacities was not very great (see notes to table 6.4). The small number of very hard-up women and the concentration of the majority in the quite fit category obviously affects the type of background factors that are associated with the capacity for independent activity in this model. As shown in table 6.5, the background factors that emerged as significant are those that—for older women in the United States today—are associated with a complex set of conditions that predict dependency, such as being married and living with an adult child, living in the center of a large metropolis, and never having worked for pay.

Regarding the second point, the scores on Capacity for Independent Activity contained two extreme "outlier" cases; that is, two women,

Mrs. Peters and Mrs. Sergio (see chapter 7), had scores that were significantly more negative than those of any other women. Mrs. Peters's score was −8.6 and Mrs. Sergio's an even more dismal −13.4. The next lowest scores on this dimension were on the order of −4.0 or less.

To check whether these extreme scores were spurious or valid results, I reanalyzed these women's responses to all the questions in their interview schedules. The comparison revealed two things of importance: First, both cases contain an unusually dense combination of conditions that are negatively associated in this study with self-management (such as the relatively recent death of a husband, sharing a household with an adult child, needing help to manage shopping and household tasks, and lack of involvement in outside activities, as measured, for example, by never having attended religious services in the past year).

Second, a number of features of the two women's circumstances, such as living arrangements, family networks, and primary sources of support were quite dissimilar. The presence of differences as well as commonalities among these two very low-scoring women points to the diversity of the conditions that have negative effects for aging, as well as those that have positive effects. Profiles of these two women's circumstances are presented in chapter 7, illustrating the variety in the types of situations that are associated with dependency in later life.

CORRELATES OF SUCCESSFUL AGING: LEVELS OF SIGNIFICANCE

A. Dimension 1: Perceived Well-being		
Name of Background Factor[a]	Level of Significance[b]	Direction of Effect on Successful Aging (– or +)
1978 Survey		
1. R[c] worried about family future in depression.	*	–
2. R rates health poor compared to others in same age group.	**	–
3. R can do the shopping without difficulty.	***	+
1987 Survey		
4. R living with husband and others.	*	–
5. R's husband died within past year.	**	–
6. R worked for pay in past 10 years (since 1987).	**	+
7. R has friends or neighbors who would help if sick.	***	+

a. In all three sections of the table (A, B, and C), items collected in the 1978 and 1987 surveys are listed separately to establish their timing in the life course of women in the sample.
b. For all three sections of the table:
   * = .05–.10
   ** = .01–.05
   *** = <.01.
c. R, respondent.

continued

Appendix 6-D CORRELATES OF SUCCESSFUL AGING: LEVELS OF
SIGNIFICANCE (continued)

B. Dimension 2: Capacity for Independent Activity

Name of Background Factor	Level of Significance	Direction of Effect on Successful Aging
1978 Survey		
1. R rates own health poor or fair compared to others in same age group.	*	−
2. R never worked for pay since her first marriage.	***	−
3. R lived in a central city, 1978.	***	−
1987 Survey		
4. R lived with stem family or nonkin, 1987.	***	−
5. R never attended church or synagogue in past year, 1987.	***	−

C. Dimension 3: Private Safety Net

1978 Survey		
1. R's year of birth, 1900–1910.	*	−
2. R never worked for pay since her first marriage.	**	−
3. R was not employed in 1978.	***	−
4. R was living with 5 or more persons in 1978.	***	−
1987 Survey		
5. R has someone to share interests and activities with.	**	+
6. R was living with husband and others, 1987.	***	−
7. R never attended church or synagogue in past year.	***	−
8. R did not change her residence in last 10 years.	***	+

Chapter Seven

THE MARKERS: SUCCESSFUL AND OPPRESSIVE AGING

I don't think I'll be here in a couple of years. I hope I am not.

—Mrs. Smith, age 84

Chapter 6 noted that a model of successful aging could be a useful aid in identifying those women most in need of help from sources outside their private means. This chapter focuses on those women. The aim is to illustrate the types of situations where unmet needs are resulting in great pain, loss of dignity, and loss of hope. The rationale is that by sharpening understanding of the conditions under which old age is particularly oppressive, we will become more aware and better able to develop new ways to alleviate the causes of preventable distress.

But what of the successful agers? For policy purposes, they deserve attention also. As described in chapter 6, a woman was defined as more or less successful on the basis of her scores compared with those assigned to all others in the sample. Thus, to know what it means to do poorly, we need to know what it means to do well. From a study of successful agers, we can learn about the kinds of opportunities that contribute to effective aging and then try to maximize them in our own and other women's lives; from those who are oppressed, we can learn about the constraints against a rewarding life in old age and try to avert their negative influence. In short, knowing something about the experiences of women at both extremes of the continuum can give us the kinds of insights on the aging process we need to actively influence the forces affecting the life chances of the very old.

SUCCESSFUL AGERS

In this study's model, successful agers were defined as women who did well relative to other women in each of the three major life domains: (1) sense of well-being, (2) independent activity, and (3) private means of support. What are the distinctive features of women who rank high on these dimensions?

Success as They See It

Because of the large subjective component, success as defined by scores on the three dimensions coincides closely with what women in this sample said they wanted themselves. They said they wanted to be contented with what they have and to have happy memories of their earlier life. They said they wanted to be able to take care of themselves and their homes for as long as possible without having to depend on their children or charity. In applying this rigorous ethos of independence, women in this sample regarded their spouse as the exception. Over all others, he was expected to be the bulwark. Women who were still married and, for whatever reason, could not call upon their husbands in case of need, tended to receive lower scores than those whose husbands were still standing by them.

Along with looking after themselves, self-determination is highly associated with a sense of well-being. Women in the follow-up study said they wanted to live as they chose in their own homes and to be the arbiters of their day-to-day lives. And finally, they wanted assurance of some kind of support in case their capacity for independent activity broke down. They wanted to be able to call upon someone in an emergency, sufficient income to be able to purchase needed services, or assets (such as a house) that could be translated into income or used as leverage to enable them to determine for themselves their future living situation.

In summary, high-scoring women are contented with their living arrangements, homes, neighborhoods, and social ties. They perceive their health as at least fairly good and not a factor strongly limiting what they want to do. At the core of their sense of well-being is that either they are capable of managing activities, such as shopping and housekeeping, on their own, or they have private means of support—relatives to help out in various practical ways (such as paying medical bills and providing financial counseling); friends for company, emotional support, and assistance with small daily tasks (such as doing errands, picking up library books, watering plants, giving lifts to shopping and social events); and resources (such as ownership of property in their own or their husband's name) to implement their desire to stay in their own home.

This composite picture of successful agers incorporates the numerous markers of the three dimensions. In real life, the combinations of the three domains are highly individual and idiosyncratic (see chapter 8). Each woman reflects a particular configuration of psychological contentment, functional capacity, and system of social supports.

Mrs. Crawford illustrates the idiosyncratic expression of the association between, for example, level of self-management and psychological well-being.

Mrs. Crawford:
High Functional Dependency, High Life Satisfaction

Although wholly dependent on her husband for personal care and household upkeep, Mrs. Crawford still scored high on a sense of well-being and contentment. In her case, this seemed partly a function of the felicitous nature of her social supports. Eighty-eight years old when I met her and one of the oldest women in the sample, she still had her husband to care for her and she saw him as an extension of herself, not as someone upon whom she was dependent. Certainly, from the light-hearted repartee between them, there was no doubt in the couple's mind as to who was in control.

A retired teacher, Mrs. Crawford had set up the kitchen to serve as a combined office and recreation area. The kitchen table was covered with her books, magazines, and tapes. When there was cooking to be done, she explained, she sat at the table in her wheelchair and gave Mr. Crawford step-by-step instructions.

One can fairly assume that Mrs. Crawford's score on a sense of well-being would not have been as high if she had had to rely for comprehensive personal care on her son, or more probably in the case of intimate tasks such as bathing and toileting, on her daughter-in-law. This is an instance where the quality of the relationship of the provider to the recipient of care accounts for the anomaly of a high level of satisfaction despite profound functional dependence (Chappell and Badger 1989).

MARKERS OF OPPRESSIVE AGING

Chapter 1 described two women at nearly opposite poles on a continuum of successful aging. Ranking among the top 5 percent, Mrs.

Silvestri radiates the markers of success. She is happy, manages her affairs for the most part on her own, has a busy social life, three children who keep in close touch, and owns her own home . . . this, despite having lost her husband over a decade ago and managing on an income in the second to lowest category ($4,000 to $5,000).

Mrs. Farnsworth, in contrast, ranks among the lowest 30 percent it terms of successful aging. She is deeply unhappy, incapacited by numerous physical complaints, alienated socially, and abjures the person she lives with, her husband, as a main bulwark of day-to-day companionship and practical help. At the same time, Mrs. Farnsworth is not wholly bereft of social supports. She has a daughter ready to take her into her home, a number of grandchildren whom she regularly telephones, and is by no means among the least well off, financially. Who, then, are the most oppressed? What are the markers distinguishing those falling at the very bottom of the range?

The Most Vulnerable: Commonalities and Differences

Three profiles of women with among the lowest scores in the sample are presented here. Mrs. Smith scored sixth from the bottom, Mrs. Peters, second from the bottom, and Mrs. Sergio was the lowest scorer of all (see Appendix 6-C). These three were selected because of their very low positions in the range, and to illustrate the different contextual features, such as living arrangements and mode of primary care, that can be associated with low scores on the multiple markers.

Two general observations emerge from a comparison of these three lives. First, there are strong similarities in the markers that put them at the extreme lower end. Second, there are profound differences in their particular life circumstances. As is true of successful aging, oppressive aging has diverse forms and faces.

The existence of differences as well as commonalities in the characteristics of those worst off complicates identifying and assisting those most in need of supplemental supports. It means that there is no easy way to remedy what is becoming an increasing social quandary for American society—how to provide assistance to vulnerable older women in a manner that addresses their needs and respects their desire for self-determination, and at the same time accounts for the concerns of the families responsible for their care? Following are the three profiles.

Mrs. Smith:
Defeated and Living Alone

In terms of morale, independent activity, and reserves of social support, Mrs. Smith is on the edge of crisis. A widow, living alone and
at some distance from her two children, she reflects depression,
hopelessness, and defeat on every count. Asked about her future expectations, she said: "I don't think I'll be here in a couple of years. I
hope I am not."

To the question about the events in the last 10 years that have
changed her life the most, she responded: "The death of my husband.
Moving into this place. You are all alone and you have to do all the
planning yourself and my eyesight is so poor."

The markers of perceived well-being show Mrs. Smith to be lonely
and remote from other people, bored, and feeling that time hangs
heavy on her hands. She felt that things get worse as you get older,
including her health, which she said was poor compared to that of
others her age. She said her health had declined over the last three
years and stands in the way a great deal of her doing what she wants
to do.

The markers of independent activity are also relentless in revealing
the deterioration in Mrs. Smith's capacities. She depends on others
for help with all daily activities—shopping, meal preparation, laundry, housework, and managing her finances. She said she needed
some help, too, with personal care, such as washing and bathing. Her
eyesight was failing, causing her to give up the activities she enjoys
the most. Asked about her favorite pastimes, she answered: "I don't
do anything. I used to do a lot of crocheting and crewel work. I can't
do it now because I can't see well."

Going beyond walking distance without help is out of the question
for her. The interviewer, in fact, wrote in the margin, "She doesn't go
out . . . sleeps on the davenport all the time." During the year of the
interview, 1987, Mrs. Smith had never attended religious services or
gone out on trips or to visit friends.

On private safety net, Mrs. Smith also revealed profound vulnerability to dependence and isolation. She said she needed more help
with all daily tasks, but had no family, friends, or neighbors to turn
to. She designated paid employees as both her primary and secondary
caregivers. However, this was clearly a precarious arrangement. Her
income was in the second to lowest category ($4,000 to $5,000), and
she rented, rather than owned, her unit in a retirement complex. She
said she had no one who would pay major medical expenses, no one
who would help if she became really ill, and no one with whom to
share interests and activities. The two children who live in another

state apparently take little interest in her welfare. Weak family support was confirmed by the employee designated as primary caregiver, who commented, "I don't think her children do enough for her."

A number of negative life changes have contributed to Mrs. Smith's oppressive experience of aging. First, there was the death of her husband and having to move from the home she had shared with him for 53 years into the rented unit she now occupies. "I couldn't keep it up any more," she says. "Too many things had to be done to it—so I sold it." Finally, she was very depressed about the recent death of her sister, as well as about her failing health and eyesight, which enforced isolation and inactivity.

Mrs. Peters:
Frail and Homebound, Living Alone

Mrs. Peters is homebound and isolated. Her very low score on capacity for independent activity is the result of frailty and weak social support. The combination of severe physical limitations and a weak "person-environment service system" bar her access to the outside world (see chapter 2).

Widowed only six years prior to the 1987 survey, Mrs. Peters received high negative scores on almost all the markers of independent management. She could not drive, needed help to go beyond walking distance, said that health problems stood in her way a great deal, was partially blind, engaged in no activities outside the home, was completely unable to do the shopping, said she needed more help with housework, and reported that, if she were ill in bed for a week, she had no one to call upon to look after her.

Mrs. Peters recognized her own vulnerability. She mentioned spontaneously (the interviewer wrote the comment in the margin), that if she became ill, she would have to go to a nursing home. She lived alone, renting her apartment from her only child, a son. However, she feels deeply estranged from him and her daughter-in-law: "My son's wife came up once and my house wasn't as clean as she liked, and she hasn't been the same since—I don't see them much anymore." Confirming the gulf between herself and her only close relatives, she passed over her son and daughter-in-law as primary caregivers and designated, instead, a woman friend living in the neighborhood.

In Mrs. Peters's case, physical dependency and weak social bonds are combined with a very low sense of well-being. Again, high negative scores on the markers for well-being tell the story. She said that she always has time on her hands, and feels lonely, depressed, and less useful as she gets older.

About the future, she said: "Would like to be stronger, but we don't always get what we want." And as for what she would really like to be doing a couple of years from now: "Getting strong so I could get out." To a question about the event that has affected her life the most in the last 10 years, Mrs. Peters replied with a stark, "Losing my husband."

Mrs. Peters's isolation and alienation from family cannot be explained simply by supposing that she is an unlikable misanthrope. The friend who was interviewed as her primary caregiver remarked that knowing Mrs. Peters has been enjoyable and has in some ways compensated for the loss of her own parents:

> "I could not be near my folks and they have died—it has built a bridge because I couldn't be with them—makes me think that I'll be that age someday—hope someone will check in on me. She also tells interesting stories and has had a very interesting life—makes me wish I had talked to my folks more."

Mrs. Sergio:
Frail and Homebound,
Living with an Adult Son

Mrs. Sergio, who had the lowest score in the entire sample on capacity for independent activity, was completely unable to do any of the IADLs (Instrumental Activities of Daily Living)—meal preparation, housework, shopping, or laundry. A daughter managed her finances. Mrs. Sergio does not drive and never goes out. At the time of the survey (1987), she had attended no religious services in the past year ("The priest comes to the house"). She says she had no friends, and spent her days smoking ("I smoke because my nerves are bad"), watching TV, and sleeping on the couch.

Mrs. Sergio's expectations about what she will be doing in a couple of years reflect her sense of helplessness and inability to control her life: "That is up to the Man upstairs. I am sitting here talking to you now, but tonight I could be dead." When asked what she would really like to be doing, she said: "I don't know what I really like. I live every day, day by day."

Like Mrs. Peters, Mrs. Sergio was recently widowed. Her husband died in 1986, and she still missed him acutely. For Mrs. Sergio, moreover, the usual traumas of losing a spouse and making the difficult transition from married woman to widow were exacerbated by two additional losses: that of her role as caregiver (her husband had been ill and dependent on her for 20 years prior to his death), and the recent death of two sons, one of whom had moved in to help her and died not long after her husband. Not surprisingly, these are the events in the last 10 years that Mrs. Sergio says have changed her life the most: "When my husband died, it changed my life. I miss him very much. Also the sudden loss of my son who lived here."

Mrs. Sergio has a full-time on-the-spot caregiver. Her 50-year-old divorced son lives in and does everything for her except attend to her most intimate personal needs, such as bathing and toileting. But their living arrangement is a burden for them both. The weight of his mother's dependency showed in Mr. Sergio's response to the question about the impact on his life of providing support: "Oh, Christ, I am going nuts. I can't go out. She says, 'You can go out for an hour or two.' But where can I go for 1 or 2 hours? I can't work because I feel that she cannot be left alone."

Mr. Sergio has been through the ropes as a caregiver. A stockhandler, packing and unloading and loading trucks, he stopped working in 1986 to take over from the brother who died suddenly, and has been looking after his mother ever since. He seldom goes out, and said he receives no help from his sisters with his mother's personal needs.

"I am on call all of the time. She wants me to be home most of the time. She won't allow me to wash and bathe her. She sponge bathes, but I don't know how she can keep herself clean that way. She cannot hold her urine and I am always cleaning up afterward. She ignores my suggestions that we do need some kind of help. I would like someone to come in to wash her, but she refuses any outside help.

My brother and sisters would leave her alone. I guess if I just went out and got a job, they would have to chip in and come down and provide some help. They all come here on Saturday nights and sit around for a couple of hours. I would like it if they would stagger their visits to give me a break."

The relationship between mother and son clearly impressed the interviewer. In one of her many marginal notes, she wrote:

"R [respondent] was lounging on the couch throughout most of the interview. She only sat up so that she could smoke a cigarette. She appears to be in rather ill health. The relationship with her son is a kind of love-hate. They were tossing barbs at each other constantly. At one point she asked him for her cane and when he gave it to her she raised it to him as if to want to hit him in a kind of serious manner."

As a parting comment on this abject situation, the interviewer wrote: "He cares very deeply for his mother even though there was quite a bit of bickering while I was there. When I left he leaned over and gave her a hug."

Contexts of Unsuccessful Aging

These three women are clearly in the grips of aging poorly. All three are unhappy, and all three see nothing meaningful in their lives.

Mrs. Smith and Mrs. Peters are similar in that they live alone and have few sustaining ties with their children who live some distance from them. Mrs. Sergio's situation is different from the other two, and the contrast with Mrs. Peters is particularly marked. There are three important differences in their circumstances: number of children, living arrangements, and relationship with the designated primary caregiver. Mrs. Peters has one child only, a son who lives in another state. In contrast, Mrs. Sergio has a large family, all of whom live close by. Counting the two sons who have died, she has had a total completed family size of eight. Only 5 percent of women in the 1978 sample had eight or more live births. In 1987, the proportion with six or more living children (the size of Mrs. Sergio's family in 1987) was only 6 percent.

Whereas the conditions that contribute to Mrs. Peters's low score consist mainly of frailty and isolation, those comprising Mrs. Sergio's low standing consist of frailty and too little time to herself. She is too much in the company of a son on whom she is wholly dependent. Her care arrangement creates what might be called "reciprocal dependency"—mother's dependence on son makes son dependent on mother. It is not just by chance that, of all the women in the sample, Mrs. Sergio had the highest negative score. She is one of a small proportion living with someone else who said they had no companion or confidant. This void in connectedness, concluded Canadian researchers Chappell and Badger (1989:S175) makes one especially vulnerable to dispiritedness. "Being one of the minority without a companion or confidant relationship can put one at risk of lower subjective well-being. Furthermore, living with someone and not having such a relationship puts one at the greatest risk of all."

In contrast, Mrs. Peters, because she lives alone and feels estranged from her family, designated a friend as primary caregiver. The friend's help is more emotional than practical; she stops in regularly to chat and to see if Mrs. Peters needs anything. As a result, the relationship is not a burden; the friend enjoys Mrs. Peters's company and cheering her up. Both women gain from the relationship. Yet, it is not sufficient to stem Mrs. Peters's sense of isolation.

In summary, the profiles of these three low-scoring women illustrate two types of extreme dependency. One sort comes from living alone and is rooted in withdrawal from social activities and estrangement from kin. Another comes from living with someone on whom one must rely for assistance, but for whom one feels no sense of companionship or sufficient trust and intimacy to confide one's deepest feelings.

The lives of these three women furthermore demonstrate how the three major life dimensions (sense of well-being, independent activity, and private means of support) are interdependent and that weakness in any one of the three substantially destabilizes a woman's prospects for retaining her current living arrangements and patterns of daily life (see chapter 3). Whether making a change will improve or worsen her sense of well-being and quality of life depends on her options and the extent of her role in making the decisions.

OPPRESSIVE AGING: OVERVIEW

Variability

In characterizing the markers of oppressive aging, it is important to again underscore the fact of variability (Dannefer 1988). The three women described here are in trouble in all three domains. They share in common unhappiness and lassitude, diminished functional capacities, dependency on others for help with the basic necessities, and negligible support from family and friends. They lack the discretionary power of owning the place where they live. For all three, these oppressive circumstances were triggered by loss of spouse, loss of physical stamina, loss of home ownership, and loss of hope in the future.

However, the commonalities end there. The three women have different living arrangements, family size, and sources of primary support. Other low-scoring women in this sample have still different combinations of circumstances. In short, the findings show that unrewarding old age is not the consequence of any one factor, such as ill health or living alone, but a confluence of negative events leading to a downward spiral in the individual's capacity to control her life.

Distinctive Features

Regardless of the particular circumstances, however, the markers of oppressive aging include depression, dependency, deterioration of functional capacity, and loss of autonomy. These markers are not particularly associated with age, but it may be harder for people in later life to withstand their devastating effects in combination. Moreover, the chances of experiencing one or another of the events that are typically associated with very low scores (i.e., loss of husband, health, home, and hope) become ever more likely as age advances.

The variables associated with a positive experience of aging are similar to these markers of oppressive aging in one clear respect: they reflect the value that women in their late 70s and 80s place on self-management, strong social ties, and continuity of residence. If these are missing, life is less than satisfactory—if they are there, one can carry on. The fact that these are more significant than measures of income and social position is important for the meaning of aging to women in modern society today, and perhaps also for women as compared to men. All of the experiences associated with aging that these women cite as being particularly traumatic relate, in one way or another, to the attenuation of intimacy and separation from their home—surroundings that represent familiarity, the seat of their special skills, and the sphere in which they have exercised the most discretion and made the most extensive and continuous contributions to others. Clearly, for women who, most of their lives have worked outside the home and held responsible positions in public life, the impact of retirement and moving into the later years may have a different meaning.

The Model: A Tool, Not a Label

The point of this model is not to label, condemn, or create invidious distinctions, but, rather, to act as a tool to help us define a hierarchy of factors that contribute to effectiveness in aging. It can be used to identify both the bright and the dark face of aging—both to increase understanding of when and under what conditions older women do particularly well, and when and under what conditions they are particularly vulnerable to social isolation and breakdown in the capacity to look after themselves.

As reiterated earlier, a low position on the continuum of successful aging is indicative of a person who is not doing well in terms of the criteria stipulated here. Such a position does not imply that the person is, in any way, personally or socially inferior to an individual at the upper end. Rather, the different positions describe something akin to degrees of vulnerability to unhappiness, dependency, and a weak system of supports from private sources, not distinctions in degrees of "making it" in any pejorative sense.

Finally, the state that I have characterized as "oppressive" does not imply that a woman is "unsuccessful" in the sense in which the term is typically applied. On the contrary, a low-scoring woman may be an extraordinary person who has fallen on hard times. She may have experienced a severe physical handicap, loss of close personal ties, or financial setbacks. She may have recently become a widow and be very distressed and, as a result of declining physical capacities, have had to move from a house she owned into a rented apartment or to the home of an adult son or daughter. The impact on sense of self of such irrevocable reversals is the stuff of fiction, drama, and biography. In The Road from Coorain (1989), Jill Ker Conway, former president of Smith College, Northampton, Mass., has vividly described such a succession of traumatic losses as the precursors of her mother's transformation from a strong, self-sufficient manager of a vast Australian sheep property into a complaining, dependent hypochondriac, mainly interested in trying to control her adult children's lives.[1]

As conditions defining success in later life, the three major life dimensions are peculiar to our times, priorities, and social institutions. But few would dismiss sense of well-being, independent activity, and private means of support as trivial or irrelevant to aging in any era or cultural milieu. Doing well in all three can confidently be taken as going a long way toward approximating what it means to age successfully. On the other hand, doing poorly in all three can distinguish quite unmistakably those women in special need of outside support.

Note

1. As described in The Road from Coorain (1989), Mrs. Conway's mother, though considerably younger, chronologically, than the women in this book's study, was prematurely aging unsuccessfully as a consequence of her profound losses.

Chapter Eight

COMING TO TERMS

You make yourself happy.

—Mrs. Silvestri, age 80

*Perhaps it is past time to acknowledge that no one ages the way
they do entirely of their own accord.*

—Robert H. Binstock, "Reviews," *The Gerontologist*

Irrespective of how successful or oppressive their circumstances, or
how good or poor their health, the 589 women in this follow-up
study are survivors. In the decade of the late 1970s and 1980s, they
outlived 304 members of their cohorts—a third of the initial sample
of 1,049 women interviewed in 1978. When followed up and reinterviewed in 1987, moreover, 7 in 10 had survived at least one husband, and over two-thirds had outlived a close relative other than
their husband.

PRESCRIPTION FOR LONG LIFE

Two questions that may occur to many readers at this point is: "How
did they do it?" and then, "What could I myself do right now to live
longer?" The Finnish demographer, Riitta Auvinen, has posed just
such questions in her work. Basing her research on the social factors
affecting the human life span, she has concluded: "If, in general, a
brief and concise answer can be given to this question, it would be:
'Love life and take good care of yourself' " (1989: 13).

This prescription for long life captures succinctly the way women
in this study described the keys to successful aging. Although, as
pointed out in chapter 2, good health and long life are by no means

the only criteria of successful aging, no one, least of all the women in this sample, would deny their fundamental importance. However, the older women in this study see health as more than merely absence of disease. For them it means not just long life, but the capacity to go on doing what they want to do, and to enjoy life for as long as they are able. Mrs. Silvestri was clear on this point: "One thing I pray when I go to bed is for the health of my children and the health of me. Never pray for money. If you are healthy you can always make money!" This way of looking at health—in terms of opportunities for, and constraints against, desired goals—is not new. In the fifth century B.C., Pericles wrote that health is "that state of moral, mental and physical well-being which enables a person to face any crisis in life with the utmost grace and facility" (cited in Furnass 1976:5).

In linking health with coping behavior, Pericles evinced concerns akin to those of ours in the United States today; that is, how can we best promote the capacities of individuals to face and deal with crises in their lives, making use, for as long as possible, of their own resources? This chapter considers this question from two perspectives: the individual and the environmental. I look first at the adaptation of individuals to events that unfold in later life, and then at the role of the environment as the context in which older people seek to meet their needs and fulfill their aspirations.

INDIVIDUAL ADAPTATIONS

How do the American women in this sample cope with crisis? How do they come to terms—with grace and facility—with changes that jeopardize their capacity to manage their affairs? Developing strategies to deal with change is a particular dilemma for women in these ages. Today, as in the time of Pericles, the transitions these women face in late life place a premium on the qualities of personal strength, self-discipline, and the ability to transcend the imputation of one's obsolescence. Today, however, many more survive into very old age, and the period of potential crisis has been greatly extended.

Coping and Stage in Life

A growing number of active, well-off couples in their late 60s and early 70s slide easily into retirement. Trading one set of activities for another, they have more discretionary time to do what they really enjoy. When asked how they are getting along, many will exclaim, "Retirement! I've never been so busy!" The emergence of this active, independent "Third Age" (Laslett 1989) has triggered a new set of stereotypes about the invincible, affluent super-elderly.

The model of successful aging shows, however, that this halcyon phase is transitory. The accumulation of losses precipitating crises gains momentum as the duration of retirement extends. As women move into their mid to late 80s, the resources they need, and the resources they have, to cope with the vicissitudes of life become increasingly out of balance. Data in chapter 6 showed that women in the oldest ages, those born in 1900 and 1901 have significantly lower capacities for independent activity and significantly thinner reserves of social supports than women born in subsequent years. Passing into the ninth decade, as we have seen, raises the likelihood of losing a lifetime partner, undergoing declines in the capacity to help oneself, having to part with people in whom one can confide, and facing uncertainty about where and how one will live in the future. Coming to terms with these kinds of changes requires patience, wisdom, and fortitude.

Revival of Ageism?

By acknowledging that moving into one's 80s is associated with a growing imbalance between good and bad events, do we run the risk of reviving stereotypes about old age that are better left to rest?[1] To avoid this risk, some might counsel suppressing discomforting realities. However, I believe that concealing the realities of older women's experience serves no one's interest. At the same time, it is not my intention here to dash new hopes for an active, independent old age with old bromides about aging as a process of inevitable loss and decline. On the contrary, a large part of this chapter affirms the resourcefulness and strength with which people adjust to late old age.

To become acquainted with women in this age group is to learn about the positive aspects of aging and the extraordinary reserves of the human spirit. Among women in these ages, refusal to admit defeat is a pervasive trait. Despite major changes in their social networks, physical capacities, and access to the mainstream of social life, a majority of women in this sample say that they are in good to excellent health, and that they have little time on their hands. Far from being glum and passively awaiting the end, some of those most battered by the toll of life events face each day as a precious gift. Mrs. Grainger is an example.

Mrs. Grainger:
Optimism in the Face of Loss

Mrs. Grainger has experienced more than her share of crises, but she remains doggedly determined to retain her exuberant persona. In 1987, she had recently undergone major surgery and was losing her sight. Her husband was in the hospital, having suffered a massive stroke, and had been given no more than a year to live. Unable to keep up their house, Mr. and Mrs. Grainger had been forced to sell their cottage by the lake and move into a home for the disabled and frail elderly. Nevertheless, Mrs. Grainger resolved to make the most of every day. Her responses to questions on the 1987 survey about her expectations and hopes for the future, and the salient events in her life, revealed humor and "the utmost grace" in coping with extensive reversals:

Expectations: "I'll probably be blind—gossiping, listening to the radio and TV, and visiting friends and children."

Hopes: "I would like to be cruising on a big ocean liner around the world."

Salient
events: "My operation that was almost fatal to me. It changed our way of living. George had to take over my care. I can't eat the things I love. I have to eat soft foods, no seasoning. I also value every day I wake up —enjoy life much more."

How do they do it? What do older women, themselves, say is the secret to maintaining oneself when everything around one seems to be falling apart?

Dictums for Daily Living

When I asked the 20 women I visited, "What, in your opinion, is the key to successful aging?" they tended to formulate their answers in terms of dictums or aphorisms that they had been taught in childhood or learned over a lifetime. These dictums consist of rules to live by, standards for conduct that have worked for them and that they believe would apply, equally, to any person negotiating the ups and downs of growing old. Some of these dictums are religious in origin: "Cast your bread upon the waters, and it shall be returned a hundred fold"; "Do unto others as you would have them do unto you." Others come from literature or folklore: "Waste not, want not"; "Neither a borrower nor a lender be"; "Live as long as you want, and don't want as long as you live."

These rules for successful aging can be clustered into six general categories (table 8.1), reflecting general orientations toward self and others: (1) Don't worry unnecessarily about the future, (2) Persevere, keep going, and never give up, (3) Don't live beyond your means, (4) Treat others right and they will treat you right, (5) Like people and get along with them, (6) Enjoy life and be content with what you have. Illuminated here are qualities of stubbornness and pride in the face of adversity, an interest in sustaining workable social relationships, and a tenacity of self in a transient world. There is recognition of the value of give and take, the importance of optimizing one's assets, and the desirability of emphasizing the quality of life—not looking for greener pastures, but enjoying the life one has in one's remaining years. Lastly, echoing Auvinen's prescription for long life (1989), there is the strong admonition "to make yourself happy." As Mrs. Porter exclaimed: "I feel good. I enjoy no matter what I do. I was never a clock watcher. No matter what I did if I'd have hated it, I wouldn't have lasted as long as I did."

What insights about older people's orientations toward coping with crisis can we draw from these dictums?

"Success"—the View from Old Age

Attitudes toward life events described in chapter 4 suggest that women in this sample have a particular definition of "success," one that differs from views typically held earlier in life. A majority said that what they would like most to be doing in a couple of years is just what they are doing now—that is, holding onto what they have and not losing any more ground (table 4.6). This is tantamount to defining success in terms of consolidating one's position and maintaining the status quo. Encountering a similar phenomenon in her research comparing younger and older women's attitudes, Lucille Bearon (1989), at the Center on Aging, Duke University Medical School, Durham, N.C., dubbed the syndrome, "No great expectations!"

However, there is another more positive way to characterize these attitudes. It is something akin to Erikson's definition of wisdom, which he saw as the crowning quality of late mid-age, the penultimate stage in human development. Wisdom, he said, is an appreciation of what really counts in life, acquired incrementally by meeting, and refusing to be undone, by the challenge of personal loss.

"WE SHALL OVERCOME"

Underlying a definition of success based on consolidation rather than growth is the tendency to combine realistic expectations about an

Table 8.1 DICTUMS FOR SUCCESSFUL AGING: WOMEN BORN 1900–1910, QUALITATIVE INTERVIEWS, 1988

1. "TAKE ONE DAY AT A TIME."

Don't worry unnecessarily—the future may never happen.

"I mean, it's no use worrying about something. Some people are such worry warts that they worry themselves to death and then it doesn't amount to anything. . . . So why worry, you know, and that is it." (Mrs. Silvestri)

"I do what I can and what I can't do will be left undone until the next time." (Mrs. Porter)

"My neighbors, they tell me: I shouldn't be doing this, I shouldn't be doing that. I says: 'What's the difference if they pick me up out of bed, or out of the garden, or out of the yard?'" (Mrs. Porter)

"I expect there will come a time when I can't drive—I'll think about that tomorrow." (Mrs. Smart)

2. "YOU CAN DO ANYTHING YOU'VE A MIND TO."

Persevere/keep going/don't give up.

"You can't lay down—you've got to keep going." (Mrs. Fleishmann)

"You can do anything, if you have to." (Mrs. Fleishmann)

"I learned to drive after my husband died (at age 57). I am a very persevering person. I took a great many more lessons than most people do—but I had made up my mind and I can do almost anything I make up my mind to do. My mother was that way. She was the strong one." (Mrs. Smart)

"Advice to older people? Well, what can you tell 'em? 'Hang in there!' If I go down, it's going to be down fightin'." (Mrs. Porter)

"I swim half a mile a day. It's what keeps me going. . . . I'm a good walker." (Mrs. Smart)

3. "WASTE NOT, WANT NOT."

Don't live beyond your means.

"I make every penny do. Pay my bill as it comes in. Check [Social Security] goes to the bank. That way you don't have to worry, see?" (Mrs. Silvestri)

"I live well, but I don't have much money. Income is just barely enough. If I have 50 cents left at the end of the month, I think, 'Phew, I made it.'" (Mrs. Smart)

"I was raised and taught all my life, 'Waste not, want not.' We never bought on credit. Never. Even today if we have the money we buy it. If not, we just do without until we get the money." (Mrs. Porter)

4. **"DO UNTO OTHERS."**

Treat others right and they'll treat you right.

"Like, treat people like the way you like to be treated, see. So that's my motto, and its worked out pretty well, believe me." [Mrs. Silvestri]

5. **"YOU CAN'T LIVE BY YOURSELF."**

Get along with people.

"You make friends and you keep 'em. Be nice to them. Be a good listener. . . . You have to live with people. You can't live by yourself, you know what I mean?" [Mrs. Silvestri]

"I like people. I like to be treated nice—and equal. I make friends wherever I go and I keep 'em." [Mrs. Porter]

6. **"YOU MAKE YOURSELF HAPPY."**

Enjoy/Be content with what you have.

"You make yourself happy." [Mrs. Silvestri]

"I feel good. I enjoy no matter what I do. I was never a clock watcher. No matter what I did if I'd have hated it, I wouldn't have lasted as long as I did. I like good eatin'. I like good music. Good programs." [Mrs. Porter]

"I enjoy living alone. I'm not a lonely person. I have a little nook upstairs. If I have that and a book, I'm happy." [Mrs. Smart]

"I love to read. I have a lot of tapes that I like to listen to." [Mrs. Crawford] uncertain future with a determination to be cheerful about the present. On the one hand, women in these ages temper their hopes with a hard look at their likely prospects—in the short and long run. On the other hand, they reflect the well-documented characteristic among older people known as a "resilient self-hood" (Borges and Dutton 1976; Campbell 1980).[2]

The success of people in late life in maintaining a sense of self in the midst of misfortune may account in part for the high levels of satisfaction found among them. Does this satisfaction derive, perhaps, from older people's pride in keeping themselves intact, and knowing that they can endure adversity? There is some evidence to suggest that it does. Margret and Paul Baltes (cited in chapter 6) observed (1988:23) that, despite the tipping of the scales in the direction of events entailing loss, "old people, on the average, do not differ from young people in their subjective reports on life satisfaction and self-related measures such as personal control and self-efficacy." The phenomenon is consistent across cultures and countries. In a 13-nation survey of human values and well-being over the adult life span, Canadian psychologists, Dorcas S. Butt and Morton Beiser (1987:87), concluded that "the oldest group shows most contentment, satisfaction, and stability in response to the questions."[3]

High levels of satisfaction are manifested in this study's sample in a number of life domains. As shown in table 8.2, some two-thirds to three-quarters of the women expressed positive feelings about their health, housing, neighborhood, and the use of their time. There was one exception to the generally resilient outlook. A smaller proportion (a little over one-half [54%]) were confident about their capacity to do their own shopping. Again, this lesser degree of optimism about functional capacities coincides with previous findings. Not surprisingly, studies show that, compared to younger age groups, older people tend to express more dissatisfaction on attitude items involving somatic complaints (Bolla-Wilson and Bleecker 1989).[4]

How is it that an age group that apparently experiences more losses than are typically found among people at the younger ages expresses equal, if not greater, contentment with life? This question goes to the heart of differences in the attitudes of old people that distinguish them from those of younger adults, and also highlights the fundamental importance of exploring subjective well-being as a component of successful aging (Whitbourne 1985). Certainly, from Erikson and Maslow onward, developmental psychologists have viewed contentment and satisfaction in old age as indicators of a positive ad-

Table 8.2 ATTITUDES TOWARD SELECTED LIFE DOMAINS: WOMEN BORN
1900–1910, 1987 SURVEY

Question	Percentage (N = 589)[a]
Compared to other people your age, would you say that your health is excellent, good, fair, or poor?	
Excellent or good	69
Do health problems stand in the way of your doing the things you want to do?	
Not at all/A little	63
Can you do the shopping for groceries without help, with some help, or are you completely unable to do the shopping for groceries?	
Without help	54
Do you think you need (more) help with shopping, doing housework, getting around the house, bathing, or managing money?	
No	87
How often do you have time on your hands that you don't know what to do with?	
Just now and then/Almost never	83
Would you say you have more space than you need in this house (or apartment or nursing home), just the right amount, or is it too small?	
Just the right amount	73
Would you say that you like this neighborhood very much, somewhat, not much, or not at all?	
Very much	77
Which of the following best describes how you (and your husband) get along on your income: can't make ends meet, just manage to get by, have enough to get along and a little extra, money is no problem?	
A little extra/Money is no problem	70

a. The reciprocal of proportions listed in the table represents the attitudes clustered
at the more negative pole: for example: 100 − 69 = 31 = fair to poor health.

aptation to the accumulation of what Judith Viorst, in her 1987 best-seller of that title, called "necessary losses." But have researchers found any more systematic approaches to adjusting to change among people moving into very old age?

MODES OF ADAPTATION

"Selective Optimization with Compensation"

From their extensive work on the psychology of successful aging, the Balteses have developed a model of the process by which adaptation in aging occurs. The process describes a general adaptation that individuals engage in throughout the life course. However, according to the Balteses (1988:22), because losses in physical and social resources intensify in very old age, the processes of adaptation described in the model acquire new significance in late life.

People's adaptation to aging, the Balteses believe, reflects two apparently conflicting tendencies. On the one hand, it shows a supreme individuality, each case of successful aging revealing a creative blending of unique individual traits with a particular combination of social attributes. On the other hand, they see adaptation among older people as the outcome of a set of recurring patterns and processes that they term, "selective optimization with compensation."

The qualitative interviews contain abundant illustrations of uniqueness as well as of recurring patterns in these women's ways of dealing with life's changes. The three women's stories described next convey the flavor of both individual responses and shared orientation to aging.

Mrs. Grainger, Mrs. Porter, and Mrs. Crawford: Uniqueness and Patterned Response to Change

"Selection," for example, involves a process of reducing the number and scope of things in which one is involved, and conserving one's skills by concentrating on a more limited number of domains. Thus, when asked what activity she most enjoys, Mrs. Grainger said: "Crocheting and knitting. But I'm partially blind . . . so I'm teaching myself to knit without looking so I'll still be able to do it when I become totally blind."

"Optimization" describes a process of enriching and augmenting one's reserves to maximize the positive features of one's chosen life course. Some women in this study, for example, said they wanted to make the most of their marriage while they still had their husband's company to enjoy. Mrs. Porter, who married at age 25 after "going with" her husband for six years, remarked: "Sometimes I fight with my husband, but we've lost so many family members—we're closer than we used to be. As we get older we appreciate each other more."

"Compensation," the third prong of the Balteses' model, refers to the process of adapting to restrictions in one's range of functional capacities by adopting props or aids of various kinds. Mrs. Crawford's interest in listening to tapes illustrates this form of adaptation. She was one of 36 women who in 1987 was using a wheelchair. Except for church services and family get-togethers over holidays, her world consists mainly of the kitchen of the stone house she and Mr. Crawford built together 43 years ago. A retired teacher, she explained that she passes the time listening to tapes. What kinds? "Personal development" tapes, such as "Nutrition for Senior Citizens" or "Strategies for Improving Memory Skills." This seems a clear instance of compensating for "the decrease in environments that are development-enhancing," a loss that gerontologist, Orville Brim (1988), in a book on the psychology of successful aging, noted is common among old people, and a very difficult aspect of aging to endure.

THE WILL TO PERSEVERE

Perseverence is another adaptive strategy. To continue to do what means the most to them, women in this sample have gone to extraordinary lengths to maintain a tight rein on their limitations (Day and Harley 1985). Mrs. Peres (chapter 4) illustrated this determination. Mrs. Hoffman, Mrs. Smart, and Mrs. Tyler were correspondingly tenacious. Mrs. Hoffman said she'd had a heart bypass operation and was taking steroids for severe rheumatoid arthritis. She told me her volunteer work in the hospital shop meant everything to her.

"The doctor says, 'Just do what you can. The days that you don't feel up to it—just lay down. Days that you feel better, go out.' And, that's what I do. I sometimes push myself to get to that hospital. I really do push myself. When you have to get dressed in relays. Take your shower and then lie down. Put on your underwear and then lie down, see. And then put on your clothes and go. Takes a lot of will power."

Mrs. Smart likes to take trips and walk. She never goes to the doctor, choosing instead to ignore inconvenient aches and pains. She commented, "When I get tired, this leg, my left leg, bothers me— But I won't listen to it. I'll say, 'You're not going to tell me where

I'm going to go or where I'm not going to go.' I've gotten to the point where I dragged it behind me."

Widowed in 1987, Mrs. Tyler lives alone and does all the work in her house and garden. A daughter and son live in other states and have asked her to come to live with them. But she wants to stay in the house that she owns. "This has been a terrible year and a half for me," she admitted. "Has it affected your health?" I asked.

"Well, it could have, but I have forced myself to eat properly, and to do things I should have because of the children. They have their own lives and I don't want them to feel they're obliged to run here. Also I want to stay here. This is where I want to be."

Downgrading of Expectations

Coming to terms with old age may involve forms of adaptation that are counterproductive to people's best interests. I refer here to a tendency, the Balteses and others have observed, for older people to lower their expectations to adjust to declines in their health, life-styles, and social resources. This could be seen as an alternative explanation for the "no great expectations" phenomenon, described earlier (Bearon 1989), and for the finding that older people express satisfaction on a par with younger people.

Although the contentment generally reported by people in the oldest ages may suggest that, in some ways, the old are more (not less) resilient to change than the young, the important point here is that the positive perceptions of older people may actually distort the quality of their living conditions relative to those of other age groups. The suggestion is that old people orient their standards of comparison to the lowest common denominator, and, thus, view their own circumstances favorably, even if they are worse off than the rest of the population.

An example from this book's study is perception of health. Over the 10-year period between the two interviews, women in this sample showed substantial consistency in rating their own health compared to that of others in the same age group. Although over a third of those in the follow-up study experienced a decline in functional capacity, virtually the same proportion of the 1987 sample as of the 1978 sample rated their health good to excellent. A total of 21 percent actually reported a rise in health status over what they had said 10 years previously (table 4.1).

THE "OBSOLETE SELF?"

The question of the standards old people use in comparing themselves with others raises again the specter of the "obsolete self." As noted in chapter 2, philosopher Esposito (1987) contends that a view of oneself as worthless results from the lack of respect for old age in modern societies. Does "the obsolete self," then, explain the tendency of the aged to downgrade expectations for themselves?

My experience has been that it does not. The men and women in their late 70s and older whom I have talked to in the United States and Australia project more of a resilient self-hood than demeaning images of old age. Most are proud that they have lived so long and are still managing reasonably well. Rather than internalizing some kind of monolithic negative view of aging, they seemed to assess their position from two quite different perspectives—society's ambivalent attitudes toward old age and their own sense of pride in who they are and what they have done. Many men and women now in their 80s, although modest about their accomplishments, have led truly extraordinary lives (see Facey 1981; also Painter and Valois 1985). Their experience has given them a sense of dignity and self-worth that remains unalloyed by social attitudes that denigrate older people.

Gender, "Generativity" and Well-being

Evaluating the self by this dual standard is perhaps even more a tendency among women, many of whom have devoted themselves largely to caregiving roles within the family, than it is among men, who are more likely to have held positions of esteem in public life. Women studied here value their nurturing roles, and are proud of the contribution they have made to rearing a new generation.

The satisfaction these older women derive from caregiving raises questions about gender differences in developing the potential for "generativity," the quality that Erikson (1982) defined as "to be careful," "to take care of," and "to care for" (chapter 2). Erikson saw this capacity to care for and about others as the pinnacle attribute of mature adults and a crucial component in the development of healthy older individuals. And Maslow (1971) felt that women might have an edge on men in finding the pathways to *self-actualization*—in his view, the ultimate marker of success at any age. Women's lifestyles and priorities, Maslow believed, fitted them better than did men's to attaining a holistic orientation to life—relating to and behaving toward others, oneself, and nature as ends rather than means.[5]

In a provocative article on social supports and mortality, Eugene Litwak and Peter Messeri (1989:61) carried this relationship between gender, caring, and well-being a step farther. Relationships involving mutual support, they suggested, can even be protective against premature mortality. Studies (e.g., Berkman and Syme 1979) have shown that, in later life, women—much more than men—have opportunities for cultivating "generativity" through their access to supportive relationships with family members and friends. One consequence of this, Litwak and Messeri concluded, is that unmarried women may be less isolated than unmarried men. This is one possible explanation, they maintained, for the finding that marriage provides a more protective environment against terminal illness and death for men than for women.

Distinctive Adaptive Patterns

In summary, three distinctive patterns of adjusting to change are found among older women in this study: (1) the blending of idiosyncratic behavior and recurring processes, (2) the juxtaposition of resiliency and high levels of life satisfaction with increasing vulnerability to personal loss, and (3) the tendency to downgrade standards of comparison with respect to life-styles and personal capacities. These patterns color the attitudes and orientations of women in this sample, and distinguish their world view from that of younger adults. They need to be borne in mind in considering the meaning of successful aging to women who are either octogenarians or soon to become so.

The discussion about gender and generativity points also to a direction for future research on the well-being of the elderly. Epidemiologists might find it fruitful to examine in more intimate detail the role of opportunities to care for and about people in contributing to lower death rates among women. An affirmative finding on the hypothesis relating mortality differentials and women's chances to "be care-ful," "take care of," and "care for," could have profound implications for the social roles of men and women and the way we rear our sons and daughters.

Unmeasured Qualities in Successful Aging

The topic of individual adaptations would be incomplete without reference to two other qualities that contribute to aging effectively: trust and a "can-do" orientation toward life. These qualities were not measured in the quantitative surveys, but they are mentioned in the literature and surfaced frequently in the open-ended questions on the 1987 survey and in the conversations I had with the women in their homes.

TRUST AND TRANSCENDENCE

In old age, the quality of trust and of liking people is the outcome of interacting with others over the entire life course. It is both a reflection of the quality of social relationships in the childhood and adult years and a determinant of the quality of social relationships in late life. Maslow (1971) and others cited earlier in this text (Baltes and Baltes 1988; Benet 1974; Inkeles and Smith 1974; Sagan 1987) concurred that—among those who have achieved a strong sense of psychological well-being—trust and the capacity to transcend their particular experience are common characteristics. Adults with this quality enjoy people and have an interest in the world outside themselves. As seen in chapter 2, the anthropologist Sula Benet (1974) detected a similar outgoing orientation among the well-adjusted, long-lived Abkhasians of the Caucasus.

A substantial proportion of women in this study had these qualities, as well, as documented by the interviewers' evaluations in 1978 and 1987 and my own encounters with the 20 women in the qualitative fieldwork.

In both surveys, interviewers were asked to rate the women according to whether they were cooperative or hostile, forthcoming or resistent. Nearly 7 in 10 (69 percent) of women in 1978 were rated "very cooperative," and in 1987, 6 in 10 (60 percent), were rated "friendly and eager." Moreover, although the surveys were conducted a decade apart and, in nearly every instance, by different interviewers, there was a high degree of consistency in ratings at the two times. Nearly 8 out of 10 (77 percent) of those found to be "friendly and eager" in 1987, had been described 10 years earlier as "very cooperative."

Personal encounters confirmed these impressions. Those rated "Friendly and Eager" on the 1987 survey readily accepted my request for a third contact, welcomed me (sometimes unannounced) into their homes, and were open about their feelings and attitudes. When I asked them about successful aging, many volunteered, "I like people." Over and over, in talking to women designated "friendly and eager" by the previous interviewer, I was struck by the quality of trust. They accepted my interest in them on my terms—as part of an ongoing effort to understand the process of aging and the situation of women in their age group in the 1980s. Those rated "cooperative but not particularly eager" in 1987 were more likely to refuse my telephone request for a third interview, and, if they did agree, were less likely to be forthcoming about themselves. Some asked: "What's this information for?" And several who refused said, in effect: "If it doesn't help me, I'm not interested."

"A 'YES' IN YOUR HEART"

Successful agers in this sample are reminiscent of the effective sales- men whom psychologist Martin Seligman chose to study because he saw them as a group constantly exposed to bad events, such as having their overtures rejected and not making a sale (Seligman and Schul- man 1986). Searching for the bases of achievement and psychological health, Seligman selected a sample of 1,000 insurance salesmen and posed a question similar to the one I have been exploring here: Among sales agents, what are the qualities that predict doing well and doing poorly? How can one determine what sort of person makes a good salesman?

Seligman concluded that, among men in his sample, the prime attribute is that of fundamental optimism. Successful salesmen have a yes in their hearts. The shoe fits women in this study, too. A majority are exposed to bad events. Most are slowing down and facing rejection—at the checkout counter in busy supermarkets, for example, or getting out their money on a crowded bus. Like the high-achieving salesmen, however, successful agers in this study are resilient and optimistic. Continuing with Seligman's theory, what seems to count in the difference between those who stand firm and those who crumble is not so much the number of bad events as "the way you construe them, what you think their significance is for your future, and how you defend against them" (Stepney 1989). In this study, women who stood firm framed their views about the future in optimistic terms. They said something like, "I'll be going to the club and bowling with my friends," rather than "I'll probably be dead" or "I hope I won't be here in a couple of years" (chapter 6).

ENVIRONMENT AS A CONTEXT OF AGING

Quality of Life in Old Age—Who's Responsible?

So far, this review of coming to terms has highlighted individual outlooks and efforts in adapting to change. I have presented data showing that a majority of women in this study have tried to help themselves and have faced life crises with grace and facility. Some, however, have not been so successful and are weighed down in old age by negative circumstances, some of which are beyond their control either to rectify or to accept with cheerful optimism. To what extent should those who are down and out be held responsible for shaping their lives in old age, and to what extent should society share the responsibility when the challenges of aging become too great and overwhelm individual will and ingenuity?

In modern societies, the social and ethical issues surrounding this question are becoming more complex and more ambiguous. At the very time when longer life is increasing both the total numbers of people at risk of being unable to cope and the average duration of exposure to that risk, actions harmful to human well-being are being practiced daily on a hitherto unimagined scale. The issue of responsiblity for the quality of life is clouded by collective behaviors that threaten the health of whole populations—disposal of poisonous wastes, extensive land development, deforestation, manufacture and distribution of toxic substances, weapons testing, and so forth. Given that the environment as a milieu supportive to human life is being thus undermined, how much responsibility for well-being in old age can be laid at the door of individual effort?

The message from this study is that individual and environmental approaches are paramount to successful aging. Personal qualities are only one facet of successful aging. Equally vital to success are the resources one has to work with (see Binstock 1990, and chapter 9 this volume). Resources mentioned previously run the gamut—from a person's financial assets (such as ownership of a house), to proximate sources of support (access to friends and neighbors), the availability of local amenities (such as free bus service for those with difficulty getting around on their own), all the way to the characteristics of the wider social and physical environment (do these foster or deter human contact and sociability?). The model proposed here views the environment as the external context in which an older person brings to bear his or her outlooks and personal choices. As such, the environment has an inescapable role in opening or closing opportunities for aging well.

Health and Individual Life-styles

To date, consideration of the balance between private and public responsibility has been directed mainly to questions about population health and the costs to individuals and society of avoidable illness and premature death. Much of the emphasis has been on raising awareness of the consequences for health of individual behavior and life-styles.

Auvinen (1989), whose research on life span was mentioned earlier here, has argued that to a much greater extent than has been acknowledged, the causes of health and well-being are social, that is, they are a by-product of people's behavior, and that the consequences for life-styles and social environments result from the way people live. In the last two decades, the list of behaviors that jeopardize well-being has lengthened appreciably and now include, among others: smoking, excessive drug use (including alcohol and drugs prescribed to old people to treat a plethora of minor and major disorders), high consumption of animal fat, sedentary work habits, sun exposure, fast driving, and heavy reliance on the private automobile. Some of these behaviors (e.g., driving while intoxicated) are risk factors in illness, trauma, and premature death. Some (e.g., drug use) foster social isolation and dependency, directly and indirectly, among the young as well as the old.

The convention today is to claim that the risks associated with these behaviors are well known and, hence, are largely the individual's affair.[6] In any case, so goes the argument, attempts to influence habits related to health in any preventive sense have largely been disappointing. This line of reasoning leads inexorably to the conclusion that, within certain limits, individuals are responsible themselves for shaping the quality of their own lives in old age.

Health and Environmental Factors

A new approach to population health is asking What are these limits?—thus shifting the locus of responsibility from individual behavior to the environmental context, that is, from personal effort to one of galvanizing collective action to seek conditions more conducive to people's needs. A number of researchers (cited in chapter 2) favor this environmental perspective, including House and colleagues (1988), who have drawn attention to the potential of demographic trends for increasing the social isolation of old people, and Lawton and colleagues (Lawton and Hoover 1981; Regnier 1981), who developed the concept of the person-environment services system.

COMING TO TERMS—EXTENDING HORIZONS

Incorporating environmental perspectives into the search for successful aging has far-reaching implications—embracing even the quality of the food supply available to urban populations. John Powles, an Australian physician, stated in 1982 that the increase in degenerative diseases, the major killers in industrial societies, is traceable in part to greater affluence and enhanced opportunities for consumption. The technical transformation of food supply from a low-fat to a high-fat diet, the adding of salt to food, and greater consumption of canned products, sugar, soft drinks, and alcoholic beverages all have a negative impact on general levels of health. Powles claimed (1982:82): "This view of degenerative disease is analogous to Freud's view of neurosis—it is in part the price to be paid for civilization!"

Pluses from the Past

Whatever the long-term effects of such consumption on people's survival, certainly, it is clear that tobacco, licit drugs, low levels of physical activity, and a high-fat diet, uncompensated for by persistent demands on human energies were much less a part of the world in which women in this study grew up than they are of the environment of their daughters and granddaughters today. In this respect, as in others to be discussed in chapter 9, women now in their 80s have something of value to pass on to future generations. As girls and young women they knew lower levels of consumption and lifestyles that made fewer demands on nonrenewable resources. People walked, cycled, or rode trams instead of driving cars. They carried goods they had purchased, unwrapped, in containers brought from home. They were self-sufficient and in many ways closer to nature and to each other. The pleasures women in this sample recall, such as reading, corresponding with friends, and attending get-togethers in community halls, were low-energy pursuits (in terms of demand on the environment), pastimes that are often unable now to compete with the lure of more high technology, electronically driven activities.

This is not to romanticize "the good old days." In many ways, life was hard and uncomfortable—houses were cold, women worked long hours to feed and clothe their families, fresh fruits and vegetables were seasonal and often hard to come by, and loved ones, especially infants and young children, sickened and died in circumstances that now would seem unnecessary (see chapter 9).

But although the not-so-distant past tends to be dismissed in preference for modern technology and modern comforts, publicizing the pluses of those earlier days needs to be encouraged, because a lower-consumption way of life (albeit in different form) is the kind we must have—and soon—if human beings and all other life is to survive even no more years into the future than the survivors in this study have come from through the past.

Ways Forward

The final chapter enlarges on these themes. Building on individual and environmental perspectives in coming to terms with aging, I suggest guidelines for action stemming from this study's findings. The guidelines are considered from two sides of the question, Who's responsible? I examine both the individual's responsibility to take command as much as possible of her own health and arrangements for care, and society's responsibility on two levels—first, to assist those unable to cope and, second, to create an environment that maximizes the opportunities for individuals to love life and look after themselves.

Notes

1. In a special issue of the Milbank Memorial Fund Quarterly devoted to "the oldest-old," Robert Binstock asked (1985:430): Does a focus on those 85 years and older present a fresh perspective on aging, or does concentration on a chronological age group threaten to revive stereotypes about morbidity, poverty, and social dependency?

2. This quality of retaining a sense of self in the midst of a shifting in the very foundations of one's physical and social world was identified as a major marker of successful aging by gerontologists, health professionals, and researchers participating in symposium on the "Markers of Aging Research," at the Gerontological Society of America's 39th annual meeting on "Markers of Successful Aging," in Chicago, Nov. 20, 1986.

3. In Butt and Beiser's study (1987), "older" was defined as 55 years of age and older. This is really too broad an age range to tell much about the orientations toward life of people in the later years. However, age 55 marks a time when individuals in many countries retire from the paid work force, a time when sociologists in the early 1960s argued that a disengagement from social roles begins.

4. Harder to explain is the fact that, in both young and old age groups, women

consistently report more symptoms of physical malfunctioning than do men. However, reporting symptoms of physical disability should not be confused with complaining or playing on sympathy as a bid for outside help. On the contrary, by far the majority of women in this study said that they wanted and expected "to do for" themselves: over four-fifths (87 percent) said they needed no (more) help in managing the shopping, housework, or their financial affairs.

5. Maslow (1971:279) described transcendence as "the very highest and most inclusive of holistic levels of human consciousness, behaving and relating, as ends rather than as means, to oneself, to significant others, to human beings in general, to other species, to nature, and to the cosmos."

6. As an example of society's attitude toward the individual's responsibility for his or her health, a T-shirt for hikers is available inscribed: "If I'd known I was going to live so long, I'd have taken better care of myself!"

Chapter Nine

CONCLUSION: LESSONS AND GUIDELINES

We need policies that promote the conviction that men and women
are irreducibly social and that we have a strong need for companionship and intimacy.
—Peter McDonald, "The 1980s: Social and Economic
Change Affecting Families"

For Americans now in their 40s, the increase in life expectancy has
transformed very old age from a rare event occurring to a few special
people to an "averagely expectable experience, to be planfully anticipated" (Erikson 1982:62). "Planfully anticipating" old age is a
new task for women, one necessitating new outlooks and new skills.
The survivors in this study face a major dilemma. Changes in their
capacity for self-management compel them to make crucial decisions
about their long-term plans, at a time when changes in their social
relationships and sources of informal support are foreclosing their
options. Recent studies have converged in finding that "there is
something that happens to octogenarians that spells fundamental
change in their lives as they find their ability to exert control di-
minishes" (Binstock 1990:274).

Much has been written about this dilemma from the standpoint
of the burden on families (the main providers of informal support)
and the costs to the society at large. As more people survive into
very old age and more require substantial care, who will provide this
care (Day 1985b)? Given the trends toward smaller family size, the
shrinking ratio of children to parents, the aging of informal caregivers
themselves (Stone, Cafferata, and Sangl 1987), and the rising demand
for institutional facilities for the elderly (Manton and Liu 1984),
policy makers increasingly are asking: What can be done to bolster
home care, shorten the length of stay in hospitals and nursing homes,

and, in general, balance private burdens and public costs (Eckholm 1990)?

Those at the vortex see the issues differently. For women already in their 80s, the trick is to play a decisive role in making arrangements for long-term care, while still preserving one's autonomy and avoiding being a burden to one's relatives and friends. This would be a difficult balancing act for people of any age. For octogenarian women, the power to implement one's choices is a diminishing opportunity. Thus, guidelines, for dealing effectively with the changing conditions and life-cycle events of modern aging—that is, with what Erikson (1982:62) called the twin facts of "developmental and historical relativity"—are essential to shaping the quality of life for both old and young generations.

The second part of this final chapter contains such a set of guidelines for action, blending both the perspectives of insiders (the women themselves) and of outsiders (professionals, policy makers, and researchers like myself). First, however, I want to underline three main lessons for research on aging derived from the study design and also to discuss the relevance of women in this study as role models for younger women.

LESSONS FROM THIS STUDY

Multiple Approaches

This study affirms, first of all, the value of multiple approaches to understanding older women's priorities and needs—in particular, the supplementing of aggregated statistical data with a closer examination of what actually happens in the lives of older people living in well-defined social settings.

This synthesis of survey methods and qualitative fieldwork illuminates a number of apparent anomalies in the behavior and attitudes of white, ever-married women born at the turn of the century. There are inconsistencies between their optimistic feelings about the present and their uncertainties about the future; between their levels of functional capacity and their receipt of help with specific tasks; between the help they say they need and the kind of support they want; and between their desire for independence and their need for interdependence.

These anomalies suggest the need to refine standard measures of dependence and independence and the circumstances under which the provision of public services is indicated. They also illustrate the pitfalls of assessing need on the basis of criteria, such as level of income or functional capacity, in isolation from other life domains. For example, what are the older woman's own interests and goals? What kinds of facilities does the local community have to support these interests, and are constraints against realizing them built into the older person's social and physical environment?

Focus on Successful Aging

A second contribution of this research is its endeavor to develop quality of life criteria through a focus on successful aging. By highlighting the strategies women in this sample use to manage transitions in late life, we can learn about how older women adapt to traumatic change. What is more, locating women along a continuum of successful aging permits us to identify life events that may be potential trouble spots. In particular, the findings show the importance to older women's well-being of a combination of contextual factors: marital status, living arrangements, home ownership, continuity of residence, and proximate social relationships. Scholars in aging have long been aware of the significance of these factors. It is hoped that the model described here illuminates how these factors work together to shape the chances for aging well or poorly.

Longitudinal Design

A third contribution of this research is its confirmation of the utility of a longitudinal design. The collection of data at three different points (i.e., the two surveys and the qualitative study) has emphasized the volatile nature of the life circumstances of women at these ages. Indeed, the changes in the women's situations between the two surveys, and again during the 16-month interval between the 1987 survey and the qualitative interviews, make it seem that today's "successful ager" may, thanks to unanticipated and unwelcome life events, become tomorrow's "oppressed ager." Accidental events undoubtedly did color these women's capacity for self-management and alter the pool of private supports available to them. However, the women's experiences suggest that aging effectively is an ongoing process over the whole life course, affected as much by internal forces such as spirit, will power, and personal resourcefulness as by arbitrary outside happenings. In reminiscing, many old people whom one would define as successful demur with the words, "I've been fortunate" (Day 1982; Facey 1981). Yet, the facts of their life stories reveal the presence of their own hands vigorously shaping their fortunes.

RELEVANCE AS ROLE MODELS

Two features shared by the women in this study—and mentioned often in this book—bear repeating for their relevance to the aging of younger women. The first is the historical setting in which these women grew up—one characterized by massive social change and technological upheaval—and the values and outlooks that they share as a result. The second is that existing alongside these common characteristics is a great diversity in the current circumstances and social backgrounds of these women.

Shared Social and Historical Conditions

Findings from this book's study suggest that women now in their 80s make both good and bad models for subsequent generations. On the one hand, because they are the first to experience in such large numbers the impact of longer life, these women have special insights about the concrete challenges of surviving into very old age. On the other hand, because the world in which they grew up and spent their adult years was so different from today's, these women may well have a different set of attitudes and orientations than those who come after them.

DURATION OF BEING "OLD"

An outstanding characteristic of women in this sample is that they are in—or close to being in—their 80s. When interviewed in 1987, these women had known what it means to be defined as "old" for some two decades. Compared to women at an earlier stage of life, the women in this study have had 20 years or more to adapt to not going out to work, to having their husbands at home, to living on a smaller income, and to thinking of the future in ever-more-foreshortened terms. The lateness of stage in their life cycle colors both the events affecting their lives and the meanings they attach to aging at this time.

TECHNOLOGICAL AND SOCIAL CHANGE

Over their lifetimes, the women in this study have both contributed to, and been affected by, accelerating technological and social change.

The momentum of population trends all over the world for example, has altered the bases of human community. The scale of demographic and health transitions over the eight decades in which these women were aging is reflected in the growth of population in absolute numbers, the shifting balance of social organization from small agricultural communities to massive urban industrial complexes, and the extension in years of life remaining after the so-called "productive" years are seen to be over (see table 9.1).

Like the very old in preliterate societies who could claim special regard because of their firsthand knowledge of past events, the same should hold true for the survivors in this study. They are the last generation of American women to have a high proportion with rural backgrounds. Half of the women in this sample lived on a farm before marriage, over one-third had fathers who were farmers, and almost 5 in 10 grew up in homes with no telephone. Seven out of 10 reported some loss of income during the depression, more than half experi-

Table 9.1 POPULATION TRENDS IN UNITED STATES, 1900–1987: POPULATION AT BIRTH OF OLDEST WOMEN IN 1900–1910 BIRTH COHORTS AND AT TIME OF 1978 AND 1987 INTERVIEWS

	At Birth (1900)	1st Interview (1978)	2nd Interview (1987)
POPULATION (millions)	84[a]	222[a]	243[a]
% TOTAL POPULATION:			
In cities of 1+ million	9[b]	47[c]	48[c]
Farm	39[d]	3[e]	2[e]
EXPECTATION OF LIFE AT BIRTH (years)			
Males	48[f]	70[g]	71[g]
Females	51[f]	77[g]	78[g]
INFANT MORTALITY RATE			
(Deaths/1,000 births)	100+[h]	14[h]	10[h]

Sources:
a. U.S. Bureau of the Census, 1988, *Statistical Abstract of the United States, 1988* (Washington, D.C.: U.S. Government Printing Office), table 2.
b. Estimated from U.S. Bureau of the Census, 1911, *Statistical Abstract of the United States, 1911* (Washington, D.C.: U.S. Government Printing Office), tables 25, 30.
c. See note a., above, table 31.
d. Estimated from U.S. Bureau of the Census, 1930, *Statistical Abstract of the United States, 1930* (Washington, D.C.: U.S. Government Printing Office), table 578.
e. See note a., above, table 1053.
f. L. I. Dublin, A. J. Lotka, and M. Spiegelman, 1949, *Length of Life*, rev. ed. (New York: Ronald Press), table 12, p. 50.
g. See note a., above, table 106.
h. See note a., above, table 81.

enced a major reduction in family income, and more than 1 in 5 experienced a job loss—their own job or that of some member of the household in which they were living. One-third grew their own food to meet their needs. These are women who have known two world wars, job scarcity, financial stringency, hard work, and strict adherence to the "Protestant ethic," with its emphasis on work as a basis of worthiness.

By no means did all in the sample grow up in households that were poor. Several of the 20 in the qualitative study described comfortable childhoods living in large houses, where mother and father sat down to dinner by candelight, served by live-in help. But all remember that one worked for what one got, and that things didn't fall into one's lap. Women in this sample know what it means to get along without many of the accoutrements of modern living that those of us in rich, industrialized countries now often take for granted: cars, telephones, motorized lawn mowers, air conditioning, washing machines, refrigerators, vacuum cleaners, and so on. A number built their retirement homes with their own hands. It was not a throwaway society—one mended, patched, and repaired. Some still do.

Health care, too, was more of a do-it-yourself affair. Hospitals, which today are the usual setting for giving birth, treating serious illness, and preparing to die, figured much less prominently in these women's early lives. Mrs. Porter, a coalminer's daughter, was delivered at home by a midwife and so were her nine siblings. Many in the sample nursed terminally ill parents at home. They made do with rudimentary medical services, and a number lost children in childbirth or infancy.

"WE CAN MANAGE"

These rugged times are imprinted on these women's attitudes toward aging now. Despite diminishing physical stamina and increasing functional disorders, a majority are living outside institutions and managing without public support. In 1987, only some 7 percent in the sample were using paid services of any kind—mostly for help with cleaning and laundry. These women have their pride. Many say they are reluctant to ask for help even from their children. "Children have their own lives to lead," they say. "[Anyway,] I have never asked for help, and I don't intend to start now." In this unflagging determination to "do for" themselves and eschew "charity," women in this study are similar to members of their age cohorts in Australia (Day, 1985a:18) and in other urban industrialized countries in the 1980s (Blythe 1979; Moen 1978; Rosenmayr 1977:132–57).

TIMING OF LIFE EVENTS

In addition to sharing a less affluent youth and young adulthood, women now in their 80s have collectively encountered a dramatic shift in the timing of major events over the life cycle. An unanticipated consequence of longer life has been the postponement of events—such as death of a husband and of living alone—from earlier into later old age. Compared with their own grandmothers at the turn of the century, for example, a higher proportion of today's older American women can expect: (1) to be primarily responsible for the long-term care of an infirm spouse (Menken 1985), (2) to live alone after reaching age 65 (Bianchi and Spain 1986; Kobrin 1976); and (3) to know some degree of frailty, necessitating dependence on others (Fulton and Katz 1984).

In this study, 159 women became widowed after they had reached age 66; 49 lost an adult son or daughter, 230 lost a brother or sister, and 189 changed their residence at least once (table 4.1). Among previous cohorts, events such as these—so painful and disruptive to the continuity of life—tended on average to occur at younger ages, when a woman might have had greater physical energy to adapt to loss and forge new bonds of intimacy. Only a third of women in this sample said they had made a new close contact over the past two or three years (but see Appendix 3-E for a possible explanation of this), while over two-thirds had known the death of a family member or close friend.

Coming to terms with these events requires personal skills for which today's cohorts of older women have had few intimate role models. The grandparents of most died before reaching these ages, and contrary to the myth of the extended family household—between the ages of 6 and 16, only 16 percent of women in this sample had a grandmother living in their family home; only 10 percent had a live-in grandfather.

On the positive side, declining mortality has extended the period of shared married life. (Although studies purport to show that widowhood is less injurious to women's health than to men's, in this study, death of one's husband within the last five years is a significant correlate of aging less well [see table 6.5]). Although the point is vigorously debated within the field, some gerontologists (Fries 1983) have forecast the extension of fit, active life well into later old age. If the phenomenon of "the youth creep" does turn out to make older people—age for age—feel and act younger, future cohorts of older women may be better able to deal with losing a husband, living alone, or changing their residence at a time when their own reserves of strength may be dwindling.

Diversity of Circumstances and Backgrounds

The existence of commonalities in attitudes in no way alters the equally significant fact of marked individual differences. The selection of the 1978 study population at random from a national sample of households made available in the follow-up study a wide range of backgrounds and social conditions. Women in this sample grew up in different-sized communities; have different educational credentials, employment histories, and patterns of family building; and in their 80s, reflect a wide range of functional capacities, support systems, and economic and social sources. Consequently, for every generalization about shared outlooks, one can point to exceptions. As one example, although a majority of the women in this study said they prefer to live separately from their children and look after themselves, Mrs. Farnsworth (chapter 1) was counting the days until she could leave her husband and move in with her daughter.

DIVERSITY AND POLICY DIRECTIONS

When it comes to developing policy guidelines, diversity has both advantages and disadvantages. On the one hand, the differences among individuals preclude simple solutions to the dilemmas women face with advancing age. On the other hand, the very diversity that confounds broad spectrum policy affords a fertile field for discovering general categories of hardship and unmet need. Diversity in personal resources and social circumstances casts into sharp relief the common challenges that confront women in this age group.

The guidelines suggested in the remainder of this chapter are a reflection of both the similarities and diversities touched upon here.

GUIDELINES FOR ACTION

Bases of Selection

Six recommendations for action are included here, based on the priorities emphasized by women in this study. They reflect insights gained from the study's findings about successful aging and from what the women said about being old and female in American society today. Primary among their concerns are the crucial importance to a sense of well-being of "doing just what I am doing now," of having friends and family members to turn to, of owning a home, and of maintaining continuity with the past by remaining in familiar surroundings.[1] These guidelines were not, however, advanced by the women themselves, either as needs or political expectations. On the contrary, as noted earlier, women in this sample come from a tradition in which one did not make demands or expect, as they see it, handouts from public charity.

The guidelines are organized to dovetail with the main approaches to successful aging described in chapter 2. They recommend the need for interventions in six main areas: (1) strengthening the capacity for self-management, (2) promoting private initiatives to build development-enhancing opportunities, (3) developing structures and programs to facilitate supportive social relations, (4) monitoring the impact of social change on linkages between older people and the physical environment, (5) broad-

Table 9.2 HOUSEHOLD INCOME IN RELATION TO 1987 WEIGHTED-AVERAGE POVERTY INDEX: NONINSTITUTIONALIZED 1987 SURVEY POPULATION, BY HOUSEHOLD SIZE

Poverty Index Ratio[a]	Household Size (including respondent)							Total	
	1	2	3	4	5	6	7	#	%
<.50	—	—	4	2	4	—	1	11	2.3
.51– .74	27	29	6	2	1	1	2	68	14.0
.75–1.24	48	25	11	—	1	—	—	85	17.5
1.25–1.74	60	31	1	4	—	—	—	96	19.8
1.75–2.50	50	27	5	1	—	—	—	83	17.1
2.51–3.50	31	—	5	2	—	—	—	38	7.8
3.51–4.50	—	33	4	—	—	—	—	37	7.6
4.51–6.50	54	17	—	—	—	—	—	71	14.6
Total	270	162	31	11	7	1	3	485	100.0
%	55.7	33.4	6.4	2.3	1.4	*[a]	1.0	100.0	

Note: Excludes income data for: Refused, 37; Don't Know, 41; and No Answer, 9.
Source: Poverty index ratios are from U.S. Bureau of the Census, "Weighted Average Poverty Thresholds in 1987," in *Money Income and Poverty Status in the United States: 1987. Current Population Reports, Consumer Income*, Series P-60, No. 161 (Washington, D.C.: U.S. Department of Commerce), table A-1, p. 41.
a. Less than 1 percent.

ening the bases of national research on aging, and (6) fostering realistic images of older women.

Guideline 1: Strengthening the Capacity for Self-management

Aged care workers—family members, doctors, social workers, and service providers—should adopt approaches that assist elderly women to manage overall functional capacities, rather than focusing piecemeal on separate health symptoms. This guideline reflects the growing concern of social scientists with what they describe as "the biomedicalization of aging" (Estes and Binney 1989), that is, the tendency to define and treat the problems of aging in medical terms. The alternative suggested here is that physicians and professionals should address the meaning of individual goals and plan health interventions specifically to enable older women to achieve them.

This recommendation addresses the powerful message in this study that older women want to stay as they are—they want to manage their own lives.

Orientations toward health afford a striking example of the distinction between insider and outsider perspectives. To the physician-epidemiologist conducting research on aging, health (morbidity) and long life (longevity) are the central focus. These are the outcome variables that professionials with a medical orientation define as ultimate goals and use to distinguish aging successfully from aging poorly (table 2.1). Not so for the women in this study. The central focus of their concerns, the goal to which they give priority, is the capacity to do things for themselves. Cataracts, for instance, are feared because they prevent reading or driving oneself to go shopping or pursuing particular hobbies or interests.

Queried about their expectations and hopes for the future, women in this survey, for the most part, said they hoped in two or three years' time to be no worse off than they are today. They fear the progressive loss of function and work hard to keep it at bay. I asked the women I visited about meals and diet. Most were well informed about nutrition and were trying to cook balanced meals and to watch their diets. A number were interested in reading about health maintenance or listening to tapes or programs on the media giving advice to the elderly on how to keep fit. This interest in self-maintenance speaks strongly for an extensive campaign to disseminate information about fitness in old age, and to make programs of rehabilitation widely available in order to conserve existing function and compensate for lost function. Specific suggested measures for accomplishing this recommendation include:

a. *Address individual goals and interests.* Women in this sample have diverse goals and interests that require different levels of functional capacity. Some are content to look after their homes, to read or watch television, and to exchange visits with family, friends, and neighbors. Others want to swim, walk, and be out and about in the community. The aim should be to raise the sights of both the elderly client and the service provider from a preoccupation with illness symptoms to an effort to maintain a level of functioning to achieve independence in desired areas.

b. *Nurture existing capacities and resources.* There is a need to work both to conserve existing capacities and to compensate for loss of function. The excuse, "just old age," is not acceptable for two reasons: first, because premature loss of function (read, "avoidable loss") fosters unnecessary dependency of the older person herself, and second, because loss of autonomy is a burden on both the older person and the people responsible for her support. Provision of informal support is a two-way process. However, dependency on the part of an older person requires extra time, effort, and financial commitment by someone else, usually a family member. Even when coming to the end of their resources, there is a tendency for family members to avoid formal support from outside agencies, such as homemaker services (Braithwaite 1990; Fulton and Katz 1984:13). Yet, studies of older people and their support systems (e.g., Edelman and Hughes 1990) have repeatedly reported that formal services provided in the home reinforce and prolong the informal help of family members and others.

c. *Promote independence in living arrangements.* In the last decade, there has been a proliferation of new kinds of living arrangements for the elderly, such as retirement communities, congregate housing, adult day care centers, and "assisted living" buildings where residents can have access to assistance as they need it (Lewin 1990:A22). Such initiatives are designed to enable frail or infirm people to stay in their homes and maintain control of their lives as long as possible. However, the programs now in place, although a vast improvement on the past, are flawed because they serve only a fraction of those in need and are aimed at a minority of the older population. For the more severely disabled, there is still a major gap in services providing personal care with bathing, dressing, and housekeeping. This gap is difficult to close, subject as it is to politics and social choice. Politicians are said to have grave doubts that the public will tolerate a tax sufficient to sustain the spiraling costs of long-term care at home (Tolchin 1990).

d. *Balance independence with help-seeking.* There is ample evidence in this study that the ethos of independence strongly colors the behavior of women in their 80s. The danger is that a cycle will be triggered of greater need and, at the same time, of greater reluctance to ask for help. The findings show that as older women become less able to do things for others, they become more reluctant to ask for outside assistance, such as to get places beyond walking distance, do errands, and attend social events. Over time, this suppression of help-seeking can undermine self-management and foster social withdrawal and premature dependency (see Appendix 3-E). Whether younger cohorts will have similar proclivities to shun help until they can no longer carry on is a question for future research. The answer will have an important bearing on the development of aged-care policies.

e. *Emphasize prevention.* In the race to keep ahead of the needs of the dependent aged, little consideration has been given to the needs of those who, like the majority of women in this sample, are slowing down, but can (and want to) look after themselves. Addressing the needs of people in this category is what I would call the prevention side of policies for the elderly. What is needed are services that forestall a breakdown in self-management, causing personal distress and necessitating more drastic intervention. In this regard, a variety of initiatives should be taken to foster access to social relationships and prolong the period of personal development and meaningful contributions to society. Like the goal of rehabilitation to prolong independent activity, prevention should aim to help the elderly and their families "manage an orderly progression of compensatory care, avoiding discontinuities and crises" (Fulton and Katz 1984:14).

Guideline 2: Promoting Private Initiatives to Build Development-Enhancing Opportunities

Major efforts should be undertaken to create development-enhancing opportunities over the whole life course (Brim 1988). Activities that spark one's intelligence and challenge one's capabilities are essential for children, young adults, and octogenarians, alike. The role of boredom and empty time as markers of less-successful aging (table 6.1) underlines the importance to older women's sense of well-being of keeping up with the times. Mrs. Carlton said about aging successfully: "The main thing you've got to remember is to keep in touch, and to keep in touch with the times, because it can outrun you in a hurry."

At least half a dozen women in the qualitative interviews explicitly mentioned keeping up an interest in the outside world as a key to successful aging. It was one reason, they said, why they liked reading so much. This strong affirmation of a continuing sense of being part of the global community reinforces Maslow's (1971) description of self-actualizing people as capable of interest in things outside themselves. The fact that women in this survey sustained this level of interest shows a remarkable resilience, and suggests that the nature of aging and the characteristics of octogenarian women are gravely misunderstood.

a. *Development-enhancing initiatives.* A number of initiatives have been developed for "young olds," such as Universities of the Third Age (see Laslett 1989, for an endorsement of the British model), Elder Hostels, and agencies that organize volunteer employment for retired people. But there is also a need to develop initiatives catering to the interests and capacities of the less active. Books, tapes, lectures, courses on current events, and contemporary issues—given at home or in senior citizens clubs and retirement and nursing homes—have a potentially large audience. Extending the horizons of people who are becoming somewhat housebound could be an important growth area for private business, at once socially useful, environmentally sound, and potentially lucrative.

Guideline 3: Developing Structures and Programs to Facilitate Supportive Social Relations

This study has underscored in numerous ways that social relationships are a cornerstone of well-being in later life. Indeed, the findings stress that much of the determination of women in this sample to not give up is motivated by their desire to sustain the give and take of the reciprocal relationships. Although, to preserve their autonomy and the rights of the younger generation to privacy, most in this sample would choose to live in their own home rather than move in with an adult child or relative, this does not mean that they want to be alone. There is strong evidence for the importance to these women of neighborhood ties and of intimacy with people living near at hand. Such bonds both substitute for the absence of close family members and supplement ties with family members who live in distant places. The mutual support exchanged also often enables a woman to remain living in her own home longer than would otherwise be possible.

As with many of the markers of successful aging in this study, this one has both a perceptual and a structural dimension. On the one hand, having close social relationships requires that the older person like people and like being around them; and on the other hand, it requires physical and social conditions that facilitate opportunities for social contact.

a. *Getting along with others.* The women I met who appeared to have a hold on life took great joy in people, and lived in environments that, if they did not facilitate congregating, at least did not discourage social intercourse. These environments varied markedly—from a small town on the periphery of a large metropolitan center, with quiet, safe neighborhoods and easy access to shopping, churches, libraries, social clubs, and doctors' offices, to a high-rise apartment for the disabled and frail elderly, where the residents could build a community, their own private safety net.

By the same token, women who appeared to be losing their hold on life tended to be less stimulated by human fellowship and living in settings that constrained casual contacts. Sometimes the constraints were self-imposed, and sometimes, they occurred as a result of functional limitations, meager financial resources, or a combination of all these disadvantages.

b. *Social relationships and community facilities.* Mrs. Tyler, whom I interviewed a year and a half following her husband's death, commented on the great comfort of living in a small community with easy access to friends and neighbors. At one point, she exclaimed: "I don't see how people who are alone survive in big cities." The finding in this study that size of community and length of time living there are correlates of capacity for independent activity and psychological well-being suggests the importance of conducting research along the three lines described in chapter 2—that is, the study of: "(i) mechanisms and processes linking social relationships to health, (ii) determinants of levels of 'exposure' to social relationships, and (iii) the means to lower the prevalence of relative social isolation in the population or to lessen its deleterious effects on health" (House, Landis, and Umberson 1988:544).

Examples of mechanisms to lower the prevalence of social isolation might include: counseling in the local community about alternative living arrangements and their possible impact on life-styles and future options; mobilization of volunteers to respond to requests for help with a host of specific home maintenance tasks (e.g., raking leaves, cleaning out the attic, reorganizing furniture to increase comfort and convenience, repairing leaky faucets); increasing the availability and convenience of public transportation so that nondrivers can continue to manage their own affairs, gain access to services, and have the chance to participate in recreational, social, or community activities; development of group activities and recreational events that go to where older people live, rather than obliging them to come out. (These points are also raised in connection with guideline 4.)

c. *Creating "artificial" extended families.* To raise the level of exposure to social relationships and lower the prevalence of relative isolation, it may be necessary to build structures in large urban areas emulating the qualities of small communities. Affordable housing by itself will not deter isolation. Housing needs to be combined with safe neighborhoods and a sense of belonging to a group who know you and care about you. A number of structures of this kind already provide relevant models, such as Sarah's Circle, a housing and living community in Washington, D.C., which provides a safe pocket of caring concern and of involvement in community activities for older individuals with meager resources and no family members to take responsibility for their needs.

Guideline 4: Monitoring the Impact of Social Change on Linkages between Older People and the Physical Environment

Increased attention needs to be given to the impact of urban development and technological change on the links between people and their physical environment. Specifically, more effort should be made to promote the integration of housing with services that foster independent activity among those categories of the population who are nondrivers or have limited access to a car, such as the frail aged, people with disabilities, young children, and suburban housewives in one-car families whose husbands drive to work (L. H. Day, forthcoming).

a. *"We have the will, but need the way."* Whether in the United States or in Australia, the consensus of older people is that so far as their capacity to look after themselves is concerned: "We have the will, but need the way (Day 1987b)." The services they want are mainly those facilitative public amenities and supports that they cannot provide for themselves, but that are essential to foster their autonomy: transportation, affordable housing in safe neighborhoods, a standard of living no worse than that of other age groups. Of particular note is the extent to which access to, and availability of, transportation determines older women's opportunities to direct their own affairs, to use services, and to participate in the recreational and social activities of the community (Victorian Women's Consultative Council 1988) The fact that a high proportion of women in the 1987 survey mentioned home-based pastimes as the activities they enjoy most, may reveal as much about their difficulties in getting around outside as it does about their social withdrawal and preference for being at home. Indeed, a number said that the reason they do not go places beyond walking distance by themselves is because they have no one to go with or cannot drive a car.

   b. *Hands-on services to promote community access.* The fundamental importance of social relationships to community access needs to be reiterated. Lawton and Hoover's observation (1981:6) cannot be stated too often: "People most frequently compose an essential link between the older person and the physical environment." Outreach services need to be organized by voluntary groups, social agencies, and formal providers to supplement the support provided by families and to counteract the cycle of isolation and encroaching dependency. Services to ease getting out and around are important for these older women, many of whom are experiencing deterioration in their vision and are concerned about changes in the road systems and shopping facilities in their communities. Organizing a service of companions to accompany older women to do errands during the day, or to attend community activities at night, would fill a need expressed by a number of women in this sample.

Guideline 5: Broadening the Bases of National Research on Aging

Aging successfully would appear to be a classic case of a goal in which the interests of the individual and of the collectivity coincide. With length of life increasing the stakes, individual women have much to gain from unlocking the secrets of effective aging. By the same token, American society has much to gain from fostering autonomy and independent activity on the part of a growing segment of the adult population. The questions I raise here are whether approaches to successful aging in current national policies and research projects go far enough, and whether they take a sufficiently comprehensive view of the range of viable actions.

   a. *National research on aging.* In the face of the rising proportion of social resources allocated to the aged, government-supported research on aging has emphasized projects that explore private initiatives in dealing with the responsibility for aged care. "An immense portion of our health and welfare effort is, in fact, devoted to the maintenance of an independent living style within one's own domicile" (Walsh 1981). National funding has concentrated, in particular, on two kinds of research directions: (a) sociobehavioral factors that promote understanding of ways to prolong the period of independent living—the period, that is, during which no extra public costs are incurred, and (b) systems of social support that facilitate informal care of the aged in private households. Current examples of the former include: study of osteoporosis to check the growing epidemic of hip fractures and broken limbs, and studies of self-directedness and self-efficacy to promote self-help in the management of daily activities. Examples of the latter include studies of informal support of the frail elderly, the findings of which can be used to develop policies to reduce the accelerating demand for nursing home facilities.[2]

Data on women born 1900–1910 confirm that prevention of osteoporosis, building self-efficacy, and nurturing the bases of informal support are all vitally important to older women's well-being. In old age, hip fracture is not only painful and disabling, but it often signals the end of self-management. The disastrous effects of hip fracture are starkly illustrated in Mrs. Farnsworth's profound sense of helplessness due, in part, to handicaps associated with painful hip replacements. Rowe and Kahn (1987:147) reported that such experiences are by no means uncommon. They cited findings, for example, that "by age 81 one-third of women and one-sixth of men will have suffered a hip fracture, often a catastrophic, if not terminal, event."

To the extent that individual and national interests do, indeed, coincide, research oriented toward exploring practicalities in the private sphere should be warmly welcomed and condoned. After asserting, as do the House Select Committee on Aging (U.S. House of Representatives 1989) and women's advocacy groups, that older women's health and social needs have been invisible for years in national priorities, it would be self-defeating, indeed, to cavil about current research directions because they happen to coincide with the national interest in devolving the costs of aged care to families and private households.

b. *Environment-oriented research and policy.* Chapter 2 called attention to the growing consensus among researchers that the answers to successful aging lie beyond the biological and psychological potential of older individuals and must be sought, as well, in the influence of broader social forces on opportunities for health and well-being. There are limits to the sort of research that focuses exclusively on individual hopes and efforts. Whether older people can have and sustain satisfying goals depends on many aspects of the social setting, such as policies with respect to housing, transportation, and amenities that cater to the emotional and physical requirements of the elderly; employment and retirement practices; access to health facilities; and services that support the work of families in caring for their dependent older members. The older women in this study endorsed this view. Asked about their priorities, they emphasized support that implements their own efforts and private resources.

c. *Public amenities and autonomy.* One consequence of the tendency to circumscribe thinking about aging issues is policy approaches that consider only one dimension of older people's needs, those needs that are essentially individual and private and for which family members are expected to take the major responsibility.[3] Such activities are those measured by the Instrumental Activities of Daily Living (IADL) and Activities of Daily Living (ADL): household maintenance and personal upkeep. Yet this study's findings suggest that even in their late 70s and 80s, only a minority of frail older people require outside help to manage these activites. A larger proportion feel that they can handle the housework by taking things more slowly and adapting their standards to their changing levels of strength and stamina.

Basically, the idea that we may have been defining older people's needs too narrowly comes down to the link between autonomy, social policy, and design of the physical environment. The concerns expressed by women in this study support the conclusion that "the extent to which autonomy and control are encouraged or denied may be a major determinant of whether aging is usual or successful on a number of physiologic and behavioral dimensions" (Rowe and Kahn (1987:146). There may be a connection between the development of greater public services to facilitate the mobility of less-active members of society, and the extension of healthier, more independent years of activity for the very old. To the extent that such services would enhance the quality of life for all ages, fostering public facilities should be promoted as ends in themselves. But to the extent that such facilities would improve health and reduce helplessness and isolation among the elderly, they might also foster a reduction in the social and economic costs of premature dependency. Again, interdependence should be recognized as a goal to be actively pursued. If such things as functional capacity, housing design, neighborhood amenities, and income are seen not as ends in themselves but as the means to achieving this goal, we will have come a long way in our attitudes about addressing the needs of old people.

Guideline 6: Fostering Realistic Images of Older Women

A redoubling of efforts is required to promote an informed, well-rounded picture of the circumstances of old women today—their interests, activities, and the contributions they make to their families and to the wider society. A collaborative and ongoing campaign should be undertaken by government committees on aging, advocacy groups, researchers, and professional organizations to counter the misconceptions that result from making the elderly "statistical ghosts" (Torrey 1988, see chapter 3). One consequence of the failure to disaggregate statistics on the very old is distorted, extreme, and contradictory images. The following are examples:

Old people are fit, active, and enjoying the best years of their lives. . . . They are frail, sedentary and isolated from the mainstream.

Old people are rich, independent, and can take care of themselves. . . . They are poor, dependent, and a drain on the public purse.

Old people contribute substantially to the community and provide support to family members. . . . They are unproductive and give nothing in return.

Old people are amply supported by their children and need no supplementary assistance from public sources. . . . They are neglected by their children, who place them in nursing homes at the first opportunity.

Sorting out myth from reality is a continuing task. In the last three decades, researchers on aging have addressed this challenge and produced a voluminous literature describing the real world of the elderly. But disseminating their findings to policymakers, politicians, and the public is slow work. In addition, scholars themselves disagree about research directions and about the policy implications significance of the findings (see, for example, Estes and Binney 1989). As a result, many misconceptions about being old in America remain locked in the conventional wisdom. Mindful that distorted images can become self-fulfilling, professionals and informed laypersons must work harder to shun loose generalities and communicate with and about old women with reference to their concrete priorities and day-to-day needs in particular social and environmental settings.

Making Old Women More Visible

"We has met the enemy and they is us!" So said Pogo sometime ago. He could have been talking about our fears of growing old.

Yet, the strength and dignity of the women in this study are inspiring. A majority have come to terms with dramatic changes in their lives and are managing on their own with a little help from their family and friends. And they reciprocate in diverse ways: helping children and grandchildren financially, volunteering in the community, and exchanging favors with friends and neighbors. They are realistic about their future and face the certainty of death with fortitude and mostly without flinching. What they like least about aging is becoming dependent; what they want most is the means to handle their own affairs. Like people in every age, they want to be "looked upon," to be respected and appreciated.

Yet, if these guidelines to a social science study have been stated in the form of advocacy, it is because what these women said (as transcribed on their questionnaires by the interviewers and in their conversations with me) also conveys a sense of quiet urgency about the looming difficulties associated with concrete aspects of their daily lives—getting the groceries, keeping up the house, getting out to social events, driving the car, remaining in close touch with family and friends, dealing with illness and disability, and above all, staying in control to the end. For a minority in the sample, aging has meant sliding into oppressive conditions from which there seems no escape and little chance of relief. Moreover, because of the growing numbers of very old women, their greater likelihood of living alone in old age and of being poor compared to men, and the increasing competition for scarce resources among different social groups, there is every possibility, that, in the future, this oppressed minority will be larger and more disadvantaged.

However, this is a social problem, not an indelible characteristic of old age or an aging society. Given a national commitment, this oppressed minority can be identified and their needs addressed. The perspectives of ill-informed outsiders are what perpetuate negative and patronizing images of aging. Fears about aging have contributed to making the situation of older women invisible, and to discounting the genuine dilemmas they face. By blocking information and obscuring the issues, fears about old age become self-fulfilling. They deter understanding about what old age entails and keep people from planfully anticipating a vigorous and satisfying senescence.

SUCCESSFUL AGING: PRIVATE STRENGTHS AND PUBLIC AMENITIES

"You Make Yourself Happy"

In the end, I return to Mrs. Silvestri—a patently successful ager. The secret of successful aging? "You make yourself happy," she said.

This study shows that for women in their 80s, there are many paths to satisfaction with life. In Mrs. Silvestri's case, the paths include good health, a "yes in her heart," a sense of trust and liking for people, knowing when and how to ask for help, and extraordinary efficacy in making the environment responsive to her self-expressed need for interdependence. Though her own income is quite small (25 percent below the weighted poverty index)—ownership of her home and three children with good incomes, give her a comfortable private safety net. Successful aging, however, as Mrs. Silvestri knows, does not come without personal effort. Making yourself happy requires good common sense and vigilance to keep yourself fit and maintain strong ties in the community.

But, finally, besides her private strengths, Mrs. Silvestri lives in a place where there are abundant public amenities for older people to help themselves: an active senior citizens club, a free bus for the elderly, quiet, safe streets to walk in, and a small enough sized community for people to have a sense of place—to know their neighbors, and to have their neighbors know them.

Mrs. Silvestri's and Mrs. Farnsworth's stories (chapter 1) vividly demonstrate that successful aging is the outcome of a nexus between personal propensities and the characteristics of the environment. Both women live in the same community, both have access to community amenities for the asking, but Mrs. Silvestri puts them to good use to implement her strong desire for autonomy and social involvement, while Mrs. Farnsworth dismisses them and withdraws into a private world of self disgust and despair.

Among women in this study, the capacity to enjoy life is a prime component of successful aging. To nurture their older populations, communities need to provide opportunities for independent activity and the creation and maintenance of intimacy. These are the conditions that will enable older women to love life and take good care of themselves.

NOTES

1. Readers will note that the guidelines deal only indirectly with income security. For one thing, although over half (54 percent) of women in this sample fall into a band of poverty or near poverty (that is, their incomes range from 50 percent below to 75 percent above the weighted poverty index [table 9.2]), only a minority specifically mentioned having financial worries. Fully 7 out of 10 (70 percent) said that money is not a problem or that they have enough to get along and a little extra. This may illustrate the tendency described in chapter 8 for older people to lower their standards to coincide with those of others in their age group worse off than themselves (Baltes and Baltes 1988). Or it may be the legacy of growing up in a less affluent society, and of learning in childhood and young adulthood to make do with what one has. To the extent that it is the latter, future cohorts may make more demands on public resources than women born at the turn of the 20th century.

Chapters 6 and 7 identified a minority of the sample for whom low income in combination with a paucity of personal resources, such as having no spouse, limited capacity for independent activity, or no primary caregiver to take responsibility for long-term care, created serious hardship. Certainly, from an outsider perspective, adequate income is an essential component of a strong private safety net. As noted in earlier chapters, the crucial importance of income is manifested through its effect on older women's choices, such as being able to afford paid services and holding onto one's house. However, in this study, housing tenure contributes substantially more to explaining differences between the respondents on Private Safety Net (dimension 3, (table 6.1, part C) than does level of income. In addition, income in 1978 was not found to be significantly correlated with a perceived sense of well-being (table 6.5). (Strategies for eliminating poverty among the elderly are discussed comprehensively by Zedlewski and Meyer [1988].)

2. A number of gerontologists (e.g., Bintock 1985; Horowitz 1985), however, question the practicality of government-funded research aimed at increasing family care of the aged. Studies show that the great proportion of the costs of basic life-supporting services is already borne by older individuals and their families (Soldo and Agree 1988).

3. Over the last decade in the United States, policies to address these individual and family needs have received increasing attention: rehabilitation to foster independent activity, programs to support caregivers in their role as providers for the profoundly disabled persons, support groups for the bereaved, counselors for financial management, and economic incentives to strengthen people's private safety nets, such as private insurance plans for long-term care in nursing homes.

REFERENCES

Antonucci, T. C., and H. Akiyama. 1987. "Social Networks in Adult Life and a Preliminary Examination of the Convoy Model." *Journal of Gerontology* 2(5):519–27.

Auvinen, Riitta. 1989. "The Human Life Span and the Social Environment." Paper presented at European Population Association conference on "Ageing Populations: Determinants and Consequences," Prague, July 3–10.

Bachrach, Christine A. 1980. "Childlessness and Social Isolation among the Elderly." *Journal of Marriage and the Family* 42:627–36.

Baltes, Margret M., and Paul B. Baltes. 1986. *The Psychology of Control and Aging.* Hillsdale, N.J.: Lawrence Erlbaum Associates.

Baltes, Paul B., and Margret M. Baltes. 1988. "Psychological Perspectives on Successful Aging: The Model of Selective Optimization with Compensation." In *Successful Aging: Perspectives from the Behavioral Sciences,* edited by Paul B. Baltes and Margret M. Baltes. New York: Cambridge University Press.

Bearon, Lucille B. 1989. "No Great Expectations: The Underpinnings of Life Satisfaction for Older Women." *Gerontologist* 29(6):772–78.

Becker, Howard S., and Blanche Geer. 1957. "Participant Observation and Interviewing: A Comparison." *Human Organization* 16(2):28–32.

Benet, Sula. 1974. *Abkhasians, The Long-Living People of the Caucasus.* In *Case Studies in Cultural Anthropology,* edited by George and Louise Spindler. New York: Holt, Rinehart & Winston.

Bengston, Vern, L. Burton, and D. Manger. 1981. "Family Support Systems and Attribution of Responsibility: Contrasts among Elderly Blacks, Mexican Americans, and Whites." Paper presented at the 34th Annual Meeting of the Gerontological Society, Toronto.

Beresford, John C., and Alice M. Rivlin. 1966. "Privacy, Poverty, and Old Age." *Demography* 3:247–58.

Berkman, Lisa F., and Leonard S. Syme. 1979. "Social Networks, Host Resistance, and Mortality: A Nine-Year Follow-up Study of Alameda County Residents." *American Journal of Epidemiology* 190(4):186–204.

Bertraux, Daniel. 1981. "From the Life-History Approach to the Transformation of Sociological Practice." In *Biography and Society: The Life History Approach in the Social Sciences*, edited by Daniel Bertraux. Beverly Hills: Sage Publications.

Bianchi, Suzanne, and Daphne Spain. 1986. *American Women in Transition*. National Committee for Research on the 1980 Census. New York: Russell Sage.

Binstock, Robert H. 1985. "The Oldest Old: A Fresh Perspective or Compassionate Ageism Revisited?" *Milbank Memorial Fund Quarterly/ Health and Society* (guest edited by Richard Suzman and Matilda White Riley) 63(2):420–51.

Binstock, Robert H. 1990. "Reviews". *Gerontologist* 30(2):273–74.

Binstock, Robert H., and Linda George, eds. 1990. *Handbook on Aging and the Social Sciences*. 3rd edition. New York: Academic Press.

Binstock, Robert H., and Ethel Shanas. 1976. *Handbook on Aging and the Social Sciences*. New York: Van Nostrand Reinhold.

Blythe, Ronald. 1979. *The View in Winter: Reflections on Old Age*. London: Allen Lane.

Bolla-Wilson, Karen, and Margit L. Bleecker. 1989. "Absence of Depression in Elderly Adults." *Journal of Gerontology* 44(2):P53–55.

Borges, M. A., and L. J. Dutton. 1976. "Attitudes toward Aging: Increasing Optimism Found with Age." *Gerontologist* 16:220–24.

Bradburn, Norman. 1969. *The Structure of Psychological Well-Being*. Chicago: Aldine.

Braithwaite, Valerie H. 1990. *Bound to Care*. Sydney: Allen & Unwin.

Branch, L. A., A. Jette, C. Evashwick, M. Polanksy, G. Rowe and P. Diehr. 1981. "Toward Understanding Elders' Health Service Utilization." *Journal of Community Health* 7(1):80–92.

Brim, Orville. 1988. *Keeping Up Ambition through the Life Span*. New York: Russell Sage.

Brody, Elaine M. 1981. "Women in the Middle." *Gerontologist* 21:471–80.

Brody, Elaine M. 1985. "Parent Care as a Normative Family Stress." *Gerontologist* 25:19–29.

Brown, Scott Campbell. 1988. "Aging, Natural Death, and the Compression of Morbidity: A Review of the Literature and Issues." Photocopy.

Butt, Dorcas Susan, and Morton Beiser. 1987. "Successful Aging: A Theme for International Psychology." *Psychology and Aging* 2(1):87–94.

Callahan, Daniel. 1988. *Setting Limits—Medical Goals in an Aging Society*. New York: Simon & Schuster.

Campbell, A. 1980. *The Sense of Well-Being in America*. New York: McGraw-Hill.

Canada. Statistics Canada. 1985. *General Social Survey*. Analysis Series. Ottawa: Statistics Canada.

Cantor, Majorie. 1979. "Neighbors and Friends: An Overlooked Resource in the Informal Support System." *Research on Aging* 1:434–63.

Cantor, Marjorie. 1980. "The Informal Support System: Its Relevance in the

Lives of the Elderly." In *Aging and Society,* edited by Edgar F. Borgatta and Neil G. McCluskey. Beverly Hills: Sage Publications.

Cantor, Majorie H. 1983. "Strain among Caregivers: A Study of Experience in the United States." *Gerontologist* 23:434–63.

Cantor, Marjorie, and Virginia Little. 1984. "Aging and Social Care." In *Handbook of Aging and the Social Sciences,* 2nd ed., edited by Robert H. Binstock and Ethel Shanas. New York: Van Nostrand Reinhold.

Chappell, Neena, and Mark Badger. 1989. "Social Isolation and Well-being." *Journal of Gerontology* 44(5):S169–76.

Cherlin, Andrew. 1983. "A Sense of History: Recent Research on Aging and the Family." In *Aging in Society: Selected Reviews of Recent Research,* edited by Matilda White Riley, Anne Foner, and Joan Waring. Hillsdale, N.J.: Lawrence Erlbaum Associates.

Cherlin, Andrew J., and F. F. Furstenberg, Jr. 1986. *The New American Grandparent: A Place in the Family, A Life Apart.* New York: Basic Books.

Clipp, Elizabeth C., and Linda K. George. 1990. "Caregiver Needs and Patterns of Social Support." *Journal of Gerontology* 45(3):S102–11.

Conway, Jill Ker. 1989. *The Road from Coorain.* New York: Alfred A. Knopf.

Cumming, Elaine, and W. E. Henry. 1961. *Growing Old: The Process of Disengagement.* New York: Basic Books.

Dannefer, Dale. 1988. "What's in a Name? An Account of the Neglect of Variability in the Study of Aging." In *Emergent Theories of Aging,* edited by James E. Birren and Vern L. Bengtson, with Donna E. Deutchman, coordinator. New York: Springer Publishing.

Dawson, Deborah A., D. J. Meny, and Jeanne Clare Ridley. 1980. "Fertility Control in the United States before the Contraceptive Revolution." *Family Planning Perspectives* 12(2):76–86.

Day, Alice T. 1982. "A Review Essay: The Fortunate Life of A.B. Facey— The Life Reviewing Process and Personal Integration." *Oral History Association of Australia Journal* 4:62–68.

Day, Alice T. 1984. " 'I Don't Need More Help—At the Moment': Orientations of the Frail Aged toward Planning for Custodial Care." In *Proceedings of Australian Family Research Conference* (Canberra), vol. 5. Melbourne: Australian Institute of Family Studies.

Day, Alice T. 1985a. *"We Can Manage": Expectations about Care and Varieties of Family Support among People 75 Years and Over.* Melbourne: Australian Institute of Family Studies.

Day, Alice T. 1985b. *Who Cares? Demographic Trends Challenge Family Care for the Elderly.* Population Trends and Public Policy Paper 9. Washington, D.C.: Population Reference Bureau.

Day, Alice T. 1986. *Women and the Challenge of Long Life.* Report prepared for the National Women's Advisory Council. Canberra, Australia: National Women's Advisory Council.

Day, Alice T. 1987a. "Characteristics of the Aged in Institutions: Current

Patterns and Future Prospects." Working Paper. Washington, D.C.: Urban Institute.

Day, Alice T. 1987b. *Put Things in One Voice and Make It Worthwhile!* Report on Consultations with Elderly Residents of New South Wales, Sydney: Premier's Department. Office of Aged Services.

Day, Alice T. 1988. "Contribution of Kin to Support of the Very Old." Working Paper. Washington, D.C.: Urban Institute.

Day, Alice T. 1989. "Kinship Networks and Informal Support in the Later Years." In *Later Phases of the Family Life Cycle: Demographic Aspects*, edited by E. Grebenik, C. Höhn, and R. Mackensen. Oxford: Oxford University Press.

Day, Alice T., and Lincoln H. Day. 1989. "Continuity and Change in Household Composition—Implications for Social Support of the Very Old." Paper presented at European Population Association conference on "Ageing Populations: Determinants and Consequences," Prague, July 3–10.

Day, Alice T., and Ann Harley. 1985. " 'I Hope that Something Will Come Out of This.' Older Women and Government Policies for the Aged." La Trobe Working Papers in Sociology, Paper 72. Bundoora, Victoria: Department of Sociology, School of Social Sciences, La Trobe University.

Day, Lincoln H. Forthcoming. *The Future of Low-Birthrate Populations.* London: Unwin Hyman.

Day, Lincoln H., and Alice Taylor Day. 1984. "Fertility and 'Life Chances'— A Comparison among 19 Countries of Controlled Fertility." *International Journal of Comparative Sociology* 25(3–4):197–225.

Diamond, Ian, and Catherine Garner. Forthcoming. "The Use of Multilevel Models to Measure the Effects of Areal Deprivation on Education." Series A. *Journal of the Royal Statistical Society.*

Doty, Pamela. 1986. "Family Care of the Elderly: The Role of Public Policy." *The Milbank Quarterly* 64(1):34–69.

Dunbar, Leslie. 1988. *The Common Interest: How Our Social Welfare Policies Don't Work and What We Can Do about Them.* New York: Pantheon Book.

Eckholm, Erik. 1990. "Haunting Issue of U.S.: Caring for the Elderly Ill." *New York Times*, March 27, p. A1ff.

Edelman, Perry, and Susan Hughes. 1990. "The Impact of Community Care on Provision of Informal Care to Homebound Elderly Persons." *Journal of Gerontology* 45(2):S74–84.

Erikson, Erik H. 1951. *Childhood and Society.* London: Imago Publishing Co.

Erikson, Erik Homburger, 1982. *The Life Cycle Completed—A Review.* New York: W. W. Norton.

Espenshade, Thomas J., and Rachel Eisenberg Braun. 1983. "Economic Aspects of an Aging Population and the Material Well-being of Older

Persons." In *Aging in Society: Selected Reviews of Recent Research,* edited by Matilda White Riley, Anne Foner, and Joan Waring. Hillsdale, N.J.: Lawrence Erlbaum Associates.

Esposito, Joseph L. 1987. *The Obsolete Self: Philosophical Dimensions of Aging.* Berkeley: University of California Press.

Estes, Carroll, and Elizabeth A. Binney. 1989. "The Biomedicalization of Aging: Dangers and Dilemmas." *Gerontologist* 29(5):587–96.

Facey, A.B. 1981. *A Fortunate Life.* Fremantle, Western Australia: Freemantle Arts Centre Press.

Fielding, Nigel G., and Jane L. Fielding. 1987. *Linking Data.* A Sage University Paper Qualitative Research Methods Series 4. Beverly Hills: Sage Publications.

Fontana, Andrea. 1977. *The Last Frontier: The Social Meaning of Growing Old.* Beverly Hills: Sage Publications.

Fries, J. F. 1983. "The Compression of Morbidity." *Milbank Memorial Fund Quarterly* 61:397–419.

Fulton, John P., and Sidney Katz. 1984. "Characteristics of the Handicapped Elderly and Implications for Rehabilitation." Paper presented at Conference on "Aging and Rehabilitation," November, Washington, D.C.

Furnass, Bryan. 1976. "Changing Patterns of Health and Disease." In *The Magic Bullet,* edited by Mark Diesendorf. Canberra, Australia: Society for Social Responsibility in Science.

George, Linda K. 1987. "Easing Caregiver Burden: The Role of Informal and Formal Supports." In *Health in Aging: Sociological Issues and Policy Directives,* edited by R. A. Ward and S. S. Tobin. New York: Springer Publishing.

Gibson, Diane M., and Wendy Aitkenhead. 1983. "The Elderly Respondent." *Research on Ageing* 5:283–96.

Hagestad, Gunnhild O. 1987. "Able Elderly in the Family Context: Changes, Chances, and Challenges." *Gerontologist* 27(4):417–22.

Harel, Zev, Edward A. McKinney, and Michael Williams. 1990. *Black Aged: Understanding Diversity and Service Needs.* London, England: Sage Publications.

Hendricks, Jon. 1984. "Lifecourse and Structure: The Fate of the Art." *Ageing and Society* 4(1):93–98.

Herzog, A. Regula, Robert L. Kahn, James N. Morgan, James S. Jackson, and Tony C. Antonnucci. 1989. "Age Differences in Productive Activities." *Journal of Gerontology* 44(4):129–38.

Hess, Beth B. 1985. "America's Elderly: A Demographic Overview." In *Growing Old in America—New Perspectives On Old Age,* 3rd. ed., edited by Beth B. Hess and Elizabeth W. Markson. New Brunswick, N.J.: Transaction Books.

Hing, E. 1987. "Use of Nursing Homes by the Elderly: Preliminary Data from the 1985 National Nursing Home Survey." In *Advance Data from*

Vital and Health Statistics, No. 135. Department of Health and Human Services (PHS)87-1250, NCHS. Washington, D.C.: U.S. Government Printing Office.

Hofland, Brian F. 1988. "Autonomy in Long Term Care: Background Issues and a Programmatic Response." *Gerontologist.* June Supplementary Issue 28:3–9.

Holden, Karen. 1988. "Poverty and Living Arrangements among Older Women: Are Changes in Economic Well-being Underestimated?" *Journal of Gerontology* 43(1):S22–27.

Horowitz, Amy. 1985. "Family Caregiving to the Frail Elderly." In *Annual Review of Gerontology and Geriatrics*, Special Volume 5, edited by M. Powell Lawton and George L. Maddox. New York: Springer Publishing 194–243.

Horowitz, Amy, and R. Dobrof. 1984. "The Role of Families in Providing Long-Term Care to the Frail and Chronically Ill Elderly Living in the Community, Final Report." Submitted to the Health Care Financing Administration, Department of Health and Human Services, Grant No. 18-P-97541/2-02, Washington, D.C.

House, James S. 1981. *Work Stress and Social Support.* Reading, Mass.: Addison-Wesley.

House, James S. 1983. "Social Support and the Quality and Quantity of Life." Paper presented at the Fourth Annual ISR Founders Symposium, University of Michigan, Ann Arbor.

House, James S., and Cynthia Robbins. 1983. "Age, Psychosocial Stress, and Health." In *Aging in Society: Selected Reviews of Recent Research*, edited by Matilda White Riley, Anne Foner, and Jean Waring. Hillsdale, NJ: Lawrence Erlbaum Associates.

House, James S., Karl R. Landis, and Debra Umberson. 1988. "Social Relationships and Health." *Science* 241:540–45.

Ingersoll, Berit. 1983. "Approaches to Combining Quantitative and Qualitative Social Support Research." Paper presented at the annual meeting of the American Psychological Association, Anaheim, Calif., August.

Inkeles, Alex, and D. Smith. 1974. *Becoming Modern: Change in Six Developing Countries.* Cambridge, Mass.: Harvard University Press.

Job, Eena Marie. 1983. "Retrospective Life Span Analysis: A Method for Studying Extreme Old Age." *Journal of Gerontology* 38(3):369–74.

Job, Eena Marie. 1984. *Eighty Plus.* St. Lucia, Queensland, Australia: University of Queensland Press.

Johnson, Denis, and Sally Hoover. 1982. "Social Indicators of Aging." In *Aging from Birth to Death.* Vol. 2 of *Sociotemporal Perspectives*, edited by M. W. Riley, R. P. Abeles, and M. S. Teitelbaum. Boulder, Colo.: Westview Press.

Karuza, Jurgis Jr., Vita C. Rabinowitz, and Michael A. Zevon. 1986. In *The Psychology of Control and Aging*, edited by Margret M. and Paul B. Baltes. Hillsdale, NJ.: Lawrence Erlbaum Associates.

Kasper, Judith D. 1988. *Aging Alone: Profiles and Projections.* Report to The Commonwealth Fund Commission on Elderly People Living Alone. Baltimore: Commonwealth Fund Commission.

Katz, S., T. D. Downs, H. R. Cash, and R. C. Gratz. 1970. "Progress in Development of the Index of ADL." *Gerontologist* 10:20–30.

Kelley, Jonathan, M.R.D. Evans, and Bruce Headey. 1989. "Moral Reasoning and Political Conflict: The Abortion Controversy." Working Paper, Department of Sociology, Institute of Advanced Studies. Canberra: Australian National University.

Kendig, Hal. "Housing, Aging, and Social Structure." In *Handbook of Aging and the Social Sciences*, 3rd ed., edited by Robert Binstock and Linda George. New York: Academic Press.

Kendig, Hal, ed. 1986. "Ageing, Families, and Social Change." In *Ageing and Families: A Social Networks Perspective*, edited by Hal L. Kendig. Sydney: Allen & Unwin: 169–185.

Kendig, H. L., D. M. Gibson, D. T. Rowland and J. M. Hemer. 1983. *Health, Welfare and Family in Later Life*. Ageing and the Family Project. Research School of Social Sciences, Australian National University.

Knopf, Olga. 1975. *Successful Aging.* New York: Viking Press.

Kobrin, Francis E. 1976. "The Fall in Household Size and the Rise of the Primary Individual in the United States." *Demography* 31:127–38.

Kobrin, Francis E. 1981. "Family Extension and the Elderly: Economic, Demographic, and Family Cycle Factors." *Journal of Gerontology* 36:370–77.

Kotlikoff, Lawrence J., and John Morris. 1987. "How Much Care Do the Aged Receive from their Children? A Bimodal Picture of Contact and Assistance." Working Paper 2391. JEL No. 918. *NBER Reporter*, Fall.

Kranz, D., and R. Schulz. 1980. "A Model of Crisis Control and Health Outcomes: Cardiac Rehabilitation and Relocation of the Elderly." In *Advances in Environmental Psychology*, edited by A. Baum and J. E. Singer. Vol. 3 of *Cardiovascular Disorders and Behavior*. Hillsdale, N.J.: Lawrence Erlbaum Associates.

Kunitz, J. Stephen. 1989. "The Quest For Anomalies: The Value of Particularism in the Study of Mortality." Paper presented to Health Transition Workshop, National Centre for Epidemiology and Population Health. The Australian National University. Canberra, May 15–19.

Langer, B. J., and J. Rodin. 1976. "The Effects of Choice and Enhanced Personal Responsibility for the Aged: A Field Experiment in an Institutional Setting." *Journal of Personality and Social Psychology* 34:191–98.

Laslett, Peter. 1984. "The Significance of the Past in the Study of Ageing." *Ageing and Society—Special Issue on History and Ageing* 4(4):379–89.

Laslett, Peter. 1989. *A Fresh Map of Life—The Emergence of the Third Age.* London: Weidenfeld & Nicolson.

Lawton, M. P, and Elaine M. Brody. 1969. "Assessment of Older People:

Self-maintaining and Instrumental Activities of Daily Living." *Gerontologist* 9:179–86.

Lawton, M. Powell, and Sally L. Hoover, 1981. "Introduction." In *Community Housing Choices for Older Americans,* edited by M. Powell Lawton and Sally L. Hoover. New York: Springer Publishing.

Lawton, M. Powell, Miriam Moss, Mark Fulcomer, and Morton H. Kleban. 1982a. "A Research and Service Oriented Multilevel Assessment Instrument." *Journal of Gerontology* 37(1):91–99.

Lawton, M. Powell, Miriam Moss, Mark Fulcomer, and Morton H. Kleban. 1982b. *Philadelphia Geriatric Center Multi-Level Assessment Instrument. Manual for Full-length MAI.* Philadelphia: Philadelphia Geriatric Center.

Levi, Primo. 1988. *The Drowned and the Saved.* New York: Summit Books.

Lewin, Tamar. 1990. "Strategies to Let Elderly Keep Some Control." *New York Times,* March 28, p. A1ff.

Litwak, Eugene. 1985. *Helping Older People: The Complementary Roles of Informal Networks and Formal Systems.* New York: Guilford Press.

Litwak, Eugene, and Peter Messeri. 1989. "Organizational Theory, Social Supports, and Mortality Rates: A Theoretical Convergence." *American Sociological Review* 54(1):49–66.

Lofland, John. 1971. *Analyzing Social Settings.* Belmont, Calif.: Wadsworth Publishing.

Longino, C. F., Jr. 1987. "The Social and Economic Characteristics of Very Old Men and Women in the United States." Paper presented at the annual meeting of the Gerontological Society of America, Washington, D.C., November.

Lowenthal, M. 1964. *Lives in Distress.* New York: Basic Books.

Maddox, George L. 1987. "Aging Differently." Presented to Gerontological Society of America, reprinted in *Gerontologist* 27(5):557–64.

Manton, K. G., and Korbin Liu. 1984. "The Future Growth of the Long Term Care Population: Projections Based on the 1977 Nursing Home Survey and the 1982 Long Term Care Survey." Paper presented at the Third National Leadership Conference on Long Term Care Issues, Washington, D.C., March.

Marcil-Gratton, Nicole, and Jacques Légaré. 1988. "Support Networks Surrounding Future Older People: Will Reduced Fertility Lead to Greater Isolation?" Groupe de recherche sur la démographie québécoise, Working Paper. Montreal: Université de Montréal.

Maslow, Abraham H. 1962. *Toward a Psychology of Being.* Princeton, N.J.: Van Nostrand.

Maslow, Abraham H. 1971. *The Farther Reaches of Human Nature.* New York: Viking Press.

Matthews, Sarah H. 1985. "Sampling Issues in Surveys of Ageing and Intergenerational relations." Paper presented at a symposium on "Methodological Issues in the Study of Ageing and Intergenerational Relations," Gerontology Research Centre, University of Guelph, Ontario, June.

McDonald, Peter. 1990. "The 1980s: Social and Economic Change Affecting Families." *Family Matters*, issue no. 26 (April):13–18.

McKinlay, John B., and Sharon L. Tennstedt. 1987. "Following a Frail Elderly Population: Methodologic Challenges of a Longitudinal Study." Background paper prepared for NIA-NICHD workshop on "Family Intergenerational Relations," Bethesda, Md., September 10–11.

Mead, Margaret. 1978 [1967]. *Culture and Commitment*, rev. ed. New York: Columbia University Press.

Menken, Jane. 1985. "Age and Fertility: How Late Can You Wait?" *Demography* 22(4):469–83.

Merton, Robert K. 1949. *Social Theory and Social Structure: Toward the Codification of Theory and Research*, Glencoe, Ill.: Free Press.

Minichiello, M. Victor. 1988. "A Patient's View of Nursing Homes." In *Ageing and Public Policy*, edited by Hal L. Kendig and John M. McCallum. Sydney: Allen & Unwin.

Mitchell, J. Clyde. 1983. "Case and Situation Analysis," *Sociological Review* 31(2, New Series):187–211.

Moen, E. 1978. "The Reluctance of the Elderly to Accept Help." *Social Problems* 25(3):293–303.

Moon, Marilyn. 1986. "Economic Issues Facing a Growing Population of Older Women." Paper presented at the annual meeting of the American Sociological Association, New York, September.

Mugford, Stephen, and Hal L. Kendig. 1986. "Social Relations: Networks and Ties." In *Ageing and Families*, edited by Hal L. Kendig. Sydney: Allen & Unwin.

Neugarten, Bernice L. 1979. "Age or Need Entitlement?" In *Aging: Agenda for the Eighties*, edited by J. Hubbard. Washington, D.C.: Government Research Corp.

Newman, Sandra J. 1986. *National Long-Term Care Policies in Australia and the United States: A Cross-National Comparison*. Baltimore: Center for Metropolitan Planning and Research, Johns Hopkins University.

Neyland, Beth, and Bruce Shadbolt. 1987. "A Comparison of the Psychological Well-being of Never-married and Married Aged Living in Urban Australia." *Australian Journal on Ageing* 6(1):24–29.

NIA-NICHD Workshop. 1987. "Family Support, Decision-Making, and Health: Intergenerational Perspectives." Bethesda, Md., September 10–11.

Novak, Mark. 1985. *Successful Aging: The Myths, Realities, and Future of Aging in Canada*. Markham, Ontario: Penguin Books, Canada.

Painter, Charlotte, and Pamela Valois. 1985. *Gifts of Age*. San Francisco: Chronicle Books.

Parker, Roy. 1988. "The Care of the Elderly by Their Spouses: Implications for Policy." Paper prepared for Committee on Family Research,

International Seminar on "Kinship and Aging," International Sociological Association, April 16–19, Balatonzamardi, Hungary.

Passuth, Patricia M., and Vern L. Bengston. 1988. "Sociological Theories of Aging: Current Perspectives and Future Directions." In *Emergent Theories of Aging*, edited by James E. Birren and Vern L. Bengston. New York: Springer Publishing.

Powles, John. 1982. "Health and the Escalation of Industrialism." In *Quarry Australia? Social and Environmental Perspectives on Managing the Nation's Resources*, edited by Robert Birrell, Doug Hill, and John Stanley. Melbourne: Oxford University Press.

Regnier, Victor. 1981. "Neighborhood Images and Use." In *Community Housing Choices for Older Americans*, edited by M. Powell Lawton and Sally L. Hoover. New York: Springer Publishing.

Ridley, Jeanne Clare, and Kerry Johnson Gruber. 1989. "Representativeness and Response Rates of a Follow-up Sample for a Health Survey. Part II: Study Reports." In *Older Women and Social Support: A Follow-up Study*, edited by Alice T. Day, Jeanne Clare Ridley, and Douglas A. Wolf. Final Report, Grant No. ROI AGO6207-01 and 02. Washington, D.C.: Urban Institute.

Ridley, Jeanne C., Deborah Dawson, Koray Tanfer, and Christine A. Bachrach. 1979. "An Assessment of Non-Response Bias." In *Proceedings of the Section on Survey Research Methods*, American Statistical Association. Washington, D.C.: American Statistical Association.

Riley, Matilda W. 1983. "The Family in an Aging Society: A Matrix of Latent Relationships." *Journal of Family Issues* 4:439–54.

Riley, Matilda White. 1987. "On the Significance of Age in Sociology." Presidential address, 1986 American Sociological Association. *American Sociological Review* 52(1):1–14.

Riley, Matilda White, ed. 1979–1982. *Aging from Birth to Death: Interdisciplinary Perspectives*. American Association for the Advancement of Science (AAAS selected symposium, 30) (v.1-2) Boulder, Colo.: Westview Press.

Riley, M. W., R. P. Abeles, and M. S. Teitelbaum, eds. 1982. *Aging from Birth to Death*, vol. 2. *Sociotemporal Perspectives*. American Association for the Advancement of Science (AAAS selected symposium) Boulder, Colo.: Westview Press.

Riley, Matilda White, Anne Foner, and Joan Waring. 1988. "Sociology of Age." In *Handbook of Sociology*, edited by Neil J. Smelser (pp. 243–90). Newbury Park, Calif.: Sage Publications.

Riley, Matilda White, Beth B. Hess, and Kathleen Bond. 1983. *Aging in Society: Selected Reviews of Recent Research*. Hillsdale, N.J.: Lawrence Erlbaum Associates.

Ringen, Stein, 1987. *The Possibility of Politics: A Study in the Political Economy of the Welfare State*. Oxford: Oxford University Press.

Rodin, Judith. 1986. "Aging and Health: Effects of the Sense of Control." *Science* 233:1271–75.

Rodin, Judith, and E. Langer. 1977. "Long-term Effects of a Control Relevant Intervention with the Institutional Aged." *Journal of Personality and Social Psychology* 35:897–902.

Rosenmayr, L. 1977. "The Family—A Source of Hope for the Elderly?" In *Family, Bureaucracy, and the Elderly*, edited by E. Shanas and M. B. Sussman. Durham, N.C.: Duke University Press.

Rosenmayr, L., and E. Kockeis. 1968. "Propositions for a Sociological Theory of Aging and the Family." *International Social Science Journal* 15:410–426.

Rosenwaike, Ira. 1985. "Demographic Portrait of the Oldest Old." *Milbank Memorial Fund Quarterly/Health and Society* (guest edited by Richard Suzman and Matilda White Riley) 63(2):187–205.

Rossi, Alice. 1980. "Ageing and Parenthood in the Middle Years." In *Life-Span Development and Behavior, Volume 3*, edited by Paul B. Baltes and Orville G. Brim. New York: Academic Press 137–205.

Rowe, J. W., and R. L. Kahn. 1987. "Human Aging: Usual and Successful." *Science* 237, (July 10): 143–49.

Rowland, Don T. 1982. "The Vulnerability of the Aged in Sydney." *Australian and New Zealand Journal of Sociology* 18:229–47.

Sagan, Leonard A. 1987. *The Health of Nations*. New York: Basic Books.

Schmidt, Mary Gwynne. 1975. "Interviewing the Old Old." *Gerontologist* 15(6): 544–47.

Seeman, Teresa, and Lisa F. Berkman. 1988. "Structural Characteristics of Social Networks and their Relationship with Social Support in the Elderly: Who Provides Support?" *Social Science and Medicine* 26(7):737–49.

Seligman, Martin E. P., and Peter Schulman. 1986. "Explanatory Style as a Predictor of Productivity and Quitting among Life Insurance Sales Agents." *Journal of Personality and Social Psychology* 50(4):832–38.

Shanas, Ethel. 1979. "The Family as a Social Support System in Old Age." *Gerontologist* 19:169–74.

Shanas, Ethel, and George Maddox. 1976. "Aging, Health, and the Organization of Health Resources." In *Handbook on Aging and the Social Sciences*, edited by Robert H. Binstock and Ethel Shanas. New York: Van Nostrand Reinhold.

Shanas, Ethel, and Peter Townsend. 1968. *Old People in Three Industrial Societies*. New York: Atherton Press.

Sieber, S. D. 1973. "The Integration of Fieldwork and Survey Methods." *American Journal of Sociology* 78(6):1335–59.

Soldo, Beth J., and Emily M. Agree. 1988. "America's Elderly." *Population Bulletin* 43(3):1–51. Washington, D.C.: Population Reference Bureau.

Soldo, Beth J., and Kenneth G. Manton. 1985. "Changes in Health Status and Service Needs of the Oldest Old: Current Patterns and Future Trends." *Milbank Memorial Fund Quarterly/Health and Society* (guest edited by Richard Suzman and Matilda White Riley) 63(2):286–319.

Soldo, Beth J., Douglas A. Wolf, and Emily M. Agree. 1986. "Family, Household and Care Arrangements of Disabled Older Women: A Structural Analysis." Paper presented at the annual meeting of the Gerontological Society of America, Chicago, November 14–21.

Stepney, Rob. 1989. "Be Happy, Have a Yes in Your Heart." *Canberra Times*, June 11, p. 8.

Stone, Robyn, Gail L. Cafferata, and J. Sangl. 1987. "Caregivers of the Frail Elderly: A National Profile." *Gerontologist* 27(2):616–26.

Streib, G. G. 1983. "The Frail Elderly: Research Dilemmas and Research Opportunities." *Gerontologist* 23(1):40–44.

Suzman, Richard, and Matilda White Riley. 1985. "Introducing the 'Oldest Old.' " *Milbank Memorial Fund Quarterly/Health and Society* (guest edited by Richard Suzman and Matilda White Riley) 63(2):177–86.

Syme, S. Leonard. 1988. "Control and Health: An Epidemiological Perspective." Paper presented at the Pennsylvania State Gerontology Conference on "Self-Directedness and Efficacy: Causes and Effects throughout the Life Course," State College, PA. October 17–18.

Symer, M. A., and B. F. Hofland. 1982. "Divorce and Family Support in Later Life—Emerging Concerns." *Journal of Family Issues* 3(1):61–77.

Tanfer, Koray. 1985. "Report on the Results of a Pilot Tracing Study of the Respondents in the 1978 Survey of Low Fertility Birth Cohorts." Unpublished Working Paper. Philadelphia: Institute for Survey Research, Temple University.

Tennstedt, Sharon L., and John B. McKinlay. 1987. "Informal Care and the Use of Formal Services: Are They Related?" Paper presented at the NIA-NICHD Workshop on "Family Support, Decision-Making, and Health: Intergenerational Perspectives," Bethesda, Md., September 10–11.

Tolchin, Martin. 1990. "Paying for Long-term Care: The Struggle for Lawmakers." *New York Times*, March 29, p. A1ff.

Torrey, Barbara Boyle. 1988. "Assets of the Aged: Clues and Issues." *Population and Development Review* 14(3):489–97.

Turner, Barbara. 1985. "Health is the Main Thing: Sex Differences, Health, and Psychological Variables in Later Life." In *Growing Old in America*, 3rd ed., edited by Beth B. Hess and Elizabeth Markson, 171–80. New Brunswick, N.J.: Transaction Books.

United Nations World Assembly on Aging. 1982. *Introductory Document: Humanitarian Issues.* Report of the Secretary-General, Item 6 of Provisional Agenda, World Assembly on Aging, Vienna, A/Conf. 113/9 v. 82-24001. New York: United Nations.

U.S. Bureau of the Census. 1987. Public Use Sample. *Current Population Survey*. Washington, D.C.: U.S. Government Printing Office.

U.S. Department of Health and Human Services. 1979. *Health Interview Survey.* Bethesda, Md.: U.S. Government Printing Office.

U.S. Department of Health and Human Services. 1982. *National Long-Term Care Survey.* Bethesda, Md.: U.S. Government Printing Office.

U.S. House of Representatives, Select Committee on Aging. 1989. *The Quality of Life for Older Women: Older Women Living Alone.* Comm. Pub. No. 100-693. Washington, D.C.: U.S. Government Printing Office.

Victorian Women's Consultative Council. 1988. *Living With Dignity: A Survey of the Needs of Older Women Victoria-June 1988.* Melbourne: Department of Premier and Cabinet.

Viorst, Judith. 1986. *Necessary Losses.* New York: Simon and Schuster.

Walsh, Thomas. 1981. In *Community Housing Choices for Older Americans,* edited by M. Powell Lawton and Sally L. Hoover. New York: Springer Publishing.

Wellman, Barry, and Alan Hall. 1986. "Social Networks and Social Support: Implications for Later Life." In *Later Life: The Social Psychology of Aging,* edited by Victor Marshall. Beverly Hills: Sage Publications.

Whitbourne, S. K. 1985. "The Psychological Construction of the Life Span." In *Handbook of the Psychology of Aging,* 2nd ed., edited by J. E. Birren and K. W. Schaie. New York: Van Nostrand Reinhold.

WHO. See World Health Organization.

Williams, Richard H., and Claudine G. Wirths. 1965. *Lives through the Years: Styles of Life and Successful Aging.* New York: Atherton Press.

Wolf, Douglas A. 1983. *Kinship and Living Arrangements of Older Americans.* Final report to the National Institute of Child Health and Human Development. Washington, D.C.: Urban Institute.

Wolf, Douglas A. 1984. "Kin Availability and the Living Arrangements of Older Women." *Social Science Research* 13(1):72–89.

Wolf, Douglas A. 1988. "Family Structure and Caregiving Portfolios." Working Paper, International Institute for Applied Systems Analysis. Laxenburg, Austria: International Institute for Applied Systems Analysis.

Wolf, Douglas A., and Beth J. Soldo. 1988. "Household Composition Choices of Older Unmarried Women." *Demography* 25(3):387–403.

World Health Organization. 1958. "The First Ten Years of the World Health Organization." Geneva: WHO.

Zarit, Steven, Pamela A. Todd, and Judy M. Zarit. 1986. "Subjective Burden of Husbands and Wives as Caregivers: A Longitudinal Study." *Gerontologist* 26:260–66.

Zedlewski, Sheila R., and Jack A. Meyer. 1988. *Toward Ending Poverty among the Elderly and Disabled: Policy and Financing Options.* Report prepared for the Villers Foundation and the Commonwealth Fund Commission on Elderly People Living Alone. Washington, D.C: Urban Institute.

ABOUT THE AUTHOR

Alice T. Day is Director of Successful Ageing, A.C.T., an Australian government-funded project to develop programs to improve the quality of life of older people in the Australian Capital Territory. She is also Chair of the Australian government's advisory committee on programs to provide home and community care services to persons of all ages who need assistance to remain living at home.

A native of New York City, she has held permanent residency status in Australia since 1973. She has a BA from Smith College, an MA from Columbia University, and a PhD (in sociology) from the Australian National University. She has taught at Mt. Holyoke College, Albertus Magnus College, Yale University, and Smith College. More recently, she has been a Mellon Fellow at the Population Reference Bureau and a Senior Research Associate at the Urban Institute. During her time at the Institute, she was Principal Investigator for the project that led to this book.

In Australia, she has been a consultant to the Australian Schools Commission, the Australian Bureau of Statistics, and the Office of Aged Services of the Australian state of New South Wales; and she was a member of the Australian National University team that conducted a large-scale survey of older persons resident in Sydney. As part of her Sydney research, she conducted semi-structured, open-ended interviews with a selection of some of the oldest men and women in the survey, publishing the results in her book, 'We Can Manage'—Expectations about Care and Varieties of Family Support among People 75 Years and Older (Melbourne: Institute of Family Studies, 1985). She is also co-author (with Lincoln H. Day) of Too Many Americans (Boston: Houghton Mifflin, 1964). In the last 10 years, her papers at conferences and articles in professional journals have focused mainly on the impact of social change on families in later life.

Alice Day has travelled widely in Australia, the United States, Europe, and China. She and her husband are members of a four-generation family: with a 90-year-old mother, a daughter, a son and daughter-in-law, and a grandchild.